Knowledge and Innovation in the New Service Economy

PREST/CRIC STUDIES IN SCIENCE, TECHNOLOGY AND INNOVATION

General Editors: Luke Georghiou, *Director, PREST* and Stan Metcalfe, *Stanley Jevons Professor of Economics and ESRC Centre for Research on Innovation and Competition, University of Manchester, UK*

This series is a forum for the outstanding research from Manchester's two leading social science research institutes – PREST (Policy Research in Engineering, Science and Technology) and CRIC (the ESRC Centre for Research on Innovation and Competition).

The books in this series reflect their concern with the economics, social and managerial implications of science and innovation. Emphasis is given to science and technology policy and the role that innovation plays in competitiveness, particularly in the new knowledge-intensive global economy.

This interdisciplinary series will include some of the best theoretical and empirical work in the field, and will be invaluable to scholars, students and policy makers.

Knowledge and Innovation in the New Service Economy

Edited by

Birgitte Andersen
Senior Lecturer, Department of Management, Birkbeck College, University of London, UK

Jeremy Howells
ESRC Senior Research Fellow, Centre for Research on Innovation and Competition (CRIC), and Co-director, Policy Research in Engineering, Science and Technology (PREST), University of Manchester, UK

Richard Hull
Lecturer in Sociology, University of Brunel, UK

Ian Miles
Professor of Technological Innovation and Social Change, and Co-director, CRIC and PREST, University of Manchester, UK

Joanne Roberts
Senior Lecturer in Economics, School of Social, Political and Economic Sciences, University of Northumbria, UK

PREST/CRIC STUDIES IN SCIENCE, TECHNOLOGY AND INNOVATION

Edward Elgar
Cheltenham, UK • Northampton, MA, USA

Published by
Edward Elgar Publishing Limited
Glensanda House
Montpellier Parade
Cheltenham
Glos GL50 1UA
UK

Edward Elgar Publishing, Inc.
136 West Street
Suite 202
Northampton
Massachusetts 01060
USA

A catalogue record for this book
is available from the British Library

Library of Congress Cataloguing in Publication Data
Knowledge and innovation in the new service economy / Birgitte Andersen ... [et al.], eds.
    p. cm. — (PREST/CRIC studies in science, technology and innovation)
Includes bibliographical references and index.
    1. Knowledge management. 2. Technological innovations–Economic aspects. 3. Information technology–Economic aspects. 4. Service industries.
I. Andersen, Birgitte, 1967– II. Series

HD30.2.K635 2000
658.4'038—dc21

ISBN 1 84064 572 5

Printed and bound in Great Britain by Bookcraft (Bath) Ltd.

Contents

Figures

Tables

List of Contributors

BIRGITTE ANDERSEN. Senior Lecturer, Department of Management, Birkbeck College, University of London, UK, and Honorary Associate Fellow, ESRC Centre for Research on Innovation and Competition (CRIC), The University of Manchester, UK

MARK BODEN. Research Fellow, Policy Research in Engineering, Science and Technology (PREST), The University of Manchester, UK

ETTORE BOLISANI. Ricercatore, Dipartimento di Tecnica e Gestione dei sistemi industriali, Università di Padova, Italy

KIERON FLANAGAN. Research Associate, Policy Research in Engineering, Science and Technology (PREST), The University of Manchester, UK

CRISTIANE HIPP. Research Fellow, Mannesmann Pilotentwicklung, Munich, Germany, and Technical University Hamburg-Harburg, Technology and Innovation Management, Hamburg, Germany.

JEREMY HOWELLS. ESRC Senior Research Fellow, Centre for Research on Innovation and Competition (CRIC), and Co-Director, Policy Research in Engineering, Science and Technology (PREST), University of Manchester, UK

RICHARD HULL. Lecturer in Sociology, University of Brunel, UK, and Honorary Associate Fellow, ESRC Centre for Research on Innovation and Competition (CRIC), UMIST, UK

IAN MILES. Professor of Technological Innovation and Social Change. Co-director, Centre for Research on Innovation and Competition (CRIC), and Policy Research in Engineering, Science and Technology (PREST), The University of Manchester, UK

JOANNE ROBERTS. Senior Lecturer in Economics, School of Social, Political and Economic Sciences, University of Northumbria, UK, and Honorary Associate Fellow, Centre for Research on Innovation and Competition (CRIC), University of Manchester, UK

BRUCE S. TETHER. ESRC Research Fellow, Centre for Research on Innovation and Competition (CRIC), UMIST, UK

MARK TOMLINSON. ESRC Research Fellow, Centre for Research on Innovation and Competition (CRIC), University of Manchester, UK.

PAUL WINDRUM. Research Fellow, Maastricht Economic Research Institute on Innovation and Technology (MERIT), Maastricht University, the Netherlands

1   Introducing the New Service Economy

Joanne Roberts, Ian Miles, Richard Hull, Jeremy Howells and Birgitte Andersen

1.1   INTRODUCTION: MOTIVATION

Service activity dominates the economies of advanced industrialised countries. In 1996 the service sector accounted for 73.3 per cent of employment and 72.9 per cent of gross domestic product in the US, and 70.6 per cent and 61.3 per cent respectively in the UK (OECD 1998). The growing importance of the service sector has been recognised for some decades, and discussions about the role of services in the economy can be traced back over several centuries (Delaunay and Gadrey 1992). Despite this, their contribution to economic activity has remained poorly understood. Until recently, services were viewed as 'laggards' within the economy, lacking scope for improved productivity, labour-intensive in nature and technologically backward. As such, services were seen very much as dependent on other sectors of the economy. But the 1990s saw much wider acknowledgement of the ways in which services can be significant contributors to wealth creating activity (Miles 1993). Knowledge-intensive services, especially knowledge intensive business services (KIBS), were identified as particularly important in the creation, and distribution of new knowledge and innovation (Miles et al. 1995; Antonelli 1999). In this new service economy highly skilled service employment is expanding. Knowledge workers and knowledge assets command high rewards, and are contributing an increasing proportion of the value of output in all sectors of the economy.

By drawing together a range of original empirical and theoretical contributions, this book provides evidence, and proposes frameworks, to

1

illuminate the complex issues, processes and structures surrounding knowledge and innovation in the new service economy. This chapter briefly explores the rise of the new service economy, before providing an overview of the chapters that follow. The key issues and themes that will be explored in these later chapters, are considered more fully in Chapter 2.

1.2   THE NATURE OF THE NEW SERVICE ECONOMY

The service sector covers a heterogeneous group of economic activities, ranging from, for example, legal and banking services, to transport, communication and cleaning services. There have been many attempts to define and classify services. Early efforts to define services as a distinctive economic activity (Fisher 1939; Clark 1957) characterise them in terms of *what they are not,* rather than what they are. For example, Clark (1957) subdivides the economy into three categories, primary, secondary and a residual tertiary or service sector. Many studies have identified the weaknesses of such a three sector typology and have proposed new classifications, which better reflect the heterogeneity of the activities considered and categorise services into various sub-groups. For example, Singelmann (1978) identifies consumer services, social services, producer services and distributive services.

An alternative method of defining the service sector is to concentrate on common features of industries as judged by the nature of their output. Hill (1977), for instance, identifies three distinct characteristics of services: first, services are *consumed simultaneously* with their production; secondly, services *cannot be stored*; and, thirdly, services are *intangible*. These features imply, furthermore, an extensive producer–consumer relationship. But there are many services which defy these descriptions: software can be consumed indefinitely (and stored), dental surgery is uncomfortably tangible, and so on. New information technologies (ITs), especially, allow some services to be separated both over time and space – for example, services can be at least partially transferred across telecommunication networks or embodied in a tangible form such as a computer disk. New technologies are enabling changes in the nature of services and bringing about the development of new services, such as those associated with the use of the Internet (Chapters 5 and 6).

It is often difficult to distinguish between goods and services. As economies grow or change their structure, technical change and economies of scale interact to splinter services from goods and goods from services. The frontier between services and goods is becoming increasingly blurred, as manufactured products contain ever-increasing amounts of services in the form of applied human capital, and require more and more services to be used in the form of complementary software, staff training, or maintenance and repairs. Many goods are an inextricable part of a total business deal that includes pre-sale and after-sales services (Nusbaumer 1987a). Moreover, increasing emphasis is being placed on delivering high quality services to consumers as a source of competitive advantage, whether a supplier is providing a manufactured good or a service. Related to this, as all sectors of the economy are becoming more knowledge- intensive in their production processes, knowledge-intensive services are becoming more intimately involved in the production of all types of commodities.

It is useful to conclude this section with a definition of services that uses the three sector classification of the economy as a springboard to a more dynamic approach. Miles (1996 pp. 3–4), drawing on the analyses of Hill (1977) and Riddle (1986), defines the tertiary sector as comprising those activities that effect transformations in:

- the state of the environment (other than those concerned with extracting raw materials) – waste management, pollution clean-up, park-keeping;
- the state of the artefacts produced by the secondary sector – repair and maintenance, goods transport, building services, wholesale and retail trade;
- the state of people – health and education services, hospitality and consumer services such as hairdressing, public transport;
- the state of symbols (that is, information) – knowledge services (which bring intelligence to bear on any of the operations already mentioned); entertainment services; communication services such as broadcasting and telecommunications, material goods themselves, or symbolic material (information).

Here, rather than being viewed as a mere residual, a more positive account of the service sector is provided. The majority of services considered in this book fall into the last category of service activity identified above. It is these services which play a central role in the new service economy where prosperity is dependent upon the creation and diffusion of knowledge and innovation.

1.3 THE RISE OF SERVICES

The twentieth century witnessed the dramatic rise of service activity as a source of employment, output, innovation and wealth creation. In the 1900s, despite employing more than 25 per cent of the work force of most advanced countries (Ott 1987), services were viewed as unproductive activities often associated with luxury and unnecessary consumption. As such they were regarded as wasteful and parasitic, depending on output in the manufacturing and extractive sectors for their survival. This view was forwarded by Adam Smith in the eighteenth century and was reinforced by Karl Marx and many others in the nineteenth century (though a close reading of Marx suggests that he was far less dogmatic about this than many later Marxists). Clearly, though, transportation and distribution services perform central functions enabling production and consumption. These services were, for instance, important factors accounting for the economic success of the Dutch and British economies from the late sixteenth century (Kindleberger 1996).

The early twentieth century saw the rise of the manufacturing sector, as mass production of consumer goods for national and international markets became widespread. And with the growth of mass production and consumption, one major class of services – domestic servants – went into sharp decline in Western societies. The creation of mass markets was facilitated by dramatic improvements in transportation, communication and distribution services brought about by the introduction and development of the railway and telegraph networks in the nineteenth century. Further technological opportunities, more sophisticated state intervention in the economy, and international co-operation contributed to a period of unprecedented growth in the post World War II period. This 'long post-war boom' saw dramatic increases in incomes and standards of living in the advanced countries – and significant growth in government investments in a wide range of public services including transportation, education and health care. In line with 'Engel's Law', as incomes grew, expenditure on essentials and staple goods declined as a percentage of income, while a higher proportion of income was devoted to the purchase of manufactured goods and more sophisticated services like entertainment, leisure and some personal services.

With the growing economic significance of the service sector, greater attention has gradually been devoted to exploring and analysing the nature and impact of services. The rise of the service sector has been interpreted in terms of alleged processes of de-industrialisation or post-industrialisation – developing either because of the decline of the manufacturing industry, or as a superior replacement for industry. Beyond these polarities, a more subtle account of the growth of services will recognise the interdependent relationship between industrial and service activity. The rise of consumer services and government-supplied services can be explained in terms of the growth of average incomes arising from increases in productivity levels in the manufacturing sector. (Though we will also need to take into account political factors behind the growth of public expenditure, and, indeed, behind the growth of wages.) The growth of transport and distributive services is closely linked both to the trade and distribution of commodities, and to personal travel associated both with leisure and new working arrangements. The fastest growing category of service activity in recent decades, producer services, has several factors behind its growth. First, in the restructuring of manufacturing activity since the 1970s, many firms have sought to develop flexible production strategies in which they focus on their primary activity (core competences) while externalising other activities including services (Chapter 12). Such externalisation and outsourcing of services means that activities which were once attributed to the manufacturing sector in national accounting systems, are now specialised activities included in the service sector. Second, the more complex economic environment, in which economic agents experience high levels of uncertainty, has stimulated the demand for services which aim to reduce risks, hence the increase in consultancy, financial, legal, insurance and related services. Third, technological change has led to IT-related producer and consumer services. As well as an increase in services bought in by firms in all sectors of the economy, new services are developing within firms arising from the acknowledgement of the contribution of, for example, marketing, distribution and after-sales maintenance and sales services to the value of a physical product. In addition, the recognition of the central role of intangible and knowledge assets in the process of production and competition has stimulated many large firms to develop internal services devoted to the management of knowledge (Chapter 9).

Clearly, services have an important role in the economies of advanced industrialised countries and to a growing extent in less developed countries. Early studies of the services sector traced the growth of service employment and considered its economic and social impact (Fuchs 1968; Singelmann 1978). There have still been several influential studies that depict services as unproductive, as laggards, as having negative impacts on economic growth and innovation (Petit 1986; Cohen and Zysman 1987). However, other studies have revealed the positive role of services in supporting and stimulating economic growth at regional, national and global levels (Riddle 1986; Nusbaumer 1987a, 1987b). Moreover, studies of producer services show them to be crucial element in economic development, as a factor that significantly influences the dynamics of growth, innovation diffusion, productivity increases and competitiveness across firms, sectors and regions (Martinelli 1991; Marshall and Wood 1995; *inter alia*). Increasingly, analyses of service activity are demonstrating the active and independent role of services, particularly producer services, as contributors to economic growth (Miles 1993). Furthermore, though services have typically not been thought of as innovative, at the beginning of the twenty-first century it is clear that services do play an important and widespread role in the process of knowledge creation and innovation in the economy.

The role of services in innovation and in particular the significance of KIBS, together with the importance of knowledge and innovation in the new service economy, are considered in detail in Chapter 2. In the remainder of this chapter we provide a brief overview of the book.

1.4   AN OVERVIEW OF THE BOOK

In Chapter 2, as stated, Joanne Roberts, Birgitte Andersen and Richard Hull provide an account of the key issues confronted in this study: the economic dimensions of knowledge, and the organisation of knowledge-intensive activity through specialised services. The rest of the book takes up these issues, and extends the analysis, through a number of specific analyses.

In Chapter 3, Mark Tomlinson uses macro-statistics to examine the contribution of services to economic activity overall. Despite the very limited detail that national accounts provide for addressing service activities, he is able to use input–output data to demonstrate a strong positive relation between the use of services and the performance of the sectors which are using them. Thus he provides evidence that suggests that the positive impact of business services, which is implicit in the use of these services by client firms, has impacts that can be demonstrated at macro-levels. Tomlinson interprets this in terms of 'knowledge flows' in the economy, with business services providing an alternative to capital and labour as knowledge-bearing inputs to production.

Chapter 4 uses firm-level survey data to address these topics in a very different way. Bruce Tether and Christiane Hipp use a German survey which provided unusually rich data on service firms and their innovation activities, to examine the nature of their relations with their clients. The specific instrument used derives from questions concerning how far the products of the service are ones that are standardised, or more specialised services produced in response to the requirements of particular clients. In terms of 'knowledge flows', the latter are liable to require far more inputs from the clients than the former, and the study investigates the implications of this form of innovation in the services. The chapter effectively challenges efforts to characterise all services as requiring high levels of client inputs, and shows how patterns of standardisation and specialisation vary across different types of service firm and sector.

The next four chapters of the book move on to provide case studies of four types of service firm (mainly business services), who are providing inputs to their clients around areas of new technological knowledge. They consider, in turn, new ecommerce, web, and computer services, all relating to the requirements of business for support in their IT use; and environmental services, which help firms confront the challenges of regulations (and litigation) around environmental topics. Some of these environmental services are also IT-based, for example supplying environmental management software, but they also draw on process engineering, energy technology, biosciences and other classes of technical knowledge.

This underlines an important point: though new IT is of pervasive importance across all services, and although many new services are IT-based, there are many other classes of technical and nontechnical knowledge underpinning KIBS. Practically every field of new technology spawns its own services, and many services employ very distinctive technologies (transport systems, pharmaceuticals, and so on). Likewise, professions involved in design, forecasting, market analysis, and the like are both represented by specialised services, and used intensively by many other services.

The next chapters consider not so much specific sorts of knowledge, but specific functions connected with knowledge. In Chapter 9, Hull considers the new discipline of 'knowledge management', which involves a wide range of approaches and tools that firms and other organisations have been implementing to cope better with the demands of a knowledge-based economy. Many business services are active in promoting knowledge management – management consultancies, of course, but also IT services, personnel and related services, and so on.

In Chapter 10, we consider one set of questions concerning knowledge management that arises *within* KIBS. How do these firms go about protecting the knowledge that is so critical to their performance and competitiveness? Drawing on surveys of three very different KIBS, Ian Miles and Mark Boden conclude that very different strategies are employed by different types of firm in different contexts. What is apparent is that governance of knowledge possessed by employees, or shared in the context of relations with suppliers and clients, is critically important. The standard IPR arrangements of patents and copyright are of much less relevance than would have been implied by most formalistic accounts of intellectual property.

In Chapter 11, Roberts considers another aspect of the strategy of KIBS: how and why do they go about extending their activities internationally? The chapter demonstrates that the vision of services as not being internationally traded is an obsolete one, and one implication is that we are witnessing much greater international competition to supply business services, with the scope for learning from others' approaches – and perhaps for importing inappropriate models? – growing.

The remaining chapters return to broader levels of analysis, addressing questions about the role of knowledge and of KIBS within economic systems – both national economies and the global economy (though we make no claim to address the developing world in this volume). In Chapter 12 Jeremy Howells examines the processes of outsourcing that have led to many firms purchasing their service inputs from external sources. Using analyses of technology and R&D support services, he explores the dynamics behind business choices to externalise or internalise such KIBS – or, rather, of how they set about to combine internal and external sources of knowledge.

In Chapter 13 Howells goes beyond the level of individual firms, to examine how services, and especially business services, fit into systems of innovation.   Recent analyses have developed the notion of innovation systems as capturing important dimensions of the innovation process, which is often crucially dependent on relations between companies, trade associations, research bodies, and what effectively constitutes an infrastructure of knowledge.

Chapter 14 examines another sort of institutional support for innovation – the IPR system. Andersen and Howells show how existing IPR instruments have developed for supporting innovation in tangible products and processes; and thus that the systems most effectively developed for protecting services – such as copyright – are not specifically attuned to innovation. In the new service economy this may hinder the diffusion of innovative ideas, and is liable to shape the innovative strategy of service firms.

Finally, we return to the global level of analysis. There has been much discussion of 'national innovation systems', but in Chapter 15 Howells and Roberts go on to consider the international elements of such systems, effectively relating the systems approach to the analysis of services internationalisation.   The study considers what constitutes globalising knowledge systems, drawing on a rich literature review and the authors' own analyses. And in Chapter 16, Howells concludes this book by reviewing the range of issues discussed in the previous chapters, and asking what the intellectual agenda should be if we are to grasp the nature of a global services economy.

These chapters provide an unusual combination of an overview of a highly important and pervasive set of phenomena, and presentation of cutting-edge research into many of the key issues and areas that it involves. We hope that it will thus prove equally relevant to researchers and students, to policymakers and business analysts. In a subsequent book we aim to take up the gauntlet which we have effectively thrown down for ourselves here, and move toward an integrated view of the role of knowledge in the new services economy – and of services in the knowledge-based economy.

2 Knowledge and Innovation in the New Service Economy

Joanne Roberts, Birgitte Andersen and Richard Hull

2.1 INTRODUCTION

Knowledge and innovation are central factors contributing to economic growth and prosperity in the new service economy. The various inter-relations between knowledge, innovation and services provide the focus for this book. The overview of the new service economy given in this chapter sets the context against which the range of contributions within this volume may be viewed. The chapter begins by examining the key features of the new service economy. This is followed by a brief review of the empirical evidence of service and knowledge-based activity. The major issues emerging from the growing importance of knowledge and innovation in the new service economy, which are considered in later chapters, are then briefly discussed. Finally, the concluding section recognises the far-reaching consequences of the rise of the new service economy and outlines several of the most significant issues that are excluded from detailed consideration in this volume.

2.2 THE ROLE OF KNOWLEDGE AND INNOVATION IN SERVICES

A number of important features that characterise the new service economy are addressed in this section. These include the role of services in the creation and dissemination of knowledge and innovation, as well as the rising

10

significance of knowledge-intensive business services (KIBS) in this process. The nature and role of knowledge in shaping and stimulating economic activity will also be addressed.

2.2.1   Services and Innovation

The relationship between services and innovation came to the fore with Gershuny's study of the 'self-service economy'. According to Gershuny (1978), the development of new service-substituting consumer goods will be encouraged in the long term by the differences in productivity levels between the service and manufacturing sectors, which, other things being equal, lead the price of services to rise relative to goods. Examples of the shift from services to goods include the move from public to private transport and from laundry services to domestic washing machines. However, the development of self-service activity creates demand for new services, for example, home shopping through the Internet or television-shopping channels require new retail systems and services such as telephone sales services.

By the 1980s a number of studies considered service innovations and the impact of technical change. Gershuny and Miles (1983), for example, argue that new information technology (IT) presents the technical inputs for a new wave of social innovation in the way of service provision in fields such as entertainment, information and education. Barras' (1986) study of the use of technology in services has been particularly influential. He argues that the process of innovation in services is preceded by the adoption of new technologies developed in other sectors. The first stage of innovation is centred on increasing the efficiency of the processes of production or delivery of existing services. The second stage involves increases in the quality of the service brought about by the new production systems. In the third stage new services are produced arising from the application of new technologies. Thus innovation takes the form of a 'reverse product cycle'. In more recent work Barras (1990) has developed a model of 'interactive innovation' to supplement the reverse product cycle approach.

Recent studies of services and innovation undermine the long held view of services as laggards of the economy (Miles et al. 1995; Miles 1996). Some services are vanguard users of technology. Indeed, 75 per cent of all expenditure on IT hardware in the UK and USA arises from services (Miles 1996). The IT revolution has increased the technology-intensity of services. Information processing is central to many service activities and consequently new ITs have great potential to assist in the efficient conduct of such activities. As noted in Chapter 1, services are heterogeneous hence they do vary considerably in the extent to which they adopt technologically-intensive methods of production.   In addition to being users of technology some services are innovators producing new IT services, such as software and databases, which they may use themselves or sell on to their clients.   Other services, particularly KIBS, play an important role in the creation and diffusion of technology and innovation (Miles et al. 1995; Antonelli 1999). This book, concerned as it is with knowledge and innovation, primarily focuses on KIBS, consequently, it is worth giving them further consideration at this point. The relationship between services and innovation will be considered further (Section 2.4) when attention is focussed on the issues emerging from the interactions between the various interrelated factors in the new service economy.

2.2.2   Knowledge-Intensive Business Services

Many services are centrally concerned with the collection, collation, creation and distribution of knowledge and information, although not all information processing services are involved in the production or supply of knowledge. For example, telecommunication and broadcasting services store and transport data and information. Knowledge-intensive services are economic activities that are intended to result in the creation, accumulation or dissemination of knowledge. Knowledge-intensive business services are an important example of these services.   Others include non-business-related public education and certain administration services.

Miles et al. (1995) identify two types of KIBS (Table 2.1).   The first consists of traditional professional services, such as accountancy and legal services, based upon specialised knowledge of administrative systems and social affairs.   These services typically help users to negotiate complex social, physical, psychological and biological systems.   These KIBS are usually users of new technology rather than agents in its development and diffusion.   The second group of KIBS consists of new services connected with technology, and with the production and transfer of knowledge about new technology. Technology-based KIBS (t-KIBS) include, for example, computer-related services and technical engineering services.

Later chapters present evidence from a variety of KIBS sectors demonstrating the full extent of their contribution to the economy at a national and, increasingly, at an international level.   The rapidly changing technological environment and increased complexity account for the increasing demand for KIBS. However, more importantly KIBS derive their significance in the emerging economy from the centrality of knowledge and innovation.

Table 2.1 Knowledge-Intensive Business Services

KIBS I: Traditional Professional Services, liable to be intensive users of new technology:

- Marketing/advertising;
- Training (other than in new technologies);
- Design (other than that involving new technologies);
- Some financial services (e.g. securities and stock-market-related activities);
- Office services (other than those involving new office equipment, and excluding 'physical' services like cleaning);
- Building services (e.g. architecture; surveying; construction engineering, but excluding services involving new IT equipment such as building energy management systems);
- Management consultancy (other than that involving new technology);
- Accounting and bookkeeping;
- Legal services;
- Environmental services (not involving new technology, e.g. environmental law; and not based on old technology e.g. elementary waste disposal services).

KIBS II: New Technology-Based KIBS:

- Computer networks/telematics (e.g. VANs, on-line databases);
- Some telecommunications (especially new business services);
- Software;
- Other computer-related services – e.g. facilities management;
- Training in new technologies;
- Design involving new office equipment;
- Office services (centrally involving new IT equipment such as building energy management systems);
- Management consultancy involving new technology;
- Technical engineering;
- Environmental services involving new technology; e.g. remediation; monitoring; scientific/laboratory services;
- R&D Consultancy and 'high-tech boutiques'.

Source: Miles *et al.* 1995.

2.2.3   Knowledge and Innovation

The significance of knowledge and innovation in economic activity has received much attention in recent years (see for example: OECD 1996c; DTI 1998; World Bank 1999). The 'knowledge-based economy' has become a popular term used to describe advanced economies. According to the OECD (1996d, p. 3) the term stems from the fuller recognition of the place of knowledge and technology in modern economies. Knowledge-based economies are directly based on the production, distribution and use of knowledge and information. Among OECD economies this is reflected in growth in high-technology investments, high-technology industries, more highly-skilled labour and associated productivity gains. The OECD estimates that more than 50 per cent of gross domestic product (GDP) in the major OECD economies is now knowledge-based (OECD 1996c,d, p. 9).

The economic significance of knowledge was raised in the nineteenth century by Marshall (1890), and, of course, the Industrial Revolution beginning in the eighteenth century drew attention to the importance of innovation. In the past, the returns of knowledge related to production techniques (including resource availability and market conditions) were of particular concern. Although these are still very central issues (Chapter 14), today 'knowledge about knowledge' has come to the forefront of the discussion. In this context the location, combination and manipulation of knowledge become increasingly central as technology and corporate competencies become more interrelated and complex (Andersen 1998).

It has even been argued that knowledge has become the only resource that can create a continuous competitive advantage for a nation (Drucker 1993). Natural resources are no longer a guarantee of competitiveness. Capital resources are highly mobile and so cannot be relied upon to secure a nation's competitiveness (Reich 1992). Systems of knowledge and innovation creation and diffusion (Chapters 13 and 15), which include knowledge workers and appropriate institutional structures, are essential assets for nations seeking to secure economic competitiveness in the twenty-first century (Lundvall 1992).

The IT revolution is central to the rising emphasis placed on knowledge in economic activity. As Castells (1996, p. 32) notes, the current technological revolution is characterised by the application of knowledge and information 'to knowledge generation and information processing/communication devices, in a cumulative feedback loop between innovation and the uses of innovation'. Consequently, innovation, science and technology, and learning are fundamental to the knowledge-based economy (Lundvall 1992; Lundvall and Johnson 1994).

In the context of the growing role of knowledge in the economy, services take on a renewed importance as both creators and distributors of knowledge and innovation. To fully appreciate the role of knowledge-intensive services in the new economy it is necessary to consider the economic nature of knowledge. An historical approach to the emerging significance of knowledge provides useful insights. In parallel with the developments in ITs there has been, since the 1960s, a separate stream of debate and commentary on the changing role and character of knowledge in contemporary societies (Machlup 1962; Bell 1974; *inter alia*). This stream of debate reflects fundamental changes in contemporary economies, not least of which is the dramatic rise of the valuations placed upon intangible assets such as brand and intellectual property.

2.2.4   Knowledge in Economic Activity

In microeconomic analysis, knowledge, like information, is characterised as a public good, since it is regarded as non-excludable and non-rival, and its production is characterised by high levels of indivisibility. However, this view of knowledge is challenged by recent developments of the Schumpeterian and Marshallian approaches, which stress the distinction between knowledge and information (Antonelli 1999), as well as the distinction between the codified and tacit elements of knowledge (Nelson 1992b).

The view of knowledge being distinct from information and data is adopted here. Data are necessary inputs into information and knowledge, and are defined as series of observations, measurements, or facts in the form of numbers, words, sounds and/or images. Data have no inherent meaning, but provide the raw material from which information is produced. Information is defined as data that have been arranged into a meaningful pattern. Data may result from the conduct of a survey, information results from the analysis of the data in the form of a report or charts and graphs that give meaning to the data. There have been extensive debates for many decades as to whether this intelligibility is unique, transcending the context, or instead dependent on the context of use. The standard distinction between information and knowledge, derived from information processing and computer science, is that knowledge is information plus problem-solving heuristics; or more broadly, information plus some means of putting it to use. Knowledge, then, is defined here as the application and productive use of information. Knowledge, however, is more than information, since it involves an awareness or understanding gained through experience, familiarity or learning.[1] Knowledge requires a relation between the 'knowing self' and the external world, and it is therefore, useful to talk of knowing as an activity or process, rather than static knowledge. However, the relationship between knowledge and information is interactive. Knowledge creation is dependent upon information, yet the development of relevant information requires the application of knowledge. The tools and methods of analysis applied to information also influence knowledge creation. The same information can give rise to a variety of different types of knowledge, depending on the type and purpose of the analysis.

A second distinction is now often made between codified or explicit knowledge and tacit or implicit knowledge. Knowledge may be codified if it can be recorded or transmitted in the form of symbols (for example, writing or drawings) or embodied in a tangible form, (for example, machinery or tools). Tacit knowledge is non-codified knowledge that is acquired via the informal take-up of learning behaviour and procedures (Howells 1996, p. 92; Nelson 1992b). Nonaka and Takeuchi (1995) identify two dimensions of tacit knowledge: the technical dimension encompassing skills or crafts; and the cognitive dimension consisting of schemata, mental models, and beliefs that shape the way individuals perceive the world around them.

Lundvall and Johnson (1994, pp. 27-8) also stress the embeddedness of knowledge in its social context. They suggest a taxonomy of economically relevant knowledge based on four broad categories: *know-what*, referring to knowledge about 'facts'; *know-why*, referring to scientific knowledge of principles and laws of motion in nature, in the human mind and in society; *know-who*, referring to specific and selective social relations; and *know-how*, referring to skills. The first two categories have the common characteristic that they can be embodied in databases. In contrast, know-who and know-how cannot be translated easily into codes understandable by other agents and therefore they are not commodities in the normal sense. Some know-who can be captured in databases listing, for example, the contact details and expertise of individuals. However, much know-who can only be obtained through the formation of special social relations that give access to experts and the efficient use of their knowledge. Similarly, some know-how can be sold as patents and as turnkey plants, but important parts remain tacit and cannot be removed from their human and social context. To some extent, such knowledge can be exchanged in the labour market, although it is often specific and related to its original context: 'One might say that important elements of tacit knowledge are collective rather than individual. Here take-overs and mergers may be regarded as attempts to gain access to tacit knowledge and know-how' (Lundvall and Johnson 1994, p. 30). It is then useful to make the distinction between tacit and codified knowledge particularly in the light of the dramatic rise in the valuations placed upon intangible assets and intellectual capital. When discussing the nature of codified versus tacit knowledge, as well as distributed knowledge resources, it is questionable whether it is at all possible to understand any type of (specialised) knowledge in isolation from its context.   Indeed, such understanding may be dependent on complex knowledge bases.

The value of knowledge is difficult for users to gauge before they have acquired and absorbed it.   This gives rise to difficulties in the market exchange of knowledge, since to reveal its value necessitates an irreversible knowledge transfer.   There are likely to be significant problems associated with the market exchange of knowledge which arise from uncertainty and risk due to information asymmetries between buyers and sellers. The exchange of knowledge gives rise to problems of adverse selection and moral hazard[2] that may prevent such transactions occurring in the open market. Furthermore, the ease with which codified knowledge can be reproduced and distributed at low or zero cost tends to undermine private ownership, hence the need for intellectual property rights. The risks and uncertainties that arise in the market exchange of knowledge are reduced by the development of networks and a relationship of trust between the parties involved. Reputation and accreditation by relevant professional bodies are important mechanisms reducing uncertainty.

Codified knowledge, with the appropriate contractual arrangements, may be transferred embodied in a tangible form as blueprints or patents, in machinery, as part of licensing and franchise agreements or trade between agents. Tacit knowledge, though, often requires time to acquire; it may, for example, be gained during an apprenticeship or a period of 'learning by doing' (Arrow 1962, drawing on Polanyi 1958). Consequently, it is not as easily traded as knowledge in codified form.   Even when knowledge is codified the tacit element remains uncodified and consequently the transfer of codified knowledge alone may fail to facilitate the successful transfer of knowledge.   The socialisation and learning procedures necessary for the successful transfer of tacit knowledge require co-presence and co-location between the transmitter and receiver.   Much tacit knowledge is developed interactively and shared within networks (Foray and Lundvall 1996). Face-to-face contact and the establishment of a relationship of trust and mutual understanding may be of particular importance to the transfer tacit knowledge (Roberts 2000).

The costs and ease of producing and distributing knowledge depend on the its nature.   As already noted, some codified knowledge can be easily reproduced and distributed at low or zero cost. By comparison, the cost and ease of reproduction and distribution of tacit knowledge (especially collective) may be high. The extent of the tacitness and collective element, relative to the codified component, of any knowledge asset or procedure has important implications for its tradability and the marginal cost of reproduction. Subsequently, this has implications for the nature of knowledge circulating in the economy.

As already stated, KIBS play a major role in the transfer of knowledge between economic agents (Miles et al. 1995). According to Antonelli (1999, p. 173) such firms perform two important functions in the economic system: first they are containers of proprietary 'quasi-generic' knowledge, extracted by means of repeated interactions with customers and the scientific community; and secondly, they act as an interface between that knowledge and the tacit knowledge buried in the routines of firms.

Knowledge assets as well as knowledge services/products have become increasingly ownership-based in modern societies, in many instances to the same extent as land and labour. However, the difficulties incurred in the market exchange of knowledge are accentuated by lack of an adequate institutional framework for the protection of knowledge assets, at a national and international level. In certain circumstances knowledge and innovations embodied in industrial processes and products or creative expressions may be protected by the patent system or by copyrights, but in other cases, the best form of protection is to keep knowledge assets within the boundaries of the firm in the form of trade secrets (Chapters 10 and 14). The creation and diffusion of knowledge and innovation in the private sector is stimulated by the profit incentive. However, for this incentive to work, an effective system for the enforcement of intellectual property rights (IPR) must exist. Currently, the effectiveness of the IPR systems is being challenged by the increasing significance of innovations embodied in intangible assets. In addition, the increased speed of new knowledge creation and innovation to some extent makes any IPR systems of protection redundant. In the past a firm might have been able to earned monopoly profits from an innovation for several years, however, now in sectors experiencing short product cycles this is not possible, even with effective IPR protection.

The differences between knowledge and other commodities have crucial implications for the way that a knowledge-based economy must be organised (Stiglitz 1999). Unlike other factors of production which experience decreasing returns in relation to their increased use, knowledge benefits from increasing returns. Stiglitz highlights the potential for new knowledge and technology to undermine competition through increasing returns to scale, 'winner-takes-all' and 'lock-in' effects. Others, such as Kay (1999), dismiss such concerns, pointing to the potential of new knowledge and technology to increase competition. Nevertheless, in a knowledge-based economy there is a clear need for government policy that not only encourages the development of knowledge creation, dissemination and application capacities, but also intervenes to ensure an appropriate level of market competitiveness. Moreover, exclusive reliance on the market for the provision of knowledge may not always result in the optimum economic or social outcome, especially given the large externalities arising from certain types of knowledge. Government intervention is essential to ensure both economic and social efficiency in the production, distribution and use of knowledge (Lundvall and Johnson 1994; Hodgson 1999).

The increasing significance of knowledge and innovation in economic activity is reflected in theoretical developments in the field of economics, most notably in studies of change and development. Until recently, changes in knowledge and technology were classified as exogenous variables and therefore excluded from models of economic growth. However, in recognition of the importance of knowledge, mainstream economists, such as Romer (1994) among others, are incorporating changes in knowledge and technology into long-term growth theory by developing endogenous growth theories. However, the mainstream economists' awkward treatment of technology (even when treated endogenously) shapes their growth theories with a static underpinning. New approaches and great contributions to economics have come from scholars taking a broader perspective. Their ideas have been integrated with the branch of economics known as 'evolutionary economics' (Nelson and Winter 1982). In their long-term theorising attention is focussed on the causes and consequences of firms' changing knowledge structures and dynamic capabilities, which evolve only in an accumulative, incremental and path-dependent manner. Along with market and price mechanisms, they are recognised as the main factors shaping corporate performance, international competitiveness, economic change and growth. However, although those new approaches may be important contributions for understanding the significance of knowledge and innovation in economic activity, they are entirely manufacturing based in their way of theorising, conceptualising and measuring. Hence, much contemporary economics on the rise of the service economy unfortunately, but justifiably, takes the form of an attack on most economics, which has been developed around problem solving for manufacturing.

2.3   SERVICE AND KNOWLEDGE-BASED ACTIVITY

The rising importance of services in the economies of advanced industrialised countries, together with their role in the process of innovation and knowledge creation and dissemination more generally has been highlighted. This section supports the analysis presented above by reviewing a range of data concerning services and knowledge. There are many problems with the *existing* conceptual and measurement framework applied in national and international statistical accounts and related literature, which have been thoroughly discussed in the services literature (for example, Griliches 1992). Griliches even argues that the current measurement methodology may be underestimating the contribution of services to innovation and output growth, which may have prevented a clear understanding of productivity and growth in the economy as a whole. Numerous reviews of these problems stress the importance of improving existing indicators and data sets and developing new ones (for example, OECD 1996a). Clearly, such literature raises important issues concerning the validity and reliability of measurements of service and knowledge based activity. Consequently, the data presented here must be viewed in the light of the weaknesses inherent within it.

2.3.1   Service Economy *Statistics*

Value added, employment and industry structures
As the figures presented in Tables 2.2 and 2.3 demonstrate, in major industrial economies total services account for more than 60 per cent of value added (with the US and UK leading with about 70 per cent), and for more than 50 per cent of employment (with the US and UK leading with about 75 per cent).   In this context 'total services' include the International Standardisation Industrial Classification, ISIC 6 (wholesale and retail trades, hotels and restaurants), ISIC 7 (transport, storage and communication), ISIC 8 (finance, insurance, real estate and business services), ISIC 9 (community, social and personal services), as well as 'producers of government services' and 'other producers'.

As argued earlier, KIBS, typically associated with 'ISIC 8', play a key role in the new service economy facilitating the flow of information and technologies between firms and sectors (Miles 1996; Miles et al. 1995; Tomlinson 2000, forthcoming). These services account for between 20 per cent and 40 per cent of services value added, and for about 20 per cent of services employment in major industrial countries, apart from in Japan and Germany (Tables 2.2 and 2.3). In these two countries, the outsourcing of KIBS is less common, consequently, employment in knowledge-based service occupation is instead incorporated within other (manufacturing) sectors. Although the degree of outsourcing differ across nations, in Chapter 3 it is illustrated how services generally are becoming essential providers of intermediate service-input to industry.

Table 2.2 Services value added (at current prices) in major industrial economies

Country	Value added: ISIC 6	Value added: ISIC 7	Value added: ISIC 8 (KIBS)	Value added: ISIC 9	Value added: producers of government services	Other producers	Value added: Total services (Share of KIBS in %)	Share of Total services in Total economy (%)
USA ($ billions – 1994)	11,27.90	411.00	1,801.60	758.70	827.00		4,926.20 (36.57)	71.10
Japan (Yen billions – 1995)	61,200.00	31,469.00	85,712.00	82,095.00	38,968.00	10,883.00	310,327.00 (27.61)	64.26
UK (£ billions – 1995)	84,706.00	50,835.00	158,224.00		*135,737.00**		429,502.00 (36.80)	71.08
Germany (DM billions – 1995)	290.86	182.57	464.24	737.16	381.86	94.67	2,151.36 (21.57)	62.22
France (FF billions – 1996)	1,177.00	442.10	1,816.00	487.70	1,309.80	61.90	5,294.50 (34.23)	67.36

Note: * Italic number contains the aggregated 'ISIC 9, producers of government services as well as other services producers'.

Source: Traced from Statistics on Value Added and Employment, Services, OECD (1997)

Table 2.3 Services employment (thousands) in major industrial economies

Country	Employment						Total services (Share of KIBS in %)	Share of total services in of total economy (%)
	ISIC 6	ISIC 7	ISIC 8 (KIBS)	ISIC 9	Producers of government services	Other producers		
USA (1994)	26,748	5,236	18,206	21,131	18,424	–	89,745 (20.28)	75.08
Japan (1995)	11,105	3,752	3,123	15,461	4,005	1782	39,228 (7.9)	58.82
UK (1995)	4,970	1,307	3,633		6,745*		16,655 (21.81)	75.62
Germany (1995)	4610	1,933	1,043	6,492	5,559	1814	21,451 (4.86)	61.53
France (1996)	3,938.50	1,295.80	2,513.30	1,613.60	6,295.60	–	15,655.80 (16.05)	70.25

Note: * Italic number contains the aggregated 'ISIC 9, producers of government services as well as other services producers'.

Source: Traced from Statistics on Value Added and Employment, Services, OECD (1997)

Services trade

Finally, the impact of services is also apparent in the trade statistics where they account for about 25 per cent of all exports in the US and France, and about 17 per cent of all exports in the UK (Table 2.4). The importance of KIBS as export or trade sectors is equally documented, with the UK leading with almost 35 per cent of all services export arising from the KIBS sector.

Table 2.4 Services trade 1990*

Country	Service sectors export out of total economy (%)	ISIC 8 (KIBS) export out of total services (%)
USA	26.39	27.90
Japan	15.42	12.27
UK	17.31	34.36
Germany	11.74	11.91
France	23.34	30.87

Note:* Services includes ISIC6, ISIC7, ISIC8, ISIC9, Producers of government services and Other producers.

Source: OECD (1995).

2.3.2   Knowledge-Based Statistics

Information and communication and global networks

The knowledge-based economy has often focused on the important role of information and communication and their capacity to generate global networks. Rising yearly US patent flows within 'Telecommunications' and 'Office equipment and data processing systems' (Figures 2.1 and 2.2) indicate the explosive pace of technological development in these sectors since about 1980. However, there are significant regional differences in the use of various forms of communication and information (Table 2.5). It is interesting to note that television is the most used media broadly defined, telephone is second, and daily newspapers third, except for the low-income countries where daily newspapers are second. From these figures, it is evident that the so-called information and communication paradigm is only relevant to the major economies of the world, other areas of the world, in particular low-income countries, are excluded.

Figure 2.1: Yearly US patent flows in Telecommunication

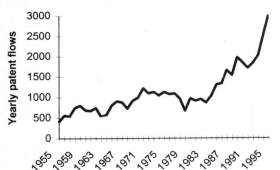

Notes: Patent classes within Telecommunication with the highest patent flows are 'Multiplex communications', 'Pulse or digital communications', 'Telephonic communications', 'Telecommunications (general)'. In 1995 they accounted for about 90 percent of the patent flows within the sector.

Source: US patent database held at the University of Reading.

Figure 2.2: Yearly US patent flows in Office equipment and data processing systems

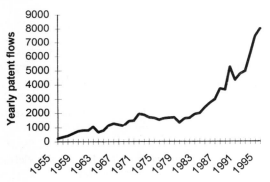

Patent classes within Office equipment and data processing systems with the highest yearly patents flows are 'Electrical/electronic computers and data processing systems', 'Static information storage and retrieval', and 'Dynamic magnetic information storage and retrieval'. In 1995 they accounted for about 82 percent of the patent flows within the sector.

Source: US patent database held at the University of Reading.

Educational capabilities and involvement in R&D

Levels and degrees of communication and information ought not to be seen isolated from educational capabilities. One of the most *basic* indicators of this is the adult illiteracy rate (Table 2.6). Although this is less than 5 per cent in high income countries, worldwide 21 per cent of males and 38 per cent of females experiences illiteracy, these figures rise to 35 per cent and 59 per cent respectively in low income countries.

Exploring tertiary enrolments related to science and technology, in the world's most developed countries, it is evident that engineering, with the exception of France, attracts the highest share of students followed by natural science or mathematics and computer science (Table 2.7). This is not surprising since, as research based on US patent data reveals, mechanical engineering is still the largest scientific base of the economy although electrical/electronics is among the fastest growing (Patel and Pavitt 1994b; Andersen 1998). Nor is it surprising that enrolments in transport and communications do not appear in the statistics, which in this International Standard Classification of Education (ISCED) scheme includes 'air crew and ships' officers programs, railway operating trades, road motor vehicle operation programs and postal service programs'. Furthermore, compared to other service sector activities, 'Transport, storage and communications' (ISIC 7) contributes the lowest value added to GNP and the lowest share of employment in most major economies today (Tables 2.2 and 2.3).

Finally, with respect to the major countries' degree of participation in science and technology research and development it is not surprising to see that Japan has the highest degree of scientists and engineers in R&D followed by US and Germany. Mansell and Wehn (1998) have recently emphasised the importance of educational capabilities and involvement in R&D, as well as the importance of regional and global information technology, communication and global networks, for sustainable regional and global development.

Table 2.5 Communication and information*

	US	Japan	UK	Germany	France	Low income	World
Daily newspapers 1994 (per 1000 people)	228	576	351	317	237	12	98
Television sets 1996 (per 1000 people)	806	700	612	493	598	47	211
Telephone main lines 1996 (per 1000 people)	640	489	528	538	564	11	133
Mobile telephones 1996 (per 1000 people)	165	214	122	71	42	0	28
Personal computers 1996 (per 1000 people)	362.4	128.0	192.6	233.2	150.7	–	50.0
Internet hosts (per 10,000 people)	442.11	75.80	149.06	106.68	49.86	0.06	34.75

Note: * These figures of course take into account the possibility of sharing communication and information channels. (No data was available on for these countries on radios.)

Source: Data traced from United Nations World Development Report 1989/99.

Table 2.6 Adult illiteracy rate 1995 (people 15 years and above)

	Male %	Female %
Low-income countries	35	59
Middle-income countries	12	25
High-income countries	Less than 5	Less than 5
World	21	38

Source: Data traced from United Nations World Development Report 1989/99.

Table 2.7 Science and technology and tertiary enrolments*

	US	Japan	UK	Germany	France
Scientists and engineers in R&D (per million people)	3732	5677	2417	3016	2537
Enrolment in natural science (% of 20–24 age group)	2.6	0.7	2.6	2.2	7.1
Enrolment in mathematics and computer science (% of 20–24 age group)	2.7	0.2	2.2	1.8	–
Enrolment in engineering (% of 20–24 age group)	4.2	9.0	4.7	5.8	1.2
Enrolment in transport and communications (% of 20–24 age group)	–	0.0	–	0.0	–

Notes:* Enrolment categories are defined in accordance with the International Standard Classification of Education (ISCED) scheme level 5 through 7 programmes (which basically covers different degrees of university programmes). Data are from the most recent year available as defined by the source.

Source: Data traced from United Nations World Development Report 1998/99.

2.4   EMERGING ISSUES

A number of new phenomena have been identified in the discussion outlined above, including the changing role of services within the economy generally and particularly within innovation processes. Moreover, the emergence of new KIBS, and the increasing importance for production in general of a number of knowledge-intensive activities and factors are apparent. Related issues concern, for example, user–supplier interactions, the intensified management of information and knowledge, and the general class of intangible assets as opposed to tangible assets of capital.

The motivation for this book, as outlined in Chapter 1, is to bring together a variety of different perspectives and recent empirical research on these phenomena. The aims include developing our understandings of the inter-connections between these phenomena, and suggesting a number of theoretical, empirical and policy-oriented approaches. The remainder of this chapter maps out the emerging issues and themes that form the basis for the succeeding chapters. In brief, these can be placed under three distinct headings:

- The New Demands for Knowledge, and New Types of Knowledge: Here consideration is given to the issues arising from the role of new technologies, and new understandings of knowledge, both as activities and as intangible assets.
- Services Firms as Innovators – Actors, Sectors, Activities, Strategies: The second set of themes and issues are those arising from consideration of the increasing importance of specific services for production and innovation, and vice versa.
- Towards Emerging Systems: The final major set of themes and issues arise when knowledge, innovation, and services are examined from a system perspective.

2.4.1   The New Demands for Knowledge, and New Types of Knowledge

The pervasive diffusion of new ICTs into many areas of economic and social activity is enabling more extensive and rapid flows of information and knowledge generally. This in turn helps to create the expectation that more detailed and rapid transfer of information and knowledge is possible and desirable, or in other words it helps to create *new demands for information and knowledge* – there is a process of positive feedback. With respect to services, the sheer scale, complexity and variety of the pervasive diffusion of ICTs is firstly enabling, and indeed demanding, the emergence of a wide variety of new service entities which either utilise ICTs for some other function, such as logistics (see Chapter 5 on ecommerce), or are required for such utilisation, such as computer maintenance, training and advice (see Chapter 6 on Web services). These service entities are sometimes separate firms or organisations, and sometimes new units or departments, such as the now ubiquitous IT department (parts of which may of course then be outsourced to a new service entity, see Chapter 8). Secondly, however, this same pervasive diffusion of ICTs is in turn generating new demands specifically for services based on the provision of information, knowledge or expertise. A classic example of this is the rapid rise in 'consultancy firms', but the rise in lobbying and pressure groups could also be considered in this light, and the emergence of environmental consultancy firms (see Chapter 7) spans the two.

In addition, there has been extensive discussion of changes in the production of scientific and technological knowledge, focussing on the new levels of complexity and variety both in the character of that knowledge and in its production. One of the classic formulations is to distinguish between 'Mode 1' and 'Mode 2' styles of knowledge production (Gibbons et al. 1994). Mode 2 knowledge, in contrast to Mode 1, is interdisciplinary or 'transdisciplinary', rather than set within traditional academic disciplines; it is governed largely by the problematics arising within the 'context of application' rather than academic problems and interests and is thus more 'reflexive'; and it is more heterogeneous and transient, and less hierarchical[3]. This reconfiguration has been enabled, at least partly, through new ICTs and/or the increasing importance assigned to user–supplier interactions. However, it is clear that this reconfiguration will create additional demands, first for new or other types of knowledge input, and secondly for new forms of organisation and co-ordination, such as information and knowledge management (see Chapter 9). It has been argued that KIBS build and support knowledge infrastructures via production, transformation, combination and accumulation of distributed knowledge resources (Miles and Boden 2000), and this is very much the essence of the mode 2 style of knowledge production. In the context of new or other knowledge inputs, the different types of knowledge which have been recognised as being important, in addition to the scientific and technological knowledge mostly considered in the literature, may be social, organisational, and strategic management knowledge, information-based knowledge, cultural knowledge and market awareness, as well as aesthetic knowledge (Andersen and Miles 1999).

2.4.2   Services Firms as Innovators - Actors, Sectors, Activities, Strategies

The complex interrelations between knowledge, innovation and services have been elaborated above. A number of issues emerge from these inter-relations, and these will be examined further, in various ways, in many of the succeeding chapters. These issues can briefly be summarised as follows:

- The issue of distinguishing between innovations developed for the clients of service firms and functions, and innovations developed for the service firm or function itself.
- The emergence of a wide variety of new service firms, functions and organisations.
- In particular, the emergence of specific types or sectors of new service firms, and especially the growth of KIBS, which are vital *intermediary actors* within innovation processes in general (Chapters 5, 6 and 7).
- The possibility that, in general, service firms are becoming more knowledge-focussed and engaging in more knowledge-type activities, as they seek to improve their own innovative potential and to enhance their central role in general innovation processes.
- This finally raises the issue of which strategies service firms might adopt, and especially strategies for managing and protecting their intellectual assets (see especially Chapters 9 and 10).

2.4.3   Towards Emerging Systems

In this section issues arising from the inter-relations discussed above are considered in a broader system perspective. The first and most obvious starting point is that of the systems of innovation approach (see Chapters 13 and 15 for extended discussions), originally developed in relation to the *national* context by Freeman, who defines a system of innovation as 'the network of institutions in the public and private sectors whose activities and interactions initiate, import, modify and diffuse new technologies' (1987, 1). Increasingly attention has focused on *sectoral, regional or local*, and *international or supra-national* systems of innovation, and on the institutions and firms shaping, engaged in, as well as affecting the knowledge-based activities central to innovation – such as learning, searching, exploring, marketing and finance.

It is clear that service firms, functions and organisations potentially play central roles within any particular system of innovation, and yet, as amply demonstrated in Chapter 13, this role has generally been ignored or side-lined. Thus, for instance, service functions and firms have always played a key role in the identification of market and competitor knowledge, and in the organisation of the delivery of new product offerings. Indeed, it is useful to consider whether the knowledge-intensive activities so central to any innovation system have begun to develop systemic features of their own, quite distinct from any surrounding system of innovation. The suggestion arising from previous extensive research is that KIBS, and especially technology-based KIBS (t-KIBS), are contributing to *a new knowledge infrastructure* (Miles et al. 1995; Antonelli 1999), an infrastructure that complements the first knowledge infrastructure largely constituted by universities together with public and semi-public research institutes of different kinds. This approach clearly has much in common with Gibbons et al. (1994) discussion of Mode 2 knowledge production, discussed above.

In this view, KIBS have come to play a central role in transferring, and in many cases creating and combining, knowledge resources in innovation systems. They are doing this directly through their provision of services, and indirectly through facilitating the mobility of highly educated personnel. The direct roles played by KIBS have much in common with the roles of organisations within the public knowledge infrastructure. There is evidence that there is a shift from the traditional public knowledge infrastructure to the private, second knowledge infrastructure. Thus, in employment terms, the knowledge services of t-KIBS are rapidly gaining in importance, while public and semi-public R&D institutes generally have become relatively less important.

There is also some evidence of a tendency towards a blurring of the boundaries between services offered by the public knowledge infrastructure and KIBS services. Nevertheless, the two infrastructures generally play different roles as providers of technological knowledge resources within innovation systems. Universities primarily have technological relations with large R&D-intensive manufacturing firms and (in the case of social and administrative knowledge) the public sector. KIBS firms have a much broader spectrum of clients, including public authorities and some smaller firms. Small and medium enterprises generally have a relatively low level of internal competence, and limited financial resources, so many of them lack capabilities for making effective use of KIBS and often rely on public or semi-public sources for external technological knowledge. Large firms and other organisations, however, benefit disproportionately from both knowledge infrastructures.

One feature that clearly has great significance for inter-relations between knowledge, innovation and services is the regulation of and accounting for intellectual capital. The term intellectual capital is derived primarily from recent developments within accounting which seek to present an account to shareholders that is more disaggregated than merely intangible assets (see Yakhlef and Salzer-Mörling 2000). It includes and specifies such elements as customer capital (such as brand and loyalty), the intellectual assets embodied in employees, as well as R&D expenditure and intellectual property such as portfolios of patents and copyrights. However, what is particular for services is that knowledge may not just be an 'asset', but also an intangible output (for example, for consultancy firms and law firms), or it may be embedded in intangible output (for example, music and software). Hence, generating and capturing rent from knowledge and intangibles (sometimes via exploitation of the IPR system) becomes central, and often determines the manner in which KIBS are provided. One of the paradoxical features of current IPR systems is that they have been developed to deal with an essentially manufacturing-based industrial structure. Consequently there are a number of mismatches between IPR systems and the new configurations of economic and industrial activity. However, as argued in Chapter 14, such mismatches cannot be understood independently from the history of technology and corporate capitalism, IPR rationales, the evolution of IPR legislation and corporate strategy, which all take part in shaping the innovation system.

Finally, then, this section has highlighted a key feature of system perspectives, namely the requirement to allow for interactions between different systems, rather than assigning any one particular system supremacy. Thus there may, as has been noted within the literature on innovation systems (see Chapter 15), be complex interactions between local, national, sectoral, international and supranational systems; and further complex interactions between the imperatives of globalisation, the activities of international capital markets, the systems of IPR regulation, and the activities of international service and manufacturing firms.

2.5   CONCLUSIONS

In concluding, it is necessary to identify several aspects of the interrelations between knowledge, innovation and services that require further analysis beyond that present in this book. These aspects are taken up more fully in Chapter 16. One of the primary difficulties facing researchers investigating knowledge, innovation and services arises from the lack of suitable information, and this is especially so with respect to service innovations and output. These problems are accentuated by the way economists theorise, conceptualise and measure, as well as the weaknesses inherent in existing data sets. This is a major issue, but one which is not addressed in this book. Nevertheless, the issue is reflected in the variety of methodological approaches applied in this volume, with some contributors conducting relatively small-scale qualitative studies (Chapters 5, 6, 7 and 9), while others have applied alternative approaches placing more emphasis on conceptual analysis (Chapter 15).

The lack of suitable information also accounts for some of the gaps in the analysis within this book. For instance, there is very little external research on the ways that *knowledge and perceptions* of the operation of capital markets and other financial aspects of innovation processes, as opposed to the brute operations of finance and equity capital, may have impacts on those innovation processes. If, as suggested above, international capital markets interact with other systemic features of the relations between knowledge, innovation and services in essentially complex, rather than simple ways, then there is clearly a requirement for further research on this complexity. This could, for instance, shed light on the continuing debates about the relative 'short-termism' of UK equity markets.

A second significant omission relates to the absence of public services, such as transport, health, social services and education, in the discussions contained within this book. Public services undoubtedly play an essential role in the new service economy. Indeed, the role of such services in supporting the infrastructures of national innovation systems, or 'the learning economy', is increasingly recognised, and although there has been extensive historical and sociological research on many of these services, there is clearly a need for further work here.

Thirdly, the suggestion of an emergent 'second knowledge infrastructure' consisting of KIBS firms and other organisations separate from the traditional public and semi-public knowledge infrastructure of universities and research bodies, clearly informs much of the discussion in some of the early chapters of this book. However, the relation emerging between these two infrastructures is not explored, but evidence suggests a possibility of significant tensions emerging between them[4]. Such relationships and tensions are worthy of investigation.

Fourthly, the issues raised by the growing significance of knowledge and innovation in the new service economy are considered throughout this book in the context of the advanced industrialised countries. Clearly, these developments do have important implications for the development process, and consequently for the fate of the developing world. Developing countries face specific challenges, for example, higher rates of adult illiteracy (Table 2.6), which not only impair their ability to absorb knowledge and innovation but also their capacity to establish successful indigenous knowledge creating competencies. The role of knowledge in the development process has attracted much attention in recent years (see for example, World Bank 1999; Mansell and Wehn 1999). Consequently, there is no attempt to contribute to this growing field of literature here. However, by analysing the issues and themes arising from the relationship between knowledge, innovation and services in advanced countries, where they are currently most apparent, insights of wide ranging relevance are gained.

Finally, the view taken on the relations between knowledge and innovation in this book is one concerned primarily with technological innovation and scientific knowledge, although with some significant amendments to take account of service innovation. However, there are good reasons for taking a broader view of knowledge and the innovation process. First, an analysis of knowing as an activity and a dynamic process in which the place of reflexivity is recognised can provide greater depth to the appreciation of knowledge. Secondly, there is a strong argument that static knowledge and knowing as an active process are in fact merely two particular forms of the many complex relations between knowledge and power. This relationship between knowledge and power is central to an understanding of the evolution of knowledge. For although knowledge may be thought of as a source of power, power itself influences the creation, dissemination and application of knowledge. The political and economic power to influence knowledge and innovation is evident in the size of government and commercial budgets devoted to R&D. Thirdly, the power to develop and use knowledge is unevenly distributed. This is most obvious in relation to the input of developing countries into the process of knowledge creation compared to that of the advanced industrialised countries. However, such inequalities also exist, and are to some extent increasing, within the advanced industrialised countries. Knowledge and innovations can, then, be seen as an expression of the social relations within a given society, and as these social relations evolve, so do the directions of efforts to create, disseminate and apply knowledge. An important issue arising from the emergence of new service economies relates to how the changes that they bring about will influence the pattern of inequality and the nature of social relations. In particular, what will the subsequent impact be on knowledge and innovation?

The overview of the new service economy provided in the chapter reveals that a full understanding of knowledge and innovation requires an analysis that draws on many disciplines such as economics, institutional theory, sociology, political economy and psychology. The chapters that follow will not be able to draw on all of these lines of work, by any means! However, they will contribute to our understanding of knowledge and innovation in the new service economy, by considering some of the perspectives that can usefully be applied from the field of innovation studies and those areas of social science that border most closely on it.

NOTES

1. See, for example, Boisot (1998), for an extended discussion of the distinction between knowledge, information and data.
2. Adverse selection is an ex ante information problem referring to a situation when one party in a potential transaction is better informed about a relevant variable in the transaction than the other party. Moral hazard is an ex post information problem referring to action which parties in a transaction may take after they have agreed to execute the transaction.
3. See also Chapter 12 for discussion of current trends in innovation outsourcing, which points out that there was a significant degree of independent R&D prior to World War II, not based within firms or academia, which then declined. This thus argues against any simplistic identification of Mode 1 with academic and in-house R&D.
4. For example, in the recent disputes over genetically modified (GM) foods in the UK, one could argue that bodies such as the Consumers' Association and environmental pressure groups such as Greenpeace are more characteristic of the second knowledge infrastructure, in that they adopt non-traditional non-disciplinary methods of knowledge generation and dissemination. One could further argue that, in the disputes over GM foods, the UK government listened initially to the 'first knowledge infrastructure' – that of established university-based traditional. In the event, of course, the UK government, like the supermarkets, listened also to the second knowledge infrastructure and acceded to the need for clear labelling.

3 The Contribution of Knowledge-Intensive Services to the Manufacturing Industry

Mark Tomlinson

3.1 INTRODUCTION

This chapter examines the contribution that certain services make to output in the manufacturing sector, using input–output tables for the UK from 1990. The methods used to explore the relationship between certain services and manufacturing sectors are: first, a production function approach to attempt to show significant relationships between different sectors; and secondly a Leontief approach to measure flows of goods and services from sector to sector.

The increasing prevalence of service sector activity in the world economy is frequently seen either optimistically or pessimistically. On the one hand the theory of post-industrial society put forward by, for example, Bell (1973) is suggestive of a brave new world where increasing wealth creation has allowed consumers to expand their purchases beyond mere material goods to a whole new realm of useful or luxurious services. For some commentators, on the other hand, (such as Cohen and Zysman, 1987), there are potentially damaging consequences to modern economies due to the uncontrolled expansion of services and the erosion of our manufacturing bases. This is obviously a caricature, but it captures the extreme poles of the debate.

Moreover, service sector growth is frequently seen in the context of wealth created by manufacturing sectors. This conception of the service sector has sometimes resulted in services being seen as unproductive laggards with little to contribute in real terms to economic growth or productivity. Also it has not been until fairly recently that the service sector has been sufficiently disaggregated in economic statistics to allow useful analysis of its constituent parts. This is despite its growing importance – such as the fact that services now constitute over 60 percent of world output in industrialised nations and around half of all output in developing countries (see Williams, 1997, Table 2.2, p. 17).

The more pessimistic 'deindustrialisation debate' suggests that the economy has been fundamentally transformed to the detriment of manufacturing output and employment, although some economists (in the US case at least) have actually argued that the proportion of output accounted for by manufacturing has not in fact deteriorated, and only the employment level in this sector has declined. If this is the case, then increases in productivity in manufacturing are more than compensation for the loss of jobs and there is probably little to worry about. However, current debates are underway in the US about the unsatisfactory way in which many essential economic statistics are calculated. For example, quality changes are not sufficiently accounted for, and figures are frequently subjected to a number of *ad hoc* adjustments that have almost certainly led to the overestimation of manufacturing output. If there is a consistent overestimation of manufacturing output as a proportion of GDP then this suggests that there may be a corresponding underestimation of output in services.

The figures used for measuring services versus manufacturing output are usually based on an uncritical reading of official national statistics, although some recalculations are possible using known errors in the calculation procedures. Mishel (1989) attempted to rectify some of the errors and recalculated the figures for the US economy between 1973 and 1987. He showed that the loss of 3 million manufacturing jobs could be completely accounted for by the previously hidden fall in manufacturing output as a proportion of GDP. The official estimates show that manufacturing output appears to be fairly constant throughout the same period at around 22 percent of all output. Mishel's revised figures show a fall from 24.0 percent in 1973 to 20.8 percent in 1987. These figures also suggest that there has been a stronger growth in manufacturing productivity in the 1980s compared with the 1970s, but the outlook remains a pessimistic one for US manufacturing.

In contrast to the pessimism of manufacturing oriented economists, Miles (1996) has argued that 'services are increasingly bound up with the activity of all sectors of the economy – "producer services" … show the most rapid growth in services employment' (p. 4). Rather than seeing services as a separate and peripheral economic factor mainly producing superfluous consumer products, emphasis is beginning to shift towards looking at services as an integrated part of a potentially dynamic economic system. Thus the distinctions between manufacturing and services can be seen as becoming blurred, especially where knowledge intensive business services (KIBS) are concerned. Manufacturing companies that may once have had their own in-house business service departments may now be using increasingly specialised professional services from outside. Many of these services were previously hidden in the official statistics within 'manufacturing' sectors.

The rapid growth of business services in the UK may in part be because they have been out-sourced by manufacturing firms. This is how Freund et al. (1997) put it with regard to the German case (where this has not yet happened to such a great extent):

> It is often stated that Germany has fallen behind in the shift from manufacturing to services and therefore we could easily create new jobs via more services. In fact, industrial production is embedded in a large volume of services, providing the infrastructure for the direct manufacturing activities. In Siemens more than 50% of labour is indirect and could be considered as a service. However, the company is in the category of manufacturing industry and therefore contributes like many other companies of similar profile to production statistics and is not accounted for under services. (Freund et al.1997; p. 220)

Furthermore, many manufacturing industries have transferred the bulk of their production to developing countries and this has also fuelled the relative growth of the service sector in first world countries. As Williams (1997) points out the new international division of labour (NIDL) has resulted in manufacturing being increasingly located in less economically developed nations:

> In this NIDL, the control and command functions are located in a network of global cities in the developed nations whilst physical production is increasingly dispersed into a host of developing countries where new and efficient technology can be allied to lower labour costs. (Williams 1997; p. 18)

So on the one hand we have a trend towards deindustrialisation in the developed world coupled with growing strength in manufacturing industry in parts of the developing world. The deindustrialisation debate needs to take this consideration on board rather than simply bemoaning the decline in domestic manufacturing.

If services are to be seen as potential drivers of the economy rather than subordinate to manufacturing, then empirical evidence should show that at least some services make a significant contribution to economic development and manufacturing in particular. Can we demonstrate that knowledge and business services' inputs significantly contribute to manufacturing output? The methods employed to do this are expounded in the next section.

3.2 DATA AND METHODOLOGY

Two methods of analysis are proposed for exploring the scale and significance of the contribution of knowledge intensive business services to manufacturing. The first of these is to use a modified form of Cobb–Douglas production function. The second is to use Leontieff input–output techniques. Both these techniques are explained below. UK data from 1990 are used in both cases.

3.2.1 The Production Function Approach

Studies by Katsoulacos and Tsounis (2000, forthcoming) and Antonelli (2000, forthcoming) outline and test a production function approach to assess knowledge and business service inputs into the economy. The additional results reported below complement their work.

Antonelli argues that the development of knowledge within industries is strongly influenced by the network structure of firms and the strengths of the relationships between them. Furthermore:

> it is here that KIBS firms, providing access to scientific and technological information dispersed in the system, are of central importance. In terms of connectivity and receptivity, KIBS function as holders of proprietary 'quasi-generic' knowledge, from interactions with customers and the scientific community. They operate as an interface between such knowledge and its tacit counterpart, located within the daily practices of the firm. (Antonelli, forthcoming)

Thus by achieving an appropriate organisational environment and developing different forms of co-operation, knowledge–intensive services provide a major platform for fruitful connectivity and receptivity between sectors and firms. So, as well as in-house R&D and so on as the base of knowledge and performance of firms, certain services should be taken into account as providers of *essential information, knowledge and technologies throughout the system.*

Antonelli splits the knowledge-based services into two types: communication services and business services. He expects to see a correlation in the rates of growth in the use of these two types of service and to see the effects of increasing value added through their use. These data are available through national accounts statistics and input–output tables for a number of European countries using different databases (Italy, UK, Germany and France are included).

His first hypothesis is demonstrated for all the countries. That is the use of business and communication services is indeed correlated across sectors, as is their rate of growth.

He also estimates (among others) a technology production function for each country. This implies that:

Log $Y = a + b \log K + c \log L + d \log$ CBS
where:
Y = sectoral value added
K = capital stock estimated from investments
L = labour costs
CBS = inputs of communications and business services
a, b, c, d are coefficients to be estimated

The results show that communication and business services are significant determinants of sectoral value added for all the countries. The units of analysis in these models were the sectors in the input–output tables for the individual years for which the tables were available.

We modify the model slightly. Following Windrum and Tomlinson (1999), the model estimated below is:

$\log Q = a + b \log M + c \log L + d \log B$
where:
Q is sectoral gross output
M is manufactured (that is, material inputs)
L is labour costs
B is communication and business service inputs (referred to collectively as KIBS)
a, b, c, d are to be estimated.

The rationale for this approach is detailed in the appendix to Windrum and Tomlinson (1999). Also we only include manufacturing sectors in the models rather than the whole economy.

3.2.2   The Leontief Framework

Katsoulacos and Tsounis (forthcoming) effectively replicated the Antonelli study to some extent using Greek data: similar results emerged, showing the significant influence of knowledge-based services on output. However, they also went further and attempted to measure direct and indirect knowledge-intensive business service (KIBS) flows to each sector with Greek input–output tables using a Leontief framework. This enables flows of commodities and services to be traced from sector to sector. Whether the flow is direct or by a more circuitous route can be ascertained. This has an advantage over production function analysis which only takes *direct* inputs into account.

Technological and knowledge diffusion is still not very well understood, especially when it comes to flows from one firm or sector to another. The understanding of the nature of these flows is extremely important. This assists us in comprehending the influences of technological advance, innovation and knowledge generation in one sector, and how they impinge on another, through the network of overlapping entities within an economy and the various degrees of interconnectedness between sectors.

New technologies and sources of knowledge do not necessarily impact on different sectors in the same way. Knowledge will diffuse at different rates depending on the receptivity of the consuming sector and the ease with which the producing sector can generate useful and generalisable information.

Papaconstantinou et al. (1996) suggest that there are basically two types of diffusion: disembodied and equipment embodied diffusion. Disembodied diffusion is the 'transmission of knowledge, technical expertise, or technology in a way that does not necessarily involve the purchase of machinery and equipment incorporating new technology' (1996, p. 9). This type of diffusion is particularly appropriate where producer services are concerned. These concepts involve two further notions: research spillovers and absorptive capacity.

Research spillovers are the means by which new technology or knowledge developed by one sector or firm becomes available in one form or another to other entities. *Absorptive capacity* is the propensity of a firm to effectively absorb the potential available through exposure to knowledge and information that is generally in the public domain.

If we think of an economic system as a set of interlaced sectors in a network, then the nodes of the network must be analysed to assess the degree to which sectors can interact with each other. As it may be the case that knowledge generated in one sector does not take a direct route to the receiving sector, but flows through one or several intermediary channels, the Leontief approach is particularly apt. Thus the network analogy of the economy is extremely useful in this context.

The Leontief approach depends on the analysis of input–output tables which detail the levels of consumption and production of goods and services from all industries to all other industries. Such tables are compiled by government statisticians typically every five years. In principle the tables provide a resource for tracing the pathways through which knowledge and/or technology originating in one sector or sectors diffuses (via consumption) to other sectors. Input–output tables are not without their problems, but they are the only real coherent source of information for the analysis of flows and interconnections between sectors. Some advantages and disadvantages are outlined below:

Some advantages of input–output tables:
- They can simultaneously take account of supply and demand factors thus overcoming some of the one-sidedness of supply–push and demand–pull approaches.
- Indirect as well as direct flows from sector to sector can be estimated.
- Similarities and differences between sectors, and the extent to which sectors are interconnected, can be revealed.

Some disadvantages:
- Sectoral output is treated as homogeneous. Thus if a million pounds worth of goods are transferred from A to B and a million pounds worth from A to C, then B and C are assumed to have received the same amount of knowledge, technology or whatever from A.
- A sector's R&D, technology and knowledge and so on is assumed to be embodied in its output.
- Tables are only available for certain time points (usually at least 5 years apart), and sectoral definitions change over time, making comparisons difficult.
- Disembodied spillovers are not necessarily captured.

More formally in a Leontief input–output system, if vector **s** represents direct knowledge-based business services inputs, then it can be shown that:

direct + indirect KIBS inputs = $\mathbf{s}^T (\mathbf{I} - \mathbf{A})^{-1}$
(for 1 unit of output)
Where **I** is the identity matrix and **A** is the matrix of input–output coefficients (see Leontief, 1986).

This is the model used by Katsoulacos and Tsounis, which we attempt to replicate using UK data.

Using Greek input–output tables for 1980 and 1988 Katsoulacos and Tsounis calculated the direct and indirect KIBS inputs per unit of output for each sector and reported them. However, the results seem far from clear or conclusive. The top ten users of KIBS in 1988, for instance, were not all high-tech or themselves knowledge-intensive: they included the drinks sector, the leather goods sector and the perfume sector. More predictable ones included pharmaceuticals and financial services. The results are not easy to interpret. An investigation using UK tables is presented below which gives potentially more comprehensible results.

3.3 INPUT–OUTPUT TABLES FOR 1990

The input–output tables for the UK in 1990 (ONS 1995) have several advantages over the tables used by Antonelli and Katsoulacos and Tsounis. For instance, they have a much more detailed sectoral breakdown of services as well as manufacturing. This results in a total of 123 sectors (including services) and their interconnections. We now turn to the replication and expansion of the above studies with this more detailed dataset.

Also, rather than just collapsing all the categories of knowledge-based business services together in the production function analysis, each one is added to the production function model separately. This allows us to assess the *relative* impact of each service on output in the manufacturing sector. Note here that only manufacturing sectors (but also including extractive industries, utilities and construction) are included in the models as the aim is to explore the extent to which knowledge-based services are drivers of manufacturing output. In contrast the aforementioned studies included all sectors in their models. The impact of services on other services is not so relevant to a discussion of deindustrialisation and is thus not pursued here. We now present the results of applying the two methods described.

3.3.1 Results from the Production Function Approach

The results of the basic production function model using manufacturing inputs, labour and communication and business services are shown in Table 3.1. Communication and business services (KIBS) here are comprised of the following sectors:

- Banking and finance
- Insurance
- Auxiliary financial services
- Estate agents
- Legal services
- Accountancy services
- Other professional services
- Advertising
- Computing services
- Other business services

- Postal services
- Telecommunications

Table 3.1 Basic production function models for UK manufacturing 1990

	Coefficient	S.E.	t-statistic
Constant	2.147	0.157	13.705**
Manufactures (M)	0.508	0.049	10.283**
Labour (L)	0.098	0.057	1.714*
KIBS (B)	0.342	0.066	5.206**

Notes: * significant at 10% level
        ** significant at 5% level

As can be seen here the basic model has significant coefficients on both manufactured inputs and a marginally significant coefficient on labour. However, there is a highly significant coefficient on the KIBS variable. This implies that, contrary to some of the deindustrialisation theories outlined above, certain business services are highly significant in determining output in manufacturing.

As we have included several sectors in the KIBS inputs we now turn to models where the components have been disaggregated to determine whether certain inputs are more influential than others. Table 3.2 shows several production functions where the KIBS variable has been disaggregated into its constituent parts (note that estate agents and auxiliary financial services are excluded as they contribute to very few sectors – that is, as the logarithm of zero cannot be computed most cases are lost).

The results in Table 3.2 demonstrate that certain services appear to have a more significant impact on manufacturing than others. The significant ones at the 1 per cent level are banking and financial, legal, accounting, advertising, other business and computing services. The largest coefficient seems to be banking and financial services at 0.340. Insurance, advertising, other business services, postal and telecommunications services appear to be less significant inputs for manufacturing output (telecommunications and postal services are actually completely insignificant). Thus communications services, peripheral services and insurance appeared to have less impact than other knowledge based business services in the UK manufacturing economy in 1990. This does not mean to say that they are insignificant with respect to other services outputs.

Table 3.2 Production function using different service inputs

Manufac-tures	0.481** (0.041)	0.612** (0.048)	0.544** (0.050)	0.553** (0.051)	0.556** (0.050)	0.632** (0.051)	0.550** (0.049)	0.620** (0.049)	0.625** (0.046)	0.619** (0.047)
Labour	0.142** (0.043)	0.166** (0.066)	0.237** (0.051)	0.229** (0.051)	0.244** (0.050)	0.248** (0.063)	0.227** (0.050)	0.216** (0.060)	0.267** (0.060)	0.264** (0.066)
Banking	0.340** (0.042)									
Insurance		0.163* (0.062)								
Legal			0.152** (0.036)							
Accoun-ting				0.153** (0.041)						
Adverti-sing					0.137* (0.035)					
Other prof						0.048** (0.062)				
Compu-ting							0.158** (0.037)			
Other business								0.096* (0.048)		
Postal									0.029 (0.038)	
Tele-comms.										0.038 (0.058)
Constant	2.49** (0.147)	2.46** (0.260)	2.72** (0.247)	2.58** (0.237)	2.51** (0.217)	2.03** (0.209)	2.64** (0.229)	2.17** (0.205)	2.10** (0.248)	2.11** (0.282)
R^2	0.97	0.94	0.95	0.95	0.95	0.94	0.97	0.94	0.94	0.94
F statistic	797**	472**	533**	511**	517**	438**	797**	456**	471**	470**

Notes: Standard errors in brackets: * significant at 5% ** - significant at 1%.

3.3.2   Results from the Leontief Approach

Moving on to the results of the Leontief approach, here the impact of direct and indirect communications services and business services have been calculated separately from the above formula. These figures show the amounts of the specific inputs required to produce one unit of output in the receiving sector. As might be expected from the production function analysis where telecommunications and postal services were not significant, the results here show that direct and indirect flows of communication services inputs are not nearly as large as in other services, although one notable exception in this regard is the insurance sector which shows substantially higher communication service inputs than other sectors.

Table 3.3 shows the top 20 users of business services (excluding communication services) in the economy as a whole in 1990. Note that this table represents relative, not absolute, use of these services; it is based on the proportion of business services input in a unit of output.

Table 3.3 Top 20 users and manufacturing users of business services (direct + indirect) in 1990

Rank	Users of business services	Manufacturing users of business services
1	Insurance	Printing and publishing
2	Owning and dealing in real estate	Oils and fats
3	Other business services	Electronic consumer goods, records and tapes
4	Computing services	Soap and toilet preparations
5	Renting of movables	Miscellaneous foods
6	Personal services	Confectionary
7	Estate agents	Animal feed stuffs
8	Other professional services	Tobacco
9	Legal services	Alcoholic drinks
10	Banking and finance	Sports goods and toys
11	Air Transport	Soft drinks
12	Ownership of dwellings	Metal doors and windows etc.
13	Auxiliary financial services	Construction
14	Advertising	Wood furniture, shop and office fittings
15	Printing and publishing	Industrial plant and machinery
16	Accountancy services	Fruit, vegetable and fish processing
17	Sea transport	Pharmaceuticals
18	Oils and fats	Textile machinery, machinery for other materials
19	Electronic consumer goods, records and tapes	Leather and leather goods
20	Distribution and repair of vehicles, filling stations and other goods	Extraction of metalliferous ores and minerals nes

It can be seen that most of these are actually services themselves showing that service sectors are in fact heavily dependent and interconnected with themselves; but there are some notable additions from manufacturing – printing and publishing, oils and fats, and electronic consumer goods. The top 20 manufacturing users of business services are shown in Table 3.3.

Table 3.3 demonstrates the wide range of manufacturing sectors that have a heavy reliance on direct and indirect knowledge based services inputs. These range from heavy manufacturing sectors such as extraction of metalliferous ores and industrial plant and machinery, to numerous food sectors, and to specialised manufacturing sectors such as pharmaceuticals and instrument engineering, although the fact remains that the top service user of KIBS (insurance) uses more than twice the volume than the top manufacturing user of KIBS (printing and publishing – the actual figures are 0.62 versus 0.27).

The results show that the reliance on KIBS tends to be concentrated in services themselves, but the explanation for the top manufacturing users of KIBS seems to require further investigation. As the results of the Katsoulacos and Tsounis study suggest, we have to explore further the uses of KIBS by certain manufacturing sectors. For instance, how can we explain the 'oils and fats' sector having higher KIBS use than 'pharmaceuticals'. Perhaps pharmaceuticals are more heavily dependent on in-house knowledge which is not revealed through the above analysis. Several other food industries also seem to be relatively heavy users, but this may be because of use of advertising and marketing services rather than knowledge impinging on production processes. Unfortunately we do not have the space to explore these issues here. Perhaps case studies or company accounts would also shed more light on this.

3.4   CONCLUSIONS

Knowledge-based business service inputs appear to be highly significant whether we look at their influence within the services or manufacturing sectors. In fact there is little evidence that these service inputs are less significant for manufacturing output than material inputs. There is therefore a convincing argument that manufacturing sectors in modern societies rely on these services. Rather than the manufacturing base being eroded away, the development of specialised services may in fact be beneficial to manufacturing and help foster the innovation in manufacturing necessary for growth. The manufacturing versus services dichotomy is then rather unhelpful. The knowledge based service sector is an integral part of the economic system rather than an unproductive or parasitic laggard.

Freund et al. of the Siemens corporation concentrate on the role of IT in manufacturing in the modern age and go as far as calling for the terms 'manufacturing' and even 'product' to be redefined.

> In many cases it is not the product itself the customer is interested in, but the services which can be provided by the product. ... The definition of manufacturing has to fall in line with this new understanding. Manufacturing means producing *all* the capabilities the customer wants to find in the product and this understanding covers *all the steps* in the value-adding chain. (Freund et al. 1997, p. 217, italics in original)

Here it can be seen that there is an acknowledged shift in the perceptions of leading manufacturers about the nature of industrial production. No longer can manufacturing be seen as the fundamental, isolated and superior branch of production in the modern western world (although the complications of third world industrial development remain to be addressed). The existence of other supporting and inextricably linked sectors and modes of activity are crucial. Freund et al. continue:

> Furthermore, manufacturing also comprises support systems, namely logistics support. Logistic objects are all kinds of material and physical components *and* all kinds of information necessary or created while pursuing the value-adding chain. (ibid., p. 217, italics in original)

In other words there is already an implicit understanding in western industry that knowledge and information contribute to value-added – as has partly been demonstrated in this chapter. The importance of services for manufacturing, especially knowledge-based services, has been shown for the UK in 1990. The importance of KIBS inputs to the output of manufacturing has also been demonstrated, confirming and reinforcing the work of other studies for other EU countries. The bleak outlook presented by arguments based on a deindustrialisation frame of reference should perhaps be viewed in the more promising light of results such as these.

4 Competition and Innovation Amongst Knowledge-Intensive and Other Service Firms: Evidence from Germany

Bruce S. Tether and Christiane Hipp

4.1 INTRODUCTION

Services dominate value added and employment in advanced industrial economies. According to Eurostat (1999), services account for two-thirds (67 per cent) of value added and employment (68 per cent – or almost 100 million jobs) in the European Union. In the United States, services account for an even higher proportion of value added (73 per cent) and employment (76 per cent). In Japan, services are less important, although they still dominate value added (62 per cent) and employment (59 per cent). Moreover, not only do services dominate economic activity, they are also increasing their dominance over time. In 1970, services accounted for less than half (46 per cent) of total employment in the European Union. In less than 30 years, therefore, services have increased their share of total employment in the European Union by 21 per cent (Eurostat, 1999); they are the only broad sector of the economy that has expanded in terms of employment. This trend will continue into the foreseeable future.

Despite their economic significance, services remain poorly understood by economists and analysts of innovation, with widely different views of services and 'the service economy'. At one extreme, services, and 'service products', are taken to be synonymous with knowledge: the service economy is 'the knowledge economy'. At the other extreme, services are characterized as dominated by highly routine (even monotonous) activities, requiring people with few skills to perform tasks that many regard as degrading.

Services are the poor relation to manufacturing, and the service economy is a low-skill, 'hamburger flipping', economy.

The truth is that services include both knowledge-intensive activities and unskilled (even demeaning) work, and much else besides. In this chapter, we examine the patterns of competition and innovation amongst German service firms. We will highlight some of the diversity within the service sector, although we are particularly concerned with comparing knowledge intensive against 'other' service firms, and technically-based services against non-technically-based services. We begin, though, with some notes from the literature on services and service innovation.

4.2   SERVICES AND INNOVATION

We began by highlighting the economic significance of services, and pointing out that, despite their significance, they have not been widely researched by economists or analysts of innovation. Recently, however, the tide has begun to turn, and considerable efforts have been made towards gaining a fuller understanding of services and service innovation. These efforts include both case study work and wide-scale surveys. We shall draw upon one of the pioneering wide-scale surveys for the analytical sections of this chapter. To contextualize our analysis, we highlight some of the main findings from the literature on services and service innovation.

Although neglected, services have not been completely ignored by economists and analysts of innovation, and Sirilli and Evangelista (1998) provide a useful summary of the main 'peculiarities of services' commonly recalled in the literature. These include:

- *The close interaction between production and consumption*, or the *coterminality* of service production and consumption. This is thought to provide difficulties in distinguishing between product and process innovation. Gallouj and Weinstein (1997) concur, pointing out that in services the term 'product' frequently denotes a process, such as a service package, a set of procedures or protocols, or an 'act'.
- *The high information content and intangible nature of the service output.* Gallouj and Weinstein (1997) point out that whilst goods usually have autonomous physical existence, exterior to their producers and consumers, this is generally not true of services. Consequently, in services there tends to be a much hazier relationship between what is produced, and the process of production, than in manufacturing.
- *The key role of human resources in the provision of services.* Service production, and service innovation, is usually thought to depend heavily

on the knowledge and skills of the people involved in the processes of production and innovation. As Gallouj and Weinstein (1997, p. 543) argue: 'One of the major features of service activities is undoubtedly the fact that the "technologies" involved usually take the form of knowledge and skills embodied in individuals (or teams) and are implemented directly when each transaction occurs, rather than in physical plant or equipment'. However, many services, such as transport and communications, banking and insurance and (large-scale) retailing depend just as heavily on physical plant and equipment technologies as do manufacturers.

- *The critical role of organisational factors in firms' performance.* This again relates to the intangible nature of most services, as well as to the question of whether 'product' innovations can be distinguished from process innovations in services. Arguably, services achieve short-term gains through 'product' innovations concerned with improving the relationship between what is provided and the service users' needs. These 'product' innovations are related to 'front-office' operations. Meanwhile, innovations in 'back-office' activities, which relate primarily to the process of service production, may be more important for the long-term efficiency of the service provider. Here, the terms 'front' and 'back office' have both figurative and literal meanings.

The above provides a summary of some of the peculiarities of services, but services are also diverse. Other contributions to the literature have provided some guideposts to this diversity. One such contribution is that by Soete and Miozzo (1989), who built upon Pavitt's (1984b) taxonomy, which was primarily concerned with technological activities within manufacturing. Using a similar approach, they identified four types of service business:

1. *Supplier dominated sectors*, for example, public and social services, such as education and administration, and personal services, together with independent retailers. These remain subject to the limitations of Pavitt's original characterisation of services as being dominated by their suppliers in terms of their technological assets and technological development trajectories. Amongst supplier-dominated firms, competition tends to be based on the skills of the workforce and price, rather than on technological advantages.

2. *Production-intensive, scale-intensive and network services.* These services, by contrast, involve considerable divisions of labour with the simplification (and co-ordination) of production (and/or delivery) tasks, and the substitution of (skilled) labour by machines. Within this group, two types of services can be distinguished:

3. *Network services*, which are heavily dependent on information communication technology (ICT) networks (for example, banks, insurance and telecommunication services). The development of ICTs has facilitated improvements in the complexity, precision and quality of services offered by these providers; ICTs have facilitated customisation, and have also had an important role in setting standards in many service activities.
4. *Scale-intensive services*. These are dependent on physical networks (for example, transport and travel services, and wholesale trade and distribution), which can provide economies of scale and of scope. There is also a heavy dependence on hardware technologies developed in the manufacturing sector.
5. *Specialised technology suppliers and science-based services*, for example, software and specialised business services. The main source of technology here is the innovative activity of the services themselves, which is itself heavily dependent on the skills and know-how of the people employed.

Soete and Miozzo emphasise that sectors, as conventionally conceived, can reside in more than one of these categories. They cite the communications sector, which is both a scale-intensive sector and a science-based, specialist supplier sector. Retailing is another example: whilst small independent shops are largely supplier dominated, the retail multiples are much less so. Large retailers use both physical and information networks to achieve economies of scale and scope.

A strength of the Soete and Miozzo taxonomy is that, like Pavitt's original, it emphasises diversity, both in relation to the (competitive) activities of firms, and in relation to the nature and purpose of innovation. For example, in routine services, or services amenable to high levels of standardisation, competition on price is intense, and thus cost reduction has often been the primary motivation for innovation. Yet there are many service activities that emphasise quality, and customer satisfaction, rather than price minimisation. An emphasis on quality and customer satisfaction tends to require closer interactions with the service user, and an increase in the variety of services provided.

A weakness of the Soete and Miozzo taxonomy is its emphasis on technology, and thus technological innovation, in a narrow sense. Non-technological innovation is overlooked. Other categorisations of service activities have not privileged technology and technological innovation in a narrow sense. For example, Silvestrou et al. (1992) differentiate service activities by the nature of their interactions with clients/customers. These authors identify two extreme categories of service organisations: (1) *Professional service organisations* – which have relatively few, highly customised, process-oriented transactions, with relatively long client contact times associated with applying considerable judgements to meeting customer needs, and (2) *Mass service organisations* – which have many customer transactions, typically involving short client contact times, little client specific judgement, and little customisation.   They also identify a third category – *service shops* – which is described as falling between these two extremes in terms of the above described features.

Also of note is de Jong's (1994) distinction between infrastructure services, value added services, pre-specified services and ad hoc services. According to de Jong, *infrastructure services* are those, such as telecommunications and transport services, which make use of fixed network facilities and provide (largely) standardised services. *Value added services* include accountancy and are highly specialised but are used by different types of businesses. *Pre-specified services* are services that use a standard approach or method in order to satisfy a general demand, such as repair, maintenance and cleaning services, whilst '*ad hoc*' services include management and engineering consultancy services and are called upon for specific, one-off problems. De Jong considers that the potential for pursuing economies of scale and scope can be represented in terms of the (potential) degree of standardisation or variety in the services offered. Consequently, it is likely that innovation dynamics will differ across these types of services – perhaps with opposing tendencies toward standardisation and flexibility.

In the analysis that follows, we do not seek to allocate firms to any of the above categorizations, but we are interested in comparing different types of services.   In particular, we are interested in comparing technically-based services with non-technically-based services, and with comparing more knowledge-intensive services with less knowledge-intensive services.   To some extent, our analysis compares what Soete and Miozzo describe as *specialised technology suppliers and science-based services*, or what de Jong identifies as *value added* or '*ad hoc*' *services*, with the general population of service firms.

4.3   THE DATA-SET AND CHARACTERISTICS OF THE SURVEYED FIRMS

The data-set we examine is the response to the 1995 survey of German service companies. This survey was carried out, on behalf of the German Ministry for Research and Technology, by the Centre for European Economic Research (ZEW), the Fraunhofer Institute for Systems and Innovation Research (FhG-ISI), and the Institute for Applied Social Research (INFAS). The survey focused on the innovative activities of the firms, and was based on the approach to surveying innovation suggested by the OECD's Oslo Manual (OECD, 1996a). The survey also served as a pilot exercise for the second European Community Innovation Surveys (CIS II), which were carried out in 1997.

The 1995 German survey covered a wide range of commercial services, including wholesaling and retailing, transport and communications, banking and insurance, other financial services, scientific and technical services, software, business services, plus cleaning and waste disposal, publishing and rental and real estate services. Public sector services were excluded, as were hotels and catering, personal services, and other non-business oriented services. More than 11,000 service companies were sent the questionnaire, of which 2,900 responded; a response rate of 27 per cent (See Licht et al., 1995 for a detailed discussion of the sample). In the analysis that follows, only firms with 10 or more employees are included.

For this chapter, we divided the firms by two dimensions. First, we divided by the firms between those active in the technically oriented sectors and those in other sectors. We did this because we were interested in whether the different types of knowledge at the heart of these firms affected their patterns of activity and innovation. *Technical Services* are here defined as including only computer software and engineering services. Of firms with 10 or more employees, 321 were classified as technical service firms. This was only 15 per cent of the total sample (with 10 or more employees). The great majority (1,882) were classified as *Other Service* firms.

Secondly, we divided the firms between those with higher and lower levels of 'knowledge intensity'. Our concern here is with disembodied rather than embodied knowledge (Evangelista, 1999). That is, we are only concerned with the knowledge possessed by people, rather than the knowledge embodied in machines, devices or computer programs. Ideally, a measure of disembodied knowledge requires information about both the education and the experience of the workforce. Unfortunately we have no evidence on the experience of the workforce within the firms. We therefore used educational attainment alone as our proxy for disembodied knowledge. More particularly, we used the proportion of employees in the firm with university degrees as our indicator of knowledge intensity. Those firms in which half or more of the employees had university degrees were classified as *High Knowledge-Intensity Firms*, whilst the remaining firms were classified as *Lower Knowledge-Intensity Firms*. We appreciate that this is not an exact measure of knowledge intensity – experience is likely to count for at least as much as education (for example, Bill Gates famously dropped out of Harvard before graduating to found Microsoft). Nonetheless, by educational attainment, 268 firms were classified as high knowledge intensity firms. This was only 12 per cent of the sample; the vast majority of firms (1,935) being classified as lower knowledge-intensity firms.

Combining these two dimensions provides a four-fold classification of the surveyed firms:

- *High Knowledge-Intensity Technical Service Firms – HKI-Technical.* These were 155 firms active in the technical service sectors of computer software or engineering services and in which half of more of the employees were university graduates.
- *Lower Knowledge-Intensity Technical Service Firms – LKI-Technical.* These were 166 firms active in the technical service sectors of computer software or engineering services but in which university graduates accounted for less than half their total employment.
- *High Knowledge-Intensity Other Service Firms – HKI-Other.* These were 113 firms not active in the technical service sectors of computer software or engineering services but in which university graduates constituted half or more of their total employment.
- *Lower Knowledge-Intensity Other Service Firms – LKI-Other.* These were 1,769 firms not active in the technical service sectors of computer software or engineering services and in which university graduates constituted less than half their total employment. This group was by far the largest, and serves as a reference group against which the behaviour of the firms in the other groups can be compared.

The first notable feature of this distribution is the high level of knowledge intensity amongst firms in the technical service firms. Almost half the technical service firms were classified as being highly knowledge-intensive, compared with just 5 per cent of the firms in the 'other' sectors. This points immediately to the importance of disembodied knowledge in technical services. Yet some technical service firms appear to get by with few highly educated workers, whilst some non-technical service companies have very high proportions of graduates in their workforce. As will be seen repeatedly in the analysis that follows, differences between groups of firms tend to be relative differences, or shades of grey, rather than absolute, black and white, differences.

Small companies with 10 to 49 employees were the largest group of survey respondents in all four of our categories of firms. In three categories small firms dominated: 65 per cent of the HKI-Technical firms were small, as were over half the LKI-Technical and HKI-Other firms. The LKI-Other firms tended to be larger, with a quarter having 250 or more employees. This pattern fits with our expectations from the literature. The LKI-Other category includes many services that are exploiting economies of scale (and scope) which tend therefore to be organized into larger firms. Economies of scale in particular do not exist to the same extent amongst many technical and knowledge-intensive activities (as defined here), and thus there is a tendency towards smaller-scale operations. However, again we note that these are tendencies, rather than absolute differences – all of our categories of firms included some small, some mid-sized, and some large firms.

Having introduced the firms and the classification we will employ, we turn to the characteristics of the firms, as revealed by the survey. Our analysis is in two parts. The first part concerns the basis of the service firms' competitiveness and the nature of the services they provide in terms of the degree to which they are adapted to users' requirements. The second part considers the innovation-related activities of the firms.

4.4   COMPETITIVENESS AND STANDARDISATION IN SERVICES

The survey asked about the sources of the firms' competitiveness. More precisely, the survey asked the firms to rank, on a scale of 1 (not relevant) to 5 (very important), each of nine possible sources of competitiveness. In the analysis that follows, we consider the proportions of firms that scored each factor 'important' (4) or 'very important' (5).

Unsurprisingly, service firms tend to derive their competitiveness from satisfying their customers' demands – this is the basis of competitiveness in services (as it is in manufacturing). Eighty-five per cent or more of the service firms declared that 'the provision of high quality services', 'delivery on time', and 'flexibility in meeting different demands' were important (or very important) to their competitiveness. Even higher proportions (94 per cent) of the technical and high knowledge-intensity service firms recognized high quality as important to their competitiveness.

These findings may seen banal, but the importance attached to quality contrasts with the much smaller proportions of firms that indicated low prices were central to their competitiveness. Low prices were considered important by half the LKI-Other firms, the largest group in our analysis. This still meant half of these firms did not identify low prices as central to their competitiveness. Amongst the technical and knowledge-intensive firms, smaller proportions indicated low prices were central to their competitiveness (36 per cent and 39 per cent respectively). Notably, the majority of the technical and knowledge-intensive service firms did not seek to compete on low prices.

Amongst the firms as a whole, low prices ranked only seventh out of the nine factors. Apart from the abovementioned 'high quality', 'flexibility' and 'timeliness of delivery', the firms were also more likely to highlight the importance of 'image and advertising' (73 per cent), 'the provision of additional support or advisory services' (63 per cent) and 'the provision of a broad service range', than low prices, as important sources of their competitiveness. The two remaining sources of competitiveness that were less frequently identified as important than low prices were the use of multiple delivery channels (24 per cent) and competing through the provision of novel services (37 per cent). This last finding is interesting, as in conjunction with the others, it suggests that novelty for its own sake is not generally important to competitiveness in services.

In general, this pattern of response highlights the importance of quality and flexibility (to meet different users' demands) as central to most service firms' competitiveness. Price obviously matters, but a large proportion of the firms do not seek to compete mainly on price. Price competition exists within a context of quality and flexibility generally geared to meeting users' demands.

Figure 4.1 Income to the firms from standardised, customised and bespoke services

Given this context, to what extent did the firms provide standardized services – that is services that were not changed to meet particular users needs, and to what extent did they provide either customized services – that is services adapted to users' requirements, or one-off, bespoke, services, designed specifically to meet individual customer's requirements?

We analyse this through a survey question that asked the firms to divide their income (in 1994) into that from standardised services, that from partially customised services and that from bespoke (or specialised) services. There are admittedly some philosophical difficulties with this question, not least in distinguishing between customised and bespoke services. We discuss the question and the results that arose from it at greater length in another paper (Tether et al. 2000). Here we just take the results and analyse them at face value.

By contrast, amongst the high knowledge-intensity technical service firms, an average of less than half the firms' income (44 per cent) was earned from standardised services. Instead, these firms tended to earn the majority of their income from services adapted or designed to suit particular user's needs. On average, these firms earned 28 per cent of their income from partially customised services, and 28 per cent of their income from bespoke services.

The other two groups of firms in this analysis, the lower knowledge-intensity technical service firms and the high knowledge-intensity other service firms lay between the two group discussed above in terms of their average division of income from standardised, partially customised and bespoke services.

The mean distribution of income from these different types of services is interesting, but it hides the variety that existed within each of the groups. Another way of examining these data is through a classification of firms by the extent to which they earned their income from standardised, partially customised and bespoke services. To make this classification, we identified the firms that earned all of their income from standardised services as 'Wholly Standardised' service providers. Those firms that earned two-thirds or more of their income, but less than all, from standardised services were classified as 'Largely Standardised' service providers. As mentioned earlier, the distinction between customised and bespoke services is problematic. The remaining firms can either be interpreted as a single group or divided up further. We divided them into two groups – 'Bespoke' service providers were those that earned at least one-third of their income from one-off, bespoke services, whilst the remaining firms, which were mainly those that derived a high proportion of their income from partially customised services, were classified as 'Largely Customised' service providers.

Comparing this classification with the groups of firms we are investigating again revealed substantial differences. Only 7 per cent of the high knowledge-intensity technical (HKI-Technical) service firms earned all of their income from standardised services; 93 per cent adapted or designed some of their services to meet individual users' needs. The proportion of less knowledge-intensive other (LKI-Other) service firms that derived all of their income from standardised services was much larger, at 26 per cent. Yet this still meant that three-quarters of these firms earned some proportion of their income from services that were adapted or designed to meet individual users' needs, even if, amongst these firms, the majority earned only a small proportion of their income from the provision of bespoke services.

How do these patterns fit with the factors the firms identified as being important to their competitiveness? Clearly, the provision of bespoke and customised services relates to the identified importance of being flexible in seeking to meet different users' demands. However, a wide variety of users' demands can also be satisfied through standardised services, so long as the range of standardised services provided is sufficiently broad. The standardisation of services relates to the creation of a fixed production routine. This also allows for the replacement of labour by machines, and/or the replacement of high cost labour by lower cost labour. It is therefore unsurprising that the lower knowledge-intensity other service firms (LKI-Other), which also tend to be larger, tend to be more orientated to the provision of standardised services than the technical or knowledge intensive firms.

Table 4.1 Investment amongst the surveyed firms

	HKI Technical	LKI Technical	HKI Other	LKI Other
Investment in ICTs per employee (median, DM)	3,000	1,800	2,400	870
Total investment per employee (median, DM)	6,500	4,850	6,650	8,000
ICT as a proportion of total investment (mean)	54%	41%	44%	24%

Flexibility can be achieved through the use of higher skilled labour and/or through greater use of flexible technologies, particularly information communication technologies (ICTs). It is interesting that the technical and high knowledge-intensity service firms tended to have both more highly educated employees and to be investing more heavily in information communication technologies than the lower knowledge-intensity other service firms, amongst which investments in ICTs tended to constitute a smaller proportion of their total investments, as the table above shows.

To summarise this section, we have found that service firms tend to concentrate on quality and flexibility rather than price, and that this is reflected in the large proportion of income many service firms earn from providing services adapted or even designed to meet individual users' needs. Knowledge-intensive and technical service firms tend to be particularly oriented towards quality and flexibility and, consequently, to providing customer-specific services. There are of course some services that focus heavily on price competition and the provision of services that are not adapted to individual users' needs, but these are a minority of service firms. However, scale economies mean that whilst these firms may be relatively rare, they also tend to be large.

4.5   INNOVATION IN SERVICES

We now analyse the patterns of innovation and innovation-related activities of the surveyed firms. The first question is whether services innovate at all, and to what extent are the categories of innovation – product, process and organizational – developed with manufacturing in mind, appropriate to services.

The survey asked three basic 'innovation questions'. These asked the firms whether, between 1993 and 1995, they had introduced:

- Any 'new or significantly improved services' (Service Innovation);
- Any 'new or significantly improved methods to produce services' (Process Innovation);
- Any 'significant organizational changes' (Organizational Innovation).

The word 'technological' was not included in these questions on innovation, and thus the definition of innovation is broader than just technological innovation.

In the event, a high proportion (76.5 per cent) of the firms claimed to have introduced an innovation (of any type) between 1993 and 1995. This varied slightly between the four categories of firms being analysed here, with the high knowledge-intensity firms being slightly more likely to claim to have innovated than their less knowledge-intensive counterparts. The higher knowledge-intensity firms were also more likely to claim they had introduced a service or process innovation than their less knowledge-intensive counterparts, but there was little difference between the types of firms in the proportions that claimed to have introduced organisational innovations.

Innovation is, however, difficult to define, and other research suggests the distinction between process and organisational innovation in services may be difficult to maintain (Hipp et al, 2000; Preissl 2000). In other research (Hipp et al. 2000), we have also shown the service 'product' innovations tend to have process innovation type effects on the innovating firms, whilst process innovations also tend to affect the nature of the services provided. Consequently, whilst a distinction can be applied to service and process/ organisational innovation in services, the effects of innovations may be less clearly demarcated than is (thought to be) the case in manufacturing.

As indicators of innovation, and innovativeness, basic questions about whether or not firms have introduced new or significantly improved services, methods to produce them, or significant organisational changes, are rather crude. A better indicator is the extent to which firms committed resources to innovation. This can, in principle at least, be measured through the financial commitments firms made to innovative activities. In practice, determining whether expenditure does or does not relate to innovation is more problematic, and obtaining accurate information from firms can also be difficult. Notwithstanding these difficulties, we are able to report the average expenditure the firms made on innovation-related activities in 1994.

Figure 4.2 Types of innovation amongst the firms

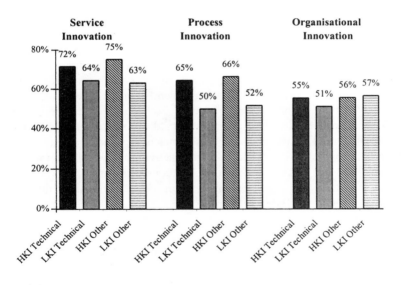

To adjust for firm size, we report this in terms of innovation expenditure per employee. The high knowledge-intensity firms tended to spend significantly more on innovation (on a per employee) basis, than their less knowledge-intensive counterparts. Both the technical and non-technical high knowledge-intensity firms spent, on average, more than 10,000 DM per employee on innovation, compared with 7,700 DM amongst the low knowledge-intensity technical service firms, and 5,400 amongst the lower knowledge-intensity other service firms. This suggests a considerably greater relative commitment to innovation amongst the technical and high knowledge-intensity firms, than amongst the general population of service firms. We should remember, however, that the category of LKI-Other firms contains many larger firms, so in absolute rather than relative terms their commitment to innovation may be considerable.

Also of interest are the components of innovation expenditure. The survey identified six categories of expenditure related to innovation. These were 'expenditures on improving production methods', 'investments in machinery and equipment linked to innovation', 'expenditures on training directly linked to innovation', 'expenditures incurred in preparing for the introduction of new services or methods to produce them', 'expenditures incurred in the market introduction of new services', and 'expenditures on R&D related to new services'. The firms were again asked to classify the importance of these on a scale of 1 (not relevant) to 5 (very important).

The category most widely recognised as important was expenditures on improved methods to produce services, but the importance of this was particularly widespread within the large group of less knowledge-intensive other service firms (LKI-Other). Investments in machinery and equipment was the second ranked category in terms of the proportion of firms identifying this as an important component of their innovation costs, and interestingly this proportion was also significantly higher amongst the less knowledge-intensive other service firms. Both these categories relate particularly to process innovation, and it would appear that this group of firms, the output of which tends to be orientated to standardised services, places a heavy emphasis on process-related activities within its innovation activities. This is in keeping with our expectations, and with the finding that these firms tend to place greater emphasis on price competition than the technical and knowledge-intensive service firms.

Cost-saving and process-related activities appear to be less significant amongst the technical and high knowledge-intensity service firms. It was shown earlier that these tend to earn a significantly larger amount of their income from customised and bespoke services. They may therefore focus more on the service provided, rather than on the process of production. There is, most probably, greater differentiation between these firms in terms of the services provided, and the quality of those services, than on the price of their services. This does not, of course, mean that the less knowledge-intensive other service firms do not also concern themselves with providing quality services, only that the relationship between quality and price is likely to be different.

Figure 4.3 Categories of innovation expenditure regarded as 'important'

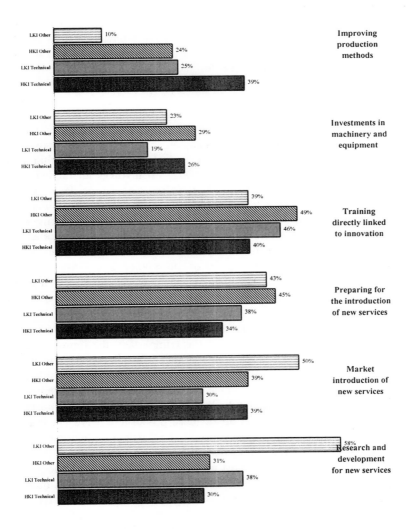

Also notable is the much greater importance of R&D activities in the innovation costs of the technical and high knowledge-intensity service firms. Amongst the less knowledge-intensive other service firms, only 10 per cent recognised R&D for new services as an important component of their innovation expenditure. Amongst the high knowledge-intensity technical service firms the proportion was four times greater, at 40 per cent, whilst a quarter of both the less knowledge-intensive technical service firms and the high knowledge-intensity other service firms also declared R&D for new services to be an important component of their innovation costs. These are remarkably high proportions, given that R&D is often erroneously considered to be the sole preserve of manufacturing. From another question on the survey we also know that half the high knowledge-intensity technical service firms conducted R&D, as did many of the firms in the other categories, including 20 per cent of the less knowledge-intensive other service firms.

Sources of information for innovation, and the extent of collaborations
We conclude our analysis with a brief investigation into the extent to which the service firms linked with other firms and organisations in their innovation activities. Successful innovation involves interactions, both within and outside the firm (for example, Rothwell 1992). It involves interacting with customers to discover how (new) products or services can be developed to suit (changing) user needs; it can also involve interacting with suppliers to source more appropriate goods or services. Other firms and institutions, such as competitors, universities and research institutions, can also be important.

To investigate these interactions, the firms were asked about the extent to which they drew upon external sources of information in undertaking their innovative activities, and the extent to which they were involved in more formal co-operative arrangements for innovation. We assess each of these questions in turn.

Concerning the sources of information used, the firms were again asked to rank, on a scale of 1 (not relevant) to 5 (very important) the significance of various sources of information for innovation. Unsurprisingly, customers were the most important external source of information. Notably, slightly more of the technical and high knowledge-intensity service firms indicated customers were important than did the less knowledge-intensive other service firms. Yet it was surprising that all of these proportions were not higher. Roughly half the firms in all four categories did not recognise their customers as being an important source of information for their innovations.

Competitors were the second most widely recognised important source of information for innovation, being identified as important by about a third of the firms. This proportion did not vary widely between the different types of service firms being investigated here. In the main, this probably relates to watching competitors and copying them, if possible, when appropriate.

Exhibitions and publications were more widely recognised as important sources of information by the more knowledge-intensive firms, as were universities and research institutes. This may be because of differences in the sorts of knowledge sought for innovation, but it may also be because these firm, with their high proportions of university graduates, are more comfortable with these sources of information than the firms with lower proportions of graduates. This said, only a small proportion of the firms of any type recognised universities, and especially research institutes, as important sources of information for innovation.

Figure 4.4 Information sources regarded as important for innovation

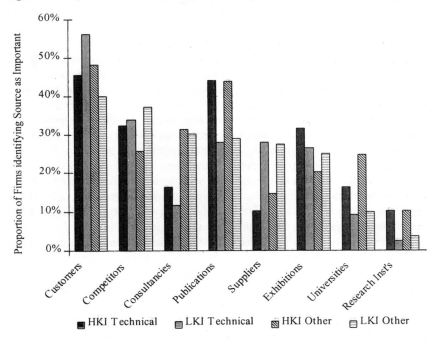

Also of note is that the less knowledge-intensive firms were more likely to identify suppliers as an important source of information for innovation, and that the non-technical service firms were more likely to recognise consultants as important sources of information. These differences may also relate to the differences in the knowledge bases of the different types of firms. Perhaps because the more knowledge-intensive firms rely heavily on their own internal knowledge assets to provide high quality services, they are less concerned with cost-reducing process innovation and exploiting suppliers (of products and services) as sources of information for innovation. The technical nature of the knowledge base of the technical service firms also seems them apart from other services in their use of marketing and other consultants. Perhaps technical service firms cannot so easily outsource those functions that non-technical services tend to outsource to consultants, or perhaps this difference reflects an inadequate understanding amongst consultants of the technical knowledge inherent to the technical service firms' activities.

With regard to collaborations, the firms were also asked whether they had engaged in any formal co-operation agreements concerning innovation projects in 1994. Some commentators suggest innovation is becoming a more highly distributed activity, and that firms are increasingly forming alliances to develop their innovations. According to our evidence, relatively few service firms have formal co-operation agreements with third parties for innovation. This proportion was lowest (at 15 per cent) amongst the less knowledge-intensive other service firms which dominate the data-set. Co-operation agreements were more common amongst the technical and more knowledge intensive service firms, and most frequent (at 38 per cent) amongst the firms with both these characteristics. This greater proportion amongst the technical and high-knowledge intensity firms, and especially amongst the firms with both these characteristics, may be due to the more complex and less standardised nature of their services.

Of the different types of organisation with which the firms may have had co-operative arrangements, customers were the most frequently identified. However, no more than 20 per cent of the firms of any type had formal co-operative agreements for innovation with their customers, or indeed any other type of external organisation. The knowledge-intensive and technical service firms, and especially the firms with both these characteristics, were more likely to have formal collaborative arrangements for innovation with their customers, as well as with their competitors, universities and research institutes, although the proportions doing so were generally small. There were no differences between the proportions of the different types of firms that had formal co-operation agreements with either their suppliers or consultants.

4.6   CONCLUSIONS

This chapter has examined the response to a widescale survey of German service firms, with particular reference to their innovation activities. Our first conclusion is that services are characterised by tremendous diversity. It is difficult to make general statements about services, and nearly impossible to make statements that apply to all services.

Our analysis showed that (in Germany at least) service firms tend to derive their competitiveness from focusing on quality and flexibility in seeking to meet the needs of different users. A significant proportion of service firms' income is earned from the customisation of services; many also provide bespoke services. Standardised services are also important, and are particularly important in more price-sensitive markets.

Most of the service firms also claimed to have innovated, in terms of new service 'products', changed production processes, and/or changed organisational arrangements. Expenditures on innovation by service firms can be high, but tend to be oriented to the process of service production in most service firms. Customers tend to be the most important source of information for innovation, which reflects the need to understand users' needs as a necessary condition for competitiveness.

Our analysis also highlighted some interesting differences between technical and non-technical service firms, and between knowledge-intensive and 'other' service firms. By the definitions employed in this chapter, these are relatively small groups of firms within the wider population of service firms – they also tend to be smaller rather than larger firms. Our analysis suggests these firms place even greater emphasis on the quality of the services they provide than the general population of service firms, and they are less concerned with price competition. They are more likely to adapt or design services to suit individual users' needs, and they are more likely to innovate. They also spend a greater amount, relative to their size, on innovation. In these firms, innovation expenditure tends to be more oriented towards improving the services provided, rather than to the process of service production or cost reductions, as is the case with services more generally. Again this is probably due to the greater complexity of the services provided, which is also reflected in the higher proportion of these firms which have co-operative arrangements for innovation with their customers and other external organisations.

Services were widely neglected by economists in the twentieth century, despite their (growing) economic importance. At the beginning of the twenty-first century greater attention needs to be paid to services, the basis of competition in services, and the nature of innovation in services. We now appreciate that services are innovative, but we need to develop a fuller understanding of the tremendous diversity that exists within the 'service sector', and that which characterises innovation in services.

5 Web Services: Knowledge of the New

Kieron Flanagan, Ian Miles and Paul Windrum[1]

5.1 INTRODUCTION

This chapter examines the knowledge-intensive business services (KIBS) active in supporting the entry of other firms into the new business environments constituted by the development of the Internet and the World Wide Web. It focuses on the professional Web design companies that have emerged to provide services to corporate clients, and on the established information providers (on-line database companies, financial information services, and publishers) that are seeking to establish themselves in the new media. It uses case studies to illustrate the important and diverse roles played by such KIBS. These case studies demonstrate the persistence of cultural and geographical determinants of business activity, even in these new environments. Before presenting this material, a little background information should be provided.

The Internet grew out of ARPANET, a distributed computer network established to support US military research (and to explore possible applications of networking more generally). This was expanded and transformed into a tool for supporting electronic communication, file transfer and remote access to computing facilities for researchers – first within the US, and later around the world. Internet-based electronic communication for businesses and, increasingly, for the general public, really took off with another innovation whose origins lie in publicly funded research – the World–Wide Web (WWW), developed by a British academic at the European Nuclear Research Centre, CERN. The WWW, and later innovations such as Web browsers, added functionalities to the Internet well beyond those envisaged by its pioneers. The user-friendly interface, means of locating and accessing information content and engaging in transactional and other communications (see Chapter 7) enabled Internet-based communications to establish a massive user base. While the WWW application was only widely released in 1991, within four years (by early 1995) it was the predominant use of the Internet.[2]

The recent expansion of the Internet is thus very much driven by WWW use, which has grown substantially faster than that of the Internet as a whole. Over the period 1993 to 1995, the proportion of traffic routed through the major Internet backbone (NSFNET) accounted for by Web use rose from 0.5 per cent to 23.9 per cent.[3] The number of 'Web sites', defined as those sites with a distinctive host name,[4] grew from 130 in mid-1993 to 650,000 by the start of 1997. Meanwhile, the share of commercial Web sites has risen dramatically. Thus, the percentage of sites with Uniform Resource Locators (URLs) ending in '.com', increased from 1.5 per cent in June 1993 to 62.6 per cent in January 1997[5] (see Figures 5.1 to 5.3).[6]

Figure 5.1 Estimated growth of Internet hosts, 1969–1999

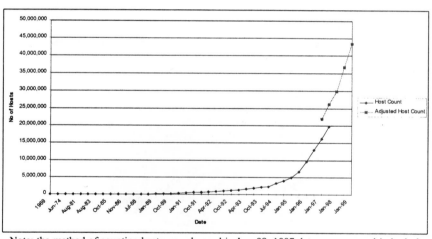

Note: the method of counting hosts was changed in Jan. 98: 1997 data are presented in both the 'old' and 'adjusted' formats, data from Jan. 98 on in the 'new' count.

Source: Network Wizards Domain Name System Survey, Jan. 1999, at http://www.nw.com/; Matthew Gray's Internet Growth Summary, Dec. 1997, at http://www.mit.edu/people/mkgray/

Commercial use of these new media is still in some sense an emerging activity. Large firms were at first mainly involved as Internet Service Providers (ISPs) and commercial bulletin board operators, whilst much of the initial WWW content was produced by computer hobbyists and academics.

But with the emergence of a large user base, and the promise of far more business and consumer use, there has been an enormous amount of commercial interest in the possibilities provided by the Web.

5.2 WEB DESIGN SERVICES

Early Websites were rarely corporate or commercial, being mainly produced by enthusiastic amateurs within organisations (generally from IT departments), and often containing little more than basic information about the company and some contact details. But with growing awareness of the technology and numbers of users, firms came to see potential commercial benefits in having a Web presence. While there is not a universal pattern, the potential features of a corporate Web presence can be seen as ranging from simple information/PR functions, through to more sophisticated catalogue and product details, through to full-blown ecommerce and aftersales support.

Figure 5.2 Distribution of hosts by top-level domain, January 1999

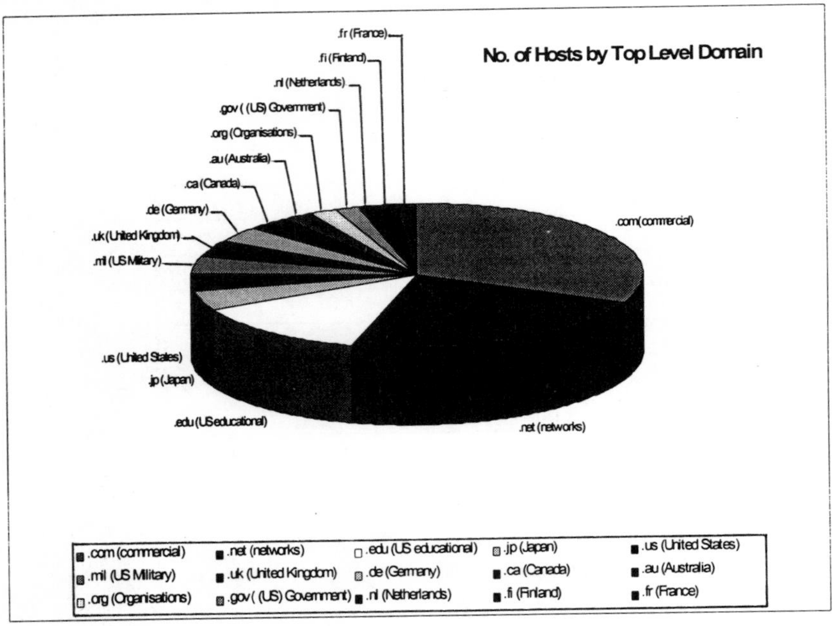

Source: Network Wizards Domain Name System Survey, Jan.. 1999, at http://www.nw.com/

Sites designed by computer technicians may have been an acceptable 'storefront' at a time when most Web users were probably also computer technicians, as the Internet became a mass-market technology, advertising and marketing concerns have come to the forefront, with attractive and functional design of Websites at a premium.

Figure 5.3 Estimated growth in number of Web sites, 1993–1997

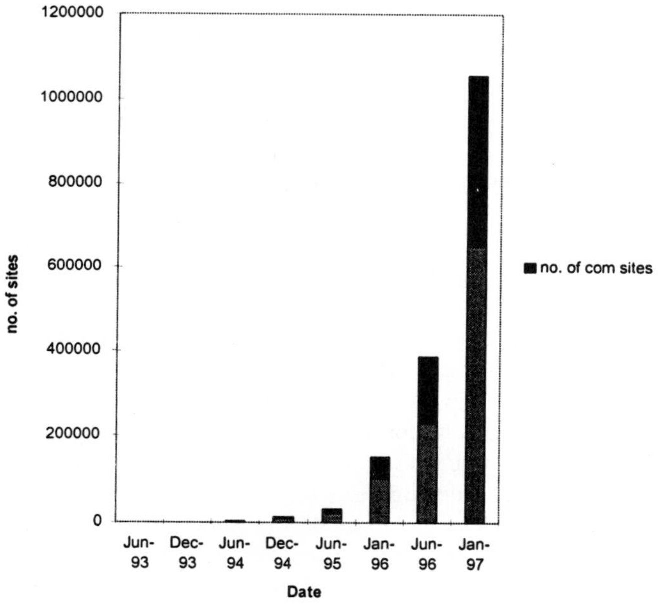

Note: Unfortunately, this survey is now discontinued, and more recent data is unavailable.

Source: Matthew Gray's Web Wanderer Survey, http://www.mit.edu/people/mkgray/ (Dec. 97).

In consequence, some entrepreneurs identified a new market niche for professional Web design services. Over recent years there has been a dramatic increase in the number of companies offering business-to-business Web design services – several hundred in the UK by the late 1990s. These Web design companies bring a variety of capabilities from a range of backgrounds – principally traditional publishing, advertising and graphic design, together with relevant IT skills. Some companies are new start-ups, sometimes consisting of little more than a single person working from their kitchen-table, others are spin-offs from established media firms. Still others are firms already established in other creative sectors, which offer Web design services to their clients as part of their portfolio of services.

It can be very expensive to develop a significant Web presence. The more complexity, functionality and interaction required, the greater the programming time and so the higher the cost. The creation and digitisation (capture) of large amounts of new content further adds to costs. More fundamentally, innovative design requires creative personnel – and the better the designers, the higher the cost. This is as true for the logical and functional design of a Website as it is for graphic design. Finally, further costs are added by maintenance and updating, periodic redesign or upgrading, the renting of server space (or connection charges), and the costs of dealing with enquiries or business generated by a Web site.

5.3   INNOVATION IN WEB DESIGN

Several broad categories of capability seem to be particularly important to innovation in Web design (and indeed to new media in general). *Form and functional* capabilities typically relate to the capture, processing and packaging of specific content asset types and to their storage and distribution. These capabilities may be both technical and creative or artistic. *Quality* capabilities include editorial and packaging expertise, skills relating to managing quality and checking for accuracy of content, capabilities relating to the generation, packaging and updating of information and capabilities relating to organising and indexing items of information. These latter logical design capabilities are also related to the level of interactivity required of the product. *Market-related* capabilities cover the detailed knowledge of the intended target market (whether large or small), knowledge of the requirements of potential users, and of the price they are willing to pay (where a charge is to be made). This knowledge frames any consideration of form and quality characteristics. Knowledge of the *area of application* is another significant set of capabilities, and one that is closely linked with market knowledge. For example, when developing a Web presence for a professional services company, knowledge of the client company's market is vital, as is an understanding of how to market to such a group. These capabilities will shape how the technical and creative skills of the Web designer are marshalled to create a site.

5.4   THE WEB IN SPACE

In order to investigate the mix of capabilities required for new media development, and their implications for the dynamics of innovation in this area, we studied several examples of small Web design services companies in the Manchester region of the UK.[7] They are relatively unusual studies of KIBS, in that we interviewed both Web service firms and their clients.

The regional focus may seem anomalous, given that so much literature on the new media suggests that IT is rendering geography irrelevant. There are certainly cases of companies who have used the Web to give themselves access to global markets that previously they could not reach, and you can order any number of traditional foodstuffs popular in a particular locale from enterprising small suppliers with a presence on the Web. However, these are truly niche services. There are also cases of firms using online services to challenge traditionally geographically-located suppliers of retail services – Amazon.com's entry into the book market is a good case in point. But where the interaction between services supplier and client needs to be intensive, propinquity still plays an important role. Indeed, much of the interchange that takes place goes on between firms located in local or regional networks.

The Greater Manchester area has a relatively large and well-established network of people and firms actively engaged in IT networks and services. Manchester has long sought to apply these technologies to regional regeneration, being the site of a pioneering (pre-Web) effort to bring telematics to small businesses and community groups (Graham 1996). A supportive structure around which an embryonic network of such firms could coalesce was provided by partially overlapping networks, linking companies working in the area's professional services, cultural and media industries. This predated the development of Internet services in Manchester, and facilitates informal knowledge exchange between members, important in a rapidly moving technology, and provides a route to knowledge acquisition through collaboration or individual recruitment. Local government, in the shape of the Manchester City Council, is generally considered by these small, creative firms to be supportive in a way that central government was not through the 1980s and early 1990s, despite its rhetoric of entrepreneurialism. But the experience of one of our case study firms in attempting to develop a Web gateway for Manchester shows that access to such support can vary enormously between different firms.

This gateway, *Virtual Manchester*,[8] was very much the product of a company called XTML (of whom more below), whose founders envisaged a skeleton Website into which local businesses, such as hotels, transport companies and others, could slot their own sites. This would constitute an effective marketing tool, and provide XTML with opportunities for new business in Web design and publishing, as companies and organisations joined *Virtual Manchester*. The site has grown rapidly, is much used, and has been widely imitated; but unlike many similar sites, it was developed entirely without government or local authority funding.   The lack of involvement by (or even blessings from) the Manchester City Council reflects its earlier commitment to the *Manchester Host*, a pre-Web local telematics initiative, and the close links this engendered between the Council and another telematics company active in Manchester, which had been responsible for development of the *Host*.

The development of networks such as this one in the Manchester area is very much influenced by the size and shape of the local economy, and of local political support.   A substantial creative services sector may not blossom in every town and city. In the (nearby) city of Liverpool, European Union grants were awarded to a local university in order to provide (free) Web design services to local firms.   Some Manchester interviewees suggested that this has reduced the opportunities for private sector Web designers, thereby undermining the formation of an indigenous Web sector in the city. (We are not in a position to substantiate this suggestion, and remain agnostic regarding it.   It is worth remembering that Liverpool (and Manchester too) is strong in another IT-based creative services sector – computer games design.) Another interesting case is *Virtual Brighton,* a successful local web resource on the model of *Virtual Manchester*. *Virtual Brighton* serves a smaller and less economically diverse community than that of Manchester, though Brighton too is located in an area with a large cluster of new media firms. Local circumstances allowed *Virtual Brighton* to grow to become the intensively used community resource which *Virtual Manchester* was originally intended to be: as well as strong local authority support, for a crucial period during the development of the site, a local cable operator's call-charging policy enabled people to make free evening calls to the local ISP.[9]

5.5   CASE STUDIES

We present three case studies below. Two concern supplier–client linkages involving Web production KIBS, and one is a success story and one a failure to enter the new media. The third case study involves a Web service supplier only (though one associated strongly with a firm creating new media content for publication).

5.5.1   Supplier–Client Case Study 1

Web Service: XTML
XTML Limited, founded in 1994, was among the first independent, dedicated Web design and publishing operations in the North West of England. A small KIBS, both in terms of employees and financial turnover, it faces many problems typical of small firms. Thus, the partners could found the company on virtually zero investment, but growth has been constrained by a lack of finance.

In its first years, the success of XTML was closely tied to that of its first major project, *Virtual Manchester*. Growth has been steady, and financial security was consolidated in June 1997 by an amalgamation with Feedback Network Communications to form two new, inter-linked firms, XTML Creative and XTML Limited. Together these provide the full range of Internet services from Web design and development to service provision – XTML is now a significant ISP in terms of bandwidth capacity despite comprising merely eight staff at the time of our research in 1997.

XTML recognises that even the largest organisation cannot hope to internalise all the competences needed in Web services – networking is vital. Informal know-how trading between technical experts in different firms, in particular, is extremely important in diffusing knowledge in this rapidly-moving field, and in developing reciprocal links which can underpin more substantive collaborations. The background skills required in this field are not provided for in existing university courses; while its two founders have college backgrounds, other staff have business/sales and 'hacking' backgrounds.

XTML's clients come from a wide range of sectors, many locating XTML through the *Virtual Manchester* site. It sees itself as often engaged in an initial effort to enhance the client's awareness of the potential of Web technology *and* of the importance of adopting a professional approach towards design and implementation. This guidance accounts for a large part of the added-value service provided. The knowledge that is handed over by XTML is expected to be of increasing importance to the client's future competitiveness – and should provide the service supplier with repeat and new business in the future. These clients are very involved in the development of their own Web pages, and XTML are keen to develop their user competences. Many clients are keen to do some updating of their own sites, though few have tried to fully internalise Web publishing to date. In some instances, the content of the site is altered automatically by the client via an automated on-line form. More technologically literate clients seek advice and assistance on more complicated aspects of Web design; for example, a subsidiary of a transnational oil company required help to develop more sophisticated tools to add to its pages on the corporate intranet – improving its competitive edge over other business units in the group's internal market.

Links with other companies, in activities such as marketing, training and technologies, allow small firms such as XTML to remain at the leading edge and to provide a broad range of products and services. XTML sometimes outsource the production of items such as speciality graphics to personal contacts with the requisite skills. Likewise, it will provide certain specialist services to fill gaps for other companies. Links with hardware and telecommunications firms are especially important in a field where systems integration is crucial and companies are plagued with problems arising from 'nearly compatible' systems that require (sometimes major) adjustments in practice.

Client: VG Elemental

VG Elemental is a Manchester-based manufacturer of mass spectrometers. It is a low volume producer of extremely specialised products for a global market (50–100 units per year is considered a high rate of output; prices range from £150,000 to £500,000 per instrument; the UK market is fairly large, as are Europe and Asia). There are a relatively low number of medium-to-large clients for such a specialised product. Client interaction (including extensive training and aftersales support) is vital to the firm, and clients are frequently heavily involved in specification, though rarely in the development phase (though sometimes clients have generated novel add-ons which can be integrated with the product). However, VG's corporate identity and visibility has suffered from being the focus of successive acquisitions: changes in name led to problems of image and brand recognition.

A Web presence would, it was hoped, constitute an effective means of advertising and customer relations to complement existing techniques. VG had been comparatively slow to investigate the Internet due to fears about the potential problems of security, and of staff time wasting, which might come with Internet access. (These fears are very widespread ones, even now.) But now VG's competitors had a Web presence, and VG was seen to be at a disadvantage.

VG turned to a local design company, in order to have face-to-face links in the set-up phase. VG also wanted a local ISP and approached U-Net, who in turn put the company in touch with XTML as one of their recommended Web developers.[10] VG found *Virtual Manchester* impressive, and XTML had some understanding of scientific instrumentation, which helped rapport develop.

Given VG's lack of experience in Web design, it wanted a supplier to initially construct the site – but, once established, it wished to be able to maintain its own site. While some Web suppliers were only interested in providing a one-off package, XTML was willing to provide assistance in training and skills development. After two months developing the general specifications for the site, the VG site was developed 'off-line' from general access. XTML would make changes to the site, and VG examined these, in a continual dialogue over the development period; interaction was intense – two or three times daily over the initial 6–8 week development period.

Though initially prompted by imitation, the resulting site is very different from VG's rivals, whose Websites tend to be large, promoting an extensive range of products and services, and thereby requiring users to actively search for the relevant pages. VG wanted its Website to tie in with its marketing and communication strategy as a specialised supplier, displaying its products and their ongoing improvement. The Website is also important to after-sales and service support as another means of communication, rather than as '*a glossy brochure*'.

VG actually has *two* Internet sites: a public site that everyone can visit, and another site for existing customers, providing aftersales support (which is marketed as a benefit to new and potential customers). The site is *not* intended to bypass the important means of interaction with the company through local service channels, which remain vital for full aftersales support. Customers with a username and password can access information such as product notes, application notes, parts and update catalogues (not pricing information, since prices vary between national markets), and access an on-line discussion group to exchange information and analyse common problems. At the time of interview, an on-line ordering service for existing customers was under consideration. There are also two 'intranet' sites. One is specially set up for agents and distributors – a sales support forum that contains detailed sales-related material. The other, an engineer support site, holds information (like electrical schematics) for VG service engineers around the world.

The company considers that, as well as improving its image and rebuilding its brand name, the Websites enable the company to disseminate information far faster than was previously possible. Given VG's small central marketing and communications department (consisting of only two people), the Web provides a good way of meeting demand for information about its products. The Web presence, in its various forms, is recognised by customers, sales people and engineers alike as the starting point to look for new information.

5.5.2   Supplier–Client Case Study 2: Millaer Seale and General Law

Millaer Seale
Millaer Seale is one of three separate but interconnected companies – the others being Northern Image, which has evolved into a supplier of digital equipment, and Manchester Net, which was set up as an ISP. The decision to operate as three distinct business entities reflects the dynamics of the sectors within which they operate: each business unit offers services to firms that are liable to be competitors of the other business units.   The solution is to develop trust relationships between different client–providers, reassuring clients that privileged information will not be utilised against them in the future. It would be commercial suicide for such KIBS to invest in long-term relationships, build up its business reputation, and then to misuse the confidential knowledge gained from client-provider relationships.

At the time of interview (late 1997) there were twelve staff working across the three companies, together with writers, photographers, set builders and model makers who are hired on a project-by-project basis to work at the Central Manchester offices.   The company has been built on tight, overlapping working groups and multi-skilling.

Millaer Seale has existed for 10 years, and is well known in the professional services, mail order and selling-off-the-page sectors. The idea for the company arose from the initial observation that the mail order market badly needed some editorial input.   Working on catalogue projects with leading UK firms (such as Next), the founders became interested in desk-top publishing, and became the first group in Manchester to produce a catalogue digitally.   This early lead on the learning curve was maintained, and after three years the company started to explore the potential of the Internet, and was able to recruit staff from Poptel, an Internet pioneer in Manchester. A recent exploratory project was a Manchester Internet shopping 'mall', developed to explore different ways by which SMEs could be encouraged to sell their products on the Web. Millaer Seale wanted to familiarise itself with the software options for Internet shopping, and to test whether SMEs' lack of general skills in IT and computing (especially in the retail sector) inhibits the development of such services.   The project received some support from Manchester City Council, as part of the EU Infocities initiative.[11]

The core competitive advantage of Millaer Seale lies in its combination of technical knowledge, design and marketing experience. The publishing background of its founders emphasises the importance of knowing the target reader and of being geared to meeting deadlines. The staff are all involved in innovation: designers work on day-to-day problems, whilst programmers develop technical solutions to these problems. Two members of staff are 'trailblazing' the new industry of Web promoting.[12] All members of staff, including clerical and administrative workers, provide input into brainstorming exercises: enthusiasm and energy count for a good deal. Millaer Seale also has an 'enforced' brainstorming session with its clients at the outset of every project. The objective is not to develop ideas but rather to give the client some insight into the difficulty of the creative process. This is very important given that there are competitors who can undercut Millaer Seale (they have fewer overheads), but offer an inferior product (they lack the range of creative skills).

Millaer Seale has gradually shifted its focus from the property market to professional services firms; a transition requiring them to learn a quite different language and to understand how these businesses work. Approximately 80 per cent of its work is gained through recommendation, with the remainder gained from active searching for new business accounts. Clients are always very keen to see that a firm has done a similar project for a customer in the same sector before enlisting their services. Once established, provider–client relationships tend to be long-lived. Some current clients have been with Millaer Seale from the outset. After-sales contacts are therefore exceedingly important.

Most current clients are located within the North West of England, with about 15 per cent elsewhere in the UK, and a few international clients. But this client mix changes over time, and reflects recent marketing effort: the company has tended to focus on national companies who have their head offices in the North West. Having been less successful in winning accounts with London-based clients, who are generally reluctant to use firms located outside the capital, Millaer Seale has an associate firm in London, which provides them with a 'presence' in the capital.

As also reported by XTML, potential clients often believe that Website 'design' is something that any teenager can quickly master. Where clients have picked up some authoring software they may think that they can do the work themselves – though most clients realise that it is better, and eventually cheaper, to pay for experts to do the work rather than wasting the time and resources of their in-house marketing team. (More of a problem for firms like Millaer Seale are competitors with low overheads or subsidised services provided through the higher education sector.) Design companies need to convince customers of the importance of good design, and to demonstrate the value of a Web site, typically by 'proving' who is visiting what sites. (The firm has forged a link with US outfit WebPromote, who can provide audited figures for banner ads on Websites. Such statistics are the only type of figures likely to convince marketing professionals.) A problem for clients is that their marketing budgets are typically set up to a year in advance, and often with little provision for a Web presence. Therefore, money needs to be squeezed from funds originally allocated elsewhere. Other organisational issues revolve around who takes responsibility for the Website within the client company – for example, is it the IT department (often initially the case) or the marketing department? Design issues must also be confronted – for example, since most North West engineering companies are selling to an international market, they cannot afford to focus their Website on a UK audience, and should consider providing text in other languages.

Millaer Seale reports that it is keen to pass knowledge on to its clients during the development process. This can range from quite general issues, such as Web directory submission procedures, to far more specific information regarding the minutiae of HTML. A distinction is made between such issues and detailed programming matters that do not directly concern the client. In principle, it is possible for a client to use the knowledge thus gained to carry out some, or all, of the work themselves. The whole issue of client knowledge can be extremely problematic: while a degree of familiarity with the Web and its underlying technology can prove useful, a little knowledge can be a dangerous thing. Clients may assume that the technical side of Web design is the main issue at hand, underestimating the difficulties involved in using the technology creatively. Generally speaking, success depends on clients first recognising that they have a marketing problem that cannot be solved in-house, and then accepting the need to pay an external provider for a solution. Again, there is a problem in the provision of an 'intangible' service product, which is one common to many creative sectors: while most companies are willing to pay for 'concrete' deliverables, such as a particular logo or piece of artwork, they are far more likely to undervalue intangible deliverables that involve creativity and the development of novel solutions.

General Law

General Law (a pseudonym) was among the first London law firms to move into the Manchester market in the 1980s. Its managers assumed that a big metropolitan firm was naturally better than the provincial competition, and that clients would flock to them. But the firm found itself shut out of the local professional services and client networks – to the extent that it was hard even to recruit good quality staff locally. General Law had to change its whole approach, and bring in new management. Millaer Seale was involved in a repositioning exercise that sought to reverse the negative impressions of General Law held by many Manchester companies, and to assure prospective customers that they were committed to the Manchester market. Millaer Seale was effectively telling key members of the law firm 'home truths', which it had to relay on to corporate leaders. The repositioning exercise worked, silencing the 'jungle drums', changing perceptions of the firm and improving the recruitment situation.

General Law's PR agency initially recommended Millaer Seale when its Manchester operation needed a specific advertisement within a very tight timescale. Millaer Seale had already worked for a number of other law firms, an important factor in selecting them. The quality of the work done by Millaer Seale was very high, and they could offer flexible timing; the first engagement led to other work. The biggest project for Millaer Seale was to work on a high-quality report on business/legal issues that General Law produced annually for senior managers in client and other firms. The document was also used as the basis for a series of press releases, several of which would be issued on the back of a particular issue in order to get more publicity mileage out of the report's contents. General Law regarded this report as the main 'selling' tool for the firm – though a sophisticated one, with high quality content and award-winning design. Millaer Seale brought an array of capabilities in publishing and production, and set itself an eight–week timescale for production (rather than the six months which it had taken in the past). Progression to a Web presence would likely have been facilitated by the continued involvement of the North West firm, but the highly favourable relations between the KIBS and client depended very much upon the General Law's Manchester Director. When this individual left to set up a new company, General Law's London staff decided to move production of the report to the capital (despite expectations of higher costs, and no assurance of improved quality of product). This demonstrates the importance of interpersonal links to many such service interrelations; in this case, the Web development was forestalled by the departure of one person.

5.5.3 Supplier Case Study 3: ArtHouse and Europress Software

ArtHouse began life in 1996 as a division of a major publisher of IT magazines. The two founders had recognised the market for commercial Web design and site management; they were joined by two other staff members in 1997, and new recruits were planned in 1998 (with a maximum of eight staff envisaged). In its first year of trading, ArtHouse has generated a turnover of £125,000. This is projected to treble or quadruple in its second year.

Europress Software, a private investor in ArtHouse, produces multimedia CD-ROMs as a core business. The two companies share premises, and the relationship goes beyond cross-ownership and colocation. ArtHouse provides Europress with access to knowledge on Internet issues (and to the competences necessary to build its own Website). Europress has given ArtHouse not only financial security in the critical start-up period, but also complementary assets such as marketing and financial experience within the general area of new media.

ArtHouse specialises in commercial Web design and Web marketing. It only offers Internet-specific forms of brand marketing, and does not carry out conventional advertising or PR activities for its clients. The company constructs and develops Websites; it is not an ISP and so does not offer 'connectivity'. Projects can vary in size, from basic 10-15 page one–off sites to larger projects that are maintained and developed on an account basis. There is no standard approach to designing a client's Website: each design is tailored to the specific requirements and objectives of the client. These vary considerably. Most assignments begin with basic research, examining issues such as the target market, the proportion of that market which has Internet access, and so on. ArtHouse sees these steps as essential in determining the success or failure of a site. This research is also instrumental to the process of designing a site, influencing the content and services to be provided. These activities constitute the R&D stage of Website development. As with Millaer-Searle, ArtHouse tends to brainstorm with its clients about their objectives for a web project, the overall design of the site, the target market, promotion, content, functionality and so on. ArtHouse puts this information into a 'client brief' which is used to communicate client requirements to ArtHouse staff.

After this process, ArtHouse puts the various elements together in order to manage the brand on-line. As well as responding to clients' needs, ArtHouse responds to the activities of competitors, learning not only from its own successes and mistakes, but also from those of its competitors. The two MDs (and joint founders) spend much time examining the Websites produced by their competitors, in an attempt to understand changing client preferences.

Rather than seeking rapid expansion, ArtHouse focused on building its own brand name during its first 12 months. This was helped enormously by landing its first contract with Granada Studios Tour, a television-themed leisure attraction in Manchester. ArtHouse produced both a Web presence and a CD-ROM for Granada Studios Tour, which forms the basis of the park's 'Futurevision' attraction. This first venture opened up a series of further projects with Granada Television, developing sites for TV programmes such as 'World in Action' and 'The Ward', which in turn led to work with other companies within the Granada Media Group (such as London Weekend Television and Granada Sky Broadcasting). Despite these high-profile media clients, the company is reluctant to be typecast as a media services firm. Seeking to maintain a broad client appeal, ArtHouse has worked hard at marketing itself to new business customers. The new company operates in a different market to its old publishing parent. In its initial 12 months, it went up a steep learning curve, deepening its marketing, image presentation, and skills in identifying and relating to business clients' needs. It places a heavy emphasis on its aftersales relationship with its clients, and is keen to keep in touch with ex-clients in order to be ready for repeat business. As part of its planned expansion at the time of our case study interviews, the company was looking at the possibility of appointing an Account Manager to oversee this process.

ArtHouse's client list now includes software and industrial/engineering companies as well as media companies. All of its current clients are UK-based, mainly from North West England and London. This reflects a strategic targeting of the local market (accounting for approximately 80 per cent of its time) and large contracts with national companies. It is simply uneconomic to chase small contracts with clients located outside the North West. Large business clients are particularly attractive to small Web designers such ArtHouse. They have greater awareness of the need to have a Web presence, and are generally willing to allocate a specific budget to its creation, maintenance and development. Larger companies tend to have a more precise view of what they want, and are keen to become actively involved. By contrast, smaller clients tend to provide little input into the site specifications and content. But interaction with the client is extremely important in the design process. The more involved the client gets, the better the product is likely to be – as ArtHouse tells its clients. Furthermore, once created, Websites need to be actively managed – hence the need to get involved.

The company's marketing limitations influenced its strategy formulation. Since its inception, the company has focused on one market niche at a time. 'Knowledge of markets is vitally important, and each market is a learning experience – after some time working in a market you get to know it better.' Such knowledge is largely gained through interactions with the market in question; 'It helps enormously to have already produced a site for a firm in the same market – not least in terms of convincing further clients'. This experience is shared by our other case study firms.

The market for Internet Web design remains immature and so client knowledge tends to be limited. This poses difficulties when pitching to clients. Each company has a different level of awareness of the potential benefits of a Web presence – it is therefore important to find the right level of explanation, and then convince them. The transfer of such knowledge is part of the package provided by the company to its client. It is noticeable that many clients are keen to gain this knowledge, and ArtHouse provides a basic grounding when initially pitching for an account. As well as being a useful means of hooking the client, this enables the client to produce a sufficiently informed design brief for them to work with. The service provider and business client are then able to work together on details regarding the content, design, marketing and technical issues.

As well as handing over any necessary development information and knowledge, ArtHouse produces a 'graphic standards manual' for many of its clients. This is common amongst advertising agencies, where a guide to managing corporate identity/brand/logo is produced. Again, this type of manual is more likely to be used by larger rather than smaller companies. Occasionally some clients have sufficient knowledge to write and maintain the Website themselves, once the design phase is completed. Still, these clients frequently return to ArtHouse for specific, or more complex, work. Other clients continue to rely on an outside agency, such as ArtHouse, to do all the construction and maintenance work for them.

The organisation of ArtHouse in turn depends on the outsourcing of some activities to other KIBS providers. In general, the company outsources services that it cannot offer itself, such as the production of specialist content or specialist market research. The company tends to give repeat business to suppliers it trusts and who understand the company's needs. 'It is important to find people who understand the market in which ArtHouse operates – from market researchers to the firm's accountants.'

5.6   CONCLUSIONS

Although Internet penetration remains low compared with more traditional broadcasting, information or communication media, and 'barriers' to electronic commerce as applied to publishing are commonly identified (revolving around the security of transaction systems and the protection of intellectual property assets), there is no doubt that the Internet has now entered a resolutely commercial phase. Though at present the only significant content publishing businesses to develop successful models for charging users for access to Web-based content are in the unlikely areas of academic publishing and pornography, it is only a matter of time before business models are successfully developed for other areas of publishing. And whilst traditional publishers and information providers are progressively exploring the opportunities opened to them by the growth of the Web, there has also grown up a sector of small, knowledge-intensive Internet design service providers, often bringing experience in design and publishing from other creative media sectors, and providing marketing and e–commerce services to a wide range of business clients.

Web design services firms, befitting a new service activity, are typically relatively small businesses, relying heavily on the technical and creative capabilities of the core personnel. They are usually new firms, led by the visions and creative abilities of their original founders. Some are new sections of established firms who provide conventional design, marketing and advertising services, and have recruited new staff able to work with the new media. Not surprisingly, initial company histories can have a long-term influence on behaviour: in particular the creative and publishing backgrounds of the founders of many of these firms seem to play a large part in shaping their approaches to Web design. While some companies come from a 'traditional' IT background (specialising in software or online services), many more seem to stem from marketing and publishing, whose creative values are apparent in their Web design, and whose capabilities influence the market niches which they have sought to develop.

Turning to the innovative strategies of the Web companies, it was interesting to see how all three service providers have used key projects, often experimental in nature, to develop longer-term knowledge and capabilities, and to simultaneously create new market niches for themselves. *Virtual Manchester* was the key to the growth and development of XTML. This provided the initial competitive space within which they could generate new business. For Millaer Seale the virtual shopping site developed in conjunction with the EU Infocities programme allowed it to experiment with electronic commerce applications and technologies. ArtHouse, for its part, has a series of developments in the pipeline, including a new approach to promoting brands on the Web.

A feature of Web design that emerges strongly in each of the case studies is the importance of the interaction between designers and their clients. All three Web design companies remarked on the generally low level of client knowledge, not only with respect to the technical aspects of the Web but also to its commercial potential. The process of bringing clients up-to-speed with the Web, and its use as a marketing tool, is considered an essential aspect of the service which these companies current providing. This is hardly a philanthropic exercise, but one which is deemed essential to developing a workable brief for a site – XTML, ArtHouse and Millaer Seale hold brainstorming sessions with clients during the initial stages of the design process. All three design companies also recognised the benefits of such interaction and knowledge transfer for the wider diffusion of commercial Web activities. Indeed both the private and wider community benefits of such 'training' were highlighted during the interviews to a notable degree. ArtHouse bemoaned the lack of a professional body which accredits Web design service providers. It argued that quality control is essential for the long-term success of what remains an infant industry.

An important question arises. Are close provider–client relationships an inherent characteristic of Web publishing, as a KIBS activity (as suggested by Miles, 1996), or are they a characteristic of the early stage of the industry's life cycle? While it is too early to answer this question, it is interesting to observe that the Web providers which we have interviewed all agreed that the commercial use of the Web was in its infancy. Web designers are keen to improve clients' general abilities to specify a brief, with a basic awareness of what is technically possible and commercially viable. Developing clients' knowledge in these domains is thought essential to the development of client preferences (and the ability of service providers to shape these developing preferences). A little imagination and appreciation of design is considered an added bonus, but not essential. However, Web designers are of course keen to maintain control over the actual problem-solving process once the basic design brief is established.

The case studies highlight a number of important factors that influence the successful development and application of Web sites by corporate clients. Several key aspects of Web design for corporate clients can be identified (which reinforces the short discussion of capabilities at the start of this chapter). Firstly, planning prior to developing and launching a corporate Web presence is essential to the success of the venture. A surprising number of corporate sites are launched without any clear idea of the business objectives to which they are intended to contribute. This involves strategic planning on the part of the client, and requires market-related capabilities on the part of the designer. ArtHouse and Millaer Seale emphasise the importance of targeting (and researching) an identifiable market for the site, and of ensuring that the market in question is one with access to the Web. This emphasises the importance of detailed market research prior to launching, and of close interactions between developer and client when developing the initial project brief. Both providers and clients observed that this stage of the development process is critical to the eventual success or failure of a project.

The design and production capabilities of the service provider are also essential to success or failure. As all our interviewees have pointed out, a Web presence is now as important a marketing tool as a conventional brochure or catalogue, and in all probability has a far wider potential circulation given the global nature of the Web. McGurran (1997) emphasises the need to harness the skills of experienced professionals in launching a Web presence, noting in particular what we have here called logical design capabilities, relating to the 'shape' or 'layout' of the site – a critical component of functionality in a Web site.

A third important factor is the continuing development and maintenance of the corporate Web presence. This requires an embeddedness of the Web within organisational structures and information management. This was best exemplified by the VG Elemental client study. VG has put a great deal of time and energy into the initial development of its Web presence(s), and is using the Web in an innovative way to compensate for its small size relative to its main competitors. However, these Web presences are not fully embedded within the existing organisational structure, with total responsibility for maintenance and development falling on the shoulders of just one person. Realising the potential of a Web site requires the development of organisational structures and routines which diffuse responsibility and input.

Another key factor is the use of the Web for marketing. This is a concept that is much on the minds of the founders of XTML, ArtHouse and Millaer Seale. The proactive use of a Web presence to interact with a visitor (ultimately in order to improve the possibility of making a sale to that customer, or to improve service to existing customers), and to register and respond to that visitor's needs is key to the evolution of Web sites away from the model of an on-line Annual Report. Business-to-business Web sites typically cater for more complex needs than business-to-consumer ones, and require greater sophistication in the presentation of service benefits not embodied in a specific product. Several of our case study firms are active in marketing professional service firms on the Web, and have developed capabilities in this regard over time.

Finally, expectations of what the Web can deliver need to be realistic. These may be quite different to the benefits delivered by marketing and other activities. For example, the use of standard advertising criteria, such as extra sales per month, may be inappropriate if improved customer service is the key benefit derived from the site. This was certainly the case with VG Elemental. The utility which can be derived from the various discussion and information forums developed by VG Elemental can be assessed by the extent to which both internal and external customers resort to using those forums. An important benefit of an interactive, commercial Web site is the opportunity to learn about the clients who visit it. Companies should therefore think carefully about the potential of a site to improve their knowledge of their customer base.

In short, professional design services, bringing specialist skills and expertise to bear, are likely to become increasingly important as corporate Web sites progressively evolve from simple on-line information services to true marketing devices. These findings are supported by McGurran's recent study (1997), which similarly considers a range of design agencies and their customers. Our research also highlights the complexity of the new media design process, and the historical path dependence of Web design companies who harness existing knowledge-based capabilities, and mobilise new ones, in order to provide a value-added service to their clients.

NOTES

1. This work was carried out as part of the SI4S project of the European Commission's TSER Programme.
2. Based on proportion of traffic distributed via NSFNET. (http://www.mit.edu/people/mkgray/, Dec. 97). For an examination of pre-Web online services, see Thomas and Miles (1989).
3. Again information provided by Matthew Gray at MIT. (http://www.mit.edu/people/mkgray/, Dec. 97). More recent data are not available since the NSFNET handed over responsibility for the provision of the primary Internet 'backbone' service to private service providers after April 1995.
4. Hence all pages under http://www.man.ac.uk/ would be counted as part of the same site, while http://les.man.ac.uk/ – where the authors are located – would constitute another.
5. Matthew Gray's Web Wanderer Survey: http://www.mit.edu/people/mkgray/ (Dec. 97). Note that the '.com' indicator excludes many commercial sites located outside the US, for example, the 'co.uk' sites in the UK. As a matter of interest, one survey of the Internet Domain Name System puts the number of hosts within the 'co.uk' domain at 585,233 in January 1999.
6. Network Wizards Domain Name System Survey: http://www.nw.com/ (Jan. 99).
7. These studies were originally undertaken as part of the SI4S investigation of KIBS (see Miles et al. forthcoming), and in the framework of Flanagan's PhD thesis (1999). For earlier work on new media services, see Bilderbeek et al. (1994).
8. http://www.manchester.com/
9. Saxenian (1991) is a classic study of the importance of location in respect of new IT industries.
10. U-Net, an ISP based in the North West, is the host for *Virtual Manchester* and owner of the 'manchester.com' domain name. XTML was its second customer, developing a close working relationship with the company, even providing some knowledge input into U-Net. Since becoming an ISP in its own right, XTML are less dependent on U-Net and could even be considered to be directly competing with U-Net. However the services being offered (such as the availability of high bandwidth), and the technologies underpinning them, differentiate the two firms.
11. The company are happy to report back to the Infocities initiative on the lessons it has learnt from the experiment – divulging such general results cannot hurt them commercially, and sharing such information across the community benefits all those concerned. For instance, one conclusion was that the available software is good but over-designed in several respects, being too secure (and too expensive), and too complicated at the back end, for SME retailers.
12. The skills needed in this business are difficult to assess (except perhaps for designers, where at least there is a portfolio to examine). Recruiting staff in order to gain specific knowledge can be difficult, and mistakes will hurt small companies. Millaer Seale tends not to advertise vacancies, but to recruit staff from other design firms or through work placements – the firm makes it a point to take people on placements from schools, colleges and universities.

6 Ecommerce: Servicing the New Economy

Ian Miles, Ettore Bolisani and Mark Boden[1]

6.1 INTRODUCTION: THE PATH TO ECOMMERCE

Electronic commerce (ecommerce) increasingly looks to be one of the important means by which new information technology (IT) will be used to transform social and economic life in the twenty–first century. In the late 1990s a remarkable explosion of stock market interest in Internet-related companies excited the US financial community; ecommerce was at the heart of this. On the one hand companies like Amazon, the online bookseller, had come from nowhere to grab sizeable portions of (in their case) the book market; on the other hand, some established companies were reporting surges of transactions through their websites – for example the mail order clothing company Land's End reported a trebling of its online sales in 1998 compared to the previous year. Market forecasters were predicting that huge volumes of consumer and business purchasing would be transacted online within a very few years.

The turning point here is evidently the growth of the Internet, and the dominance of the Web as a framework for hosting all kinds of information product and communication activity. Over the course of the 1990s the diffusion of PCs had continued, and an increasing share of them are now networked and, most importantly, connected to Internet Service Providers of one kind or another. At the end of the century we are beginning to see devices like mobile phones and televisions also gaining the ability to communicate with websites.

But the notion – and indeed much practical experience – of ecommerce dates back well before the Internet. Videotex services of the early 1980s, like the UK's Prestel and the much more widely diffused French Minitel system – were already being used for making bookings and reservations, ordering goods and services, and the like.   Indeed, the case of the tour operator Thompsons, who increased their share of the UK travel agents' business substantially at that time by being the first to offer videotex rather than telephone booking, was held up at the time as an example of the need to consider how new IT could be used to revolutionise business.   But at the time videotex only seemed suitable for a few business-to-business markets in the UK (there was little consumer usage to build on), though a range of videotex businesses did thrive in France.

Videotex had been designed with the TV in mind (in the UK), or with the specialised Minitel terminal (in France).   It was intended for use by ordinary people with no computer knowledge or training, and national systems operated in a variety of incompatible standards.   Businesses, meanwhile, were proceeding with a range of their own efforts to institute interfirm communications. As early as the 1960s there was automated transfer of large routine transactions in the US automobile industry, and by the end of that decade a number of bodies were being established to deal with issues of exchanging trade data – for example, the TDCC (Transportation Data Co-ordinating Committee), and the well-known SWIFT (the Society for Worldwide Interbank Financial Telecommunication).   As business use of computer-communications grew, there was an emergence in the 1970s and 1980s of Value Added Networks (VANs) offering sophisticated computing and data transmission services. The 1980s saw the first major expansion of EDI, with government promotion and intergovernmental standardisation efforts underway in many industrial countries.   According to the UK Department of Trade and Industry, EDI is

> computer-to-computer exchange of structured data between two or more companies, sent in a form that allows automatic processing, with no manual intervention. It is relevant to any business that regularly exchanges information such as client or company records, but is especially relevant when they send and receive orders, invoices, statements and payments.
>
> EDI remains the dominant term in the UK for electronic trading, although some people consider the term electronic data interchange to be too narrow to describe the full potential of electronic trading. Electronic Commerce (EC) encompasses techniques such as PC- based fax and e-mail, as well as EDI. (DTI 1997, p. 3)

6.2   ELECTRONIC DATA INTERCHANGE

The exchange of transactional and other product-related information is of course an activity performed across all sectors of the economy. It is one of the service functions which necessarily surrounds the diverse core activities of producing and delivering goods and services in all of these sectors. EDI is thus a case of new technology being applied to a pervasive service function, which in principle has many similar features whatever the specific goods and services involved.   It does not seem to be a dramatic extension of technological capabilities to move these service functions into electronic form, and the examples of pioneering successes in the early 1980s would seem to bear this out. Thus for many years EDI was expected to achieve rapid growth, albeit almost entirely as a business-to-business application.

However, this has not been the case. The number of companies using EDI has risen steadily over two decades, but the number of actual users is much lower than expected. The number of EDI users is generally estimated on the basis of data from service providers, and data from different sources may differ according to definitions and means of production. Thus estimates diverge, but suggest that the number of worldwide users in 1996 probably falls between 80,000 and 150,000. Whichever is most accurate, the figure is well below forecasts made in the late 1980s and early 1990s.

The diffusion of EDI has thus been considerably slower than most of its proponents ever anticipated, even in those sectors for which the technology seems to be particularly suitable. Especially in such cases, this is in large part because of the many different kinds of knowledge – and associated exchanges of knowledge resources – that are involved in EDI implementations.

One obvious issue here is the organisation of knowledge about the particular products that are being dealt with. For EDI systems to work automatically, without human beings having to be on hand to interpret just what is being meant by enquiries and orders, it is necessary for the computers at both ends of the 'conversation' to have similar languages in which to describe products and their properties. Businesses frequently have developed their own classificatory and descriptive systems, however. When they have already computerised a large part of their internal operations, these frameworks are liable to be crystallised in the parameters of their software. Chances are high that neither the product codes nor the underlying classifications will be recognised by the software systems of trading partners. Moving to the use of EDI thus means adopting frameworks that others can understand, with the implication that one's own IT systems will sooner or later have to be re-engineered (quite possibly at high cost) to accommodate these. Clearly the scale of the problem will depend to a great extent on the nature of the firm and its product range; but automation is rendered difficult on account of the considerable amount of knowledge routinely utilised by the human agents traditionally undertaking transactions.

However, this is not the only way in which the use of knowledge is important in shaping the form and uptake of EDI, and the size and nature of EDI-associated service industries. The remainder of this chapter will draw especially on the insights developed by Ettore Bolisani. At this point we should note that while this chapter focuses on the role of KIBS, there are also many public sector bodies important in EDI uptake. Other important external sources of knowledge include standardisation bodies, operating at national and international levels (right up to the UN); national governments and intergovernmental promotion of EDI through awareness and other programmes; and university-based support groups and trade associations.

6.3   EDI KNOWLEDGE AND SERVICES

A useful way to approach the different kinds of knowledge involved in EDI use, is to consider particular services associated with the various OSI levels of computer-communications activities. This approach leads us to distinguish such services as:

▪ *Telecommunication services.* These involve large-scale standard telecommunication networks with a wide geographical extension, and the basic services provided over these. Leased-line services have been provided to businesses that are heavy telecommunications users, mainly for intrafirm communications. A strong formal technical competence is required to provide telecommunications network services, as well as substantial capital equipment. In general, only large operators can afford the costs of network implementation, though longstanding ideas about there being 'natural monopolies' in telecoms network services have been substantially dented by the liberalisation policies in most Western countries, and the emergence of mobile telecoms networks. In principle EDI (and other computer-to-computer) communications can be undertaken by means of one computer, interfacing with the telecoms network via a modem, dialling up another one (as if it were a telephone), and exchanging data with it. In practice this approach has been relatively rarely used for EDI.

▪ *Value added services.* In the 1980s many specialised value added networks (VANs) providers emerged, and by the 1990s these were the main channels for EDI communications in countries like the UK. Rather than having to call up each computer with whom one needs to communicate, a single call to the VANS provider is required to access the services it supplies, such as mailboxing, message store-and-forward, and so on. Access to EDI systems – and from early days, videotex-based systems in fields such as travel reservations and insurance brokerage – is among these services. VANS provision requires not only technical assets and network management skills, but also the capability of understanding customers' application needs. Established VANs have now been joined by Internet Service Providers (ISPs) providing access to Internet and Web services. Most VANS providers are large, although in some cases smaller flexible providers supply specific services not provided by the larger companies which require a more careful attention to customers' needs.

- *Communication software and EDI translators.* Software is vital for computer-to-computer communications, forming a fundamental link of the chain between users and the communication network, and enabling 'handshakes' between computers. EDI software provides additional functions required for these specific applications. Such software handles EDI files, and translates EDI standards between the various formats required for telematic systems. The software may be provided by VANs or large software suppliers, though in some cases smaller suppliers provide effective support for particular problems of implementation.
- *User applications.* Within user firms, data have to be managed on leaving or entering the external EDI network. Standard EDI platforms need to be combined with user software (some of which may be widely diffused – such as spreadsheets, databases, and so on). The data need to be presented and achieve effects to fit the specific requirements of users or classes of users – specific types of screen presentations, LAN solutions, and so on. Due to the variety of requirements across different sectors, providers may well specialise in particular niches or markets, developing and using knowledge about the needs of any particular user or class of user.
- *Consulting services; implementation support.* These services range across specific consulting services for SMEs, technical support and training, support for implementation, and the management of large EDI communities or more dispersed systems (as in the case of VANs). To supply such services typically requires strong organisational competence as well as technical skill and access to relevant equipment.

As we move down this list, a shift in the sorts of knowledge that are central is apparent, even though it is equally visible that even within any of these classes there are likely to be numerous different fields of expertise and specific types of specialism. Some of these services, especially in the earlier groups in the list, involve applying knowledge to create tangible products or 'formal' media (equipment, codes and procedures). (This is often interpreted as involving the transfer of explicit technical knowledge 'embodied' in products; but users typically gain knowledge of how to use the products, and only limited understanding of their construction and internal processes.) Services at the higher level (development of user applications, implementation support, consulting, training, and so on) are liable to be based more on the development and interchange of tacit knowledge. Some standardised services (for example, data communication, or standard software), in some cases supported by the sale of equipment (hardware, network connections), can be simply 'supplied' with little or no customisation. But more customised and bespoke services (for example, consultancy, or customised or novel software packages) typically require complex interaction and direct contact.

The wide range of EDI services that are required in the market has led to the creation of different companies specialising in different areas. Despite the smaller-than-expected market size, then, there is still a considerable division of labour among service providers. And there is no clear evidence of a trend, at present, toward concentration or conversely toward further specialisation in EDI services. Large operators, providing a wide range of services, coexist with small, specialised suppliers.

The distinction between explicit and tacit knowledge is helpful in understanding the twofold nature of EDI. EDI effectively aims at the complete automation of transactions, which necessarily requires the formalisation of transactional procedures, and their embedding into equipment, software and codes, and in some cases formal agreements, between partners. Effective technical solutions also require the explication and formalisation of tacit knowledge about communication needs, organisational arrangements, and even social-political configurations, and so on. The generation and conversion of these forms of knowledge involves a variety of actors (users, on one side, and various kinds of services providers, on the other side) who possess different competences.

This variety of competencies and knowledge makes the implementation of the various solutions possible. The variety of services providers, specialising in different fields, supports a wider range of services, suitable for different users and needs. The two-way flow of knowledge between (and within groups of) users and services providers enables the process of the 'collective learning' needed in EDI implementation, and facilitates the diffusion of EDI from one sector or industrial cluster to another.

6.4 KNOWLEDGE, SERVICE SUPPLIERS AND USERS

6.4.1 Interchanges among EDI Users

In most countries and sectors, EDI diffusion to date has largely relied on the growth of EDI communities around a leading company. This leader, usually a large customer whose importance to its suppliers is such that it is more or less able to demand that its business partners conform to its wishes, requires that the partners be capable of exchanging EDI messages. In some cases the leader assists its partners in implementing the requisite systems.

Especially in manufacturing sectors and retailing, this has resulted in so called 'hub-spoke' EDI networks, which are effectively 'closed' communities around the leader (Zwass 1996). Such hub-spoke networks are limited in flexibility: changes in connected partners, message formats, and transaction procedures may be very difficult, as may be interconnection with other hub-spoke networks. Though EDI is claimed to offer great potential for small business, the role of SMEs in hub-spoke networks is often marginal. In many cases they are simply embedded in a closed system of relationships; cases still exist of firms having to run two different EDI systems on different equipment, in order to participate in more than one network!

It is possible that new EDI services may be able to satisfy ongoing and emerging requirements from hub-spoke communities – for instance where a large hub seeks to extend the number of partners, in order to increase the percentage of electronic transactions, and/or to extend the scope of EDI applications. On the other hand, new EDI applications might substantially support different kinds of communication, suitable for non-hub-spoke communities. In this latter case, there might be a migration from the hub-spoke framework, though social factors (such as disapproval of the 'leader', the learning required to master new practices, and so on) are liable to impede this.

6.4.2 Interchanges Between EDI Service Suppliers and Users

The variety of activities and services involved in EDI is reflected in a wide range of interactions between EDI users and services providers. These involve the application and exchange of numerous kinds of knowledge resources in manifold ways. EDI implementation is a process of interactive learning, so the exchange of such resources is continual and changing. Put another way, an evolving process of knowledge conversion unfolds between users and service providers.

The 'theory of organisational knowledge creation' by Nonaka and colleagues (1995, 1998), builds on Polanyi's (1967) distinction between *explicit and tacit knowledge*, proves helpful here.[2] It highlights issues of the *transferability* of knowledge and the mechanisms employed for this, and while it was developed to examine intra-organisational knowledge transfer, it can be applied to interorganisational relations.

Nonaka distinguishes between *individual knowledge*, owned by single operators, and *organisational knowledge*, which includes both knowledge of individuals and procedures, routines, strategies, and so on. The latter is developed at a corporate level and shared by the members of the organisation. The process of knowledge generation is then described as a *never-ending spiral*, involving four modes of converting tacit and explicit knowledge.

1. *From tacit to tacit knowledge* ('socialisation'): to share experience and thereby create and exchange tacit knowledge such as mental models and technical skills (for example, to teach somebody how to use a machine). Generally speaking, an individual can develop tacit knowledge through observation, imitation and practice (that is even without using language).
2. *From tacit to explicit knowledge* ('externalisation'): to rationalise tacit knowledge and articulate it into explicit concepts and formal models (for example, to write an instruction manual). Externalisation is the core of the knowledge creating process, given that tacit knowledge becomes explicit. Nevertheless, the formalisation of tacit knowledge necessarily implies its selection and reduction, since tacit knowledge can not be codified explicitly.
3. *From explicit to tacit knowledge* ('internalisation'): to convert explicit knowledge into specific know-how (for example, how to use a piece of equipment for specific or new needs). In particular, internalisation may be associated with 'learning by doing'.
4. *From explicit to explicit knowledge* ('combination'): to systematise and convert a system of formalised concepts into another one (for example, how to obtain a new formula, procedure, or software from existing ones).

Recent UK case studies[3] indicate that explicit or 'formal' exchanges - in the form of knowledge resources embedded in equipment and/or technical specifications – are highly significant in the EDI field.   Small firms in particular, although highly expert in their own 'core' activities, often lack the experience or technical problem-solving capabilities needed to move into the EDI world. They may be supplied with equipment, software and training (Nonaka's 'combination' and 'internalisation').

But use of EDI also requires the development of 'implicit' knowledge on the part of users.   Much of this is required because it goes beyond applications of technical knowledge which can be readily translated into formal language or embedded in equipment. This is typical of 'configurational' technologies. Implementation requires complex application not only of 'formal or explicit knowledge' but also that of 'tacit' or informal knowledge (such as know-how about how to handle incoming data, know-why about what the key objectives of EDI implementation should be, and so on). Though it may seem that EDI is simply a new artefact or system, a great deal of tacit knowledge has to be transformed into technical requirements for it to be operational in practice. In this, the lessons learned are like those repeatedly confronted by users of other computer technologies. Despite claims to 'user-friendliness', in reality considerable effort at mastery is required, and this often goes beyond simple technical skills.

EDI implementation also requires that users who are linked together should interchange details of their 'implicit' or tacit knowledge. One way in which this may happen is by making some of this knowledge explicit in the form of technical requirements (Nonaka's 'externalisation'). A case in point is complex "Trading Partners Agreements" which are used to regulate many detailed issues involved in EDI communication. Such agreements are the result of a long process of negotiation and mutual learning, and usually require long-term alliances.

In these situations, the support of service providers proves fundamental. For example, large VANs have facilitated the diffusion of EDI in large communities. They play roles in solving such problems as the development and diffusion of sectoral standards, the technical interface between different internal information systems, and the diffusion of common agreements on information use and procedure. The particular challenges posed by multi-trading EDI systems (when different standards and/or VANs have to be handled) also have their implications for the task of software development; and other problems for software developers arise where EDI systems are to be interfaced with complex internal applications. The software products act as an interface between the specific internal applications of an organisation and the standard environment represented by the EDI network. Thus they tend to combine standard components and customised functions, and their development combines explicit and tacit knowledge. Effectively, software providers and their systems analysts have to be able to convert both technical and organisational aspects of user organisations into formal codes and software applications.

Small specialised suppliers of EDI software and services are also important, especially where specific problems (within single companies, or in sets of interacting users) require highly customised solutions. The challenges here relate to the configurational and network nature of the technologies and applications being implemented; the need to fit the data processing systems into organisational routines, and to present material in comparable ways –

which means moving away from local inventory and design systems to more standard ones.

Whatever the case, a knowledge-based analysis suggests that providers are bringing their technical competences to the challenges, and receiving information about the needs and characteristics of customers as a necessary input to dealing with them. The accumulated experience 'in the field' is particularly important as a source of tacit knowledge that is converted into new forms of tacit and explicit knowledge. In many cases providers are able to develop new equipment, software or services as a result of information and understanding acquired through 'learning by interacting' with users. EDI service providers (especially the larger ones, but also the smaller ones) acquire knowledge while working with a sector or group of customers, and are next able to transfer that knowledge in new sectors or embed it in new services for other customers. Therefore, the transfer of innovation *between* sectors involves a transfer of knowledge *about* sectors on the part of the service providers themselves.

In general, the more customised the services (for example, consultancy, or customised software packages) the greater the requirement for complex interaction and direct contact. In such cases, customers and providers might need 'joint teams' to face the specific problems of implementation.

6.4.3 Interchanges Among EDI Service Suppliers

Exchanges of knowledge resources *between* EDI services providers are also significant, since a single project may require the commitment of more than one provider. Interactions between different providers of EDI support services can be vital – a single project may require the commitment of more than one provider, and this is commonplace for larger projects. The interaction between different providers may take different forms, according to the particular nature of the knowledge being employed and the knowledge resources that are required. Interaction can range from simple 'market' relationships (when equipment or software is exchanged), to more complex agreements or alliances centred on a specific project. Alliances between different providers are also liable to be important when providers are confronted by rapid technological developments (such as the rise of the Web). Many companies specialising in EDI have not yet acquired the competences that are probably going to prove critical in this field, and a likely result is the formation of strategic alliances to allow firms specialising in different fields to combine their different capabilities.

6.5 FROM EDI TO ECOMMERCE

The emergence of the Internet as a near-universal network context, and of the Web as a common platform for presenting and exchanging information, has had a major impact on practically all telematics services. It is even having an impact on electronic services more generally, as Internet telephony, Internet music downloads, and Internet video and radio broadcasts and narrowcasts bear witness. But the immediate reactions are most profound on the part of those who have been struggling with or successfully mastering the art of online provision of information and communication services. Online databases and news services, computer conferences and groupware systems, bulletin boards and messaging services, have widely recognised and 'migrated to' Web formats. Even financial information services like Reuters, which only a few years ago was content to rely on its proprietary system and to argue that the Internet was an insecure playground for techno-freaks, is now offering Web-based services (and in the process developing new lines of business).

The same wave is hitting EDI, with the complicating factor that a large number of ecommerce sites are appearing – mainly consumer-oriented – that have little to do with established EDI use. Many of these successful sites are able to use their own classification frameworks and indexing systems, to offer even inexperienced users a rapid service in locating and ordering valued items (typically such things as books, CDs, and clothes, though just about everything is online – and there is heavy activity in Internet auctions and other less standard modes of transaction too). The key to this success is that only part of the process is automated – that at the service supplier's end. At the consumer end the PC is effectively serving only as a text-based mouthpiece for a human agent who is almost always acting in real time (at present, anyway). Thus the common language interface is ordinary language, organised in ways which draw on familiar experiences (like the 'shopping basket' metaphor used in several websites). Neither party has to reorganise their knowledge of the product area to any great extent, which makes uptake of the services that much easier.

The decentralised and open structure of the Internet means that it has been notorious for security breaches, ranging from computer viruses to hacking. Such problems are of obvious concern for electronic commerce users, and there are thus major efforts to develop security mechanisms. Some of these mechanisms operate at the level of communication protocols, based for instance on encryption and return receipts. Others directly operate at the level of specific applications, such as specific systems for credit card payments. In addition to worries about the security of the Internet, there are concerns about its performance (especially its speed, but also its vulnerability to 'crashes' and outages). Many large users prefer resorting to 'protected' niches of the Internet, called Intranets, which represent an increasingly important market for services providers. But many service providers have developed security services for those willing to enter the Internet.

In particular, as concerns business-to-business electronic commerce, a major impact of Internet and Web applications is expected on the diffusion of EDI itself. According to recent studies, it is predicted that the Internet and related technologies will be the key infrastructure of the future EDI, and the driving force of the further diffusion of that technology.

At present, there are two main forms of 'Internet EDI' (Senn 1998):

- *Mail-based EDI.* Here, the functions of the traditional VANs are substituted by Internet email, reducing the need of 'intermediaries' for EDI communication, and allowing for more flexible solutions which could move toward the concept of an 'open' EDI to which much more users could have access (ISO 1994). In practice, for new users ISPs may be substituting for established VANs – and they are often far cheaper.
- *Web EDI.* This represents a more novel approach to EDI communication. It is particularly suitable for connecting a (large) partner to small firms which cannot (or do not wish to) integrate the EDI application into their internal systems, and for outreach to consumers. In such applications of the Web, EDI 'documents' (typically orders) are manually entered onto user-friendly Web forms, and then directly translated into EDI messages.

The major benefit of Web EDI is improved flexibility and user-friendliness. But its development is likely to be accompanied by the diffusion of other new Web services (for example, electronic catalogues and other applications integrated into the EDI transaction system), thus resulting in a new concept of electronic commerce. Business-to-business communications using the Web are attracting less media attention than consumer applications and outreach, but, as mentioned, are bound to become increasingly significant. We can expect Internet EDI and Web EDI to be more thoroughly integrated with other ecommerce and traditional EDI, though this will remain incomplete for a long time for a variety of practical reasons. We likewise anticipate development of more completely computerised transactions using Web pages or their analogues.

This is reflected in a flurry of activity in service firms. Many EDI consultancies are now specifically offering Web conversion and other Web services – warranting a whole section in a recent directory of UK EDI service suppliers. We are also seeing software tools being developed by software houses, allowing users to create their own ecommerce sites on the Web. No doubt such packages will often be applied and implemented by specialised service firms working for clients; and we can expect new entrants to join existing Web and EDI firms in offering such services. The scale of the eventual market is likely to be very large, even if consumer use of ecommerce takes of less rapidly than expected. Websites have become a symbol of prestige for firms, over and above their strategic value (see Chapter 6).

6.6   CONCLUSIONS

As befits a complex innovation like EDI, the types of knowledge being applied, and the communication about such knowledge among and between suppliers and users of EDI services, are complicated. EDI innovations which are clearly important for many service sectors (for example, retail, finance), and KIBS firms are playing important roles in the generation, transfer and use of the new technologies and the knowledge that underpins the artefacts and software. However, there have been many obstacles to the rapid diffusion of the technology. Much of the deployment in hub-spoke systems is forced upon smaller users, and possibly providing them with suboptimal solutions (though they might not otherwise adopt the system at all). A flourishing supply of service providers would help reduce lock-in and the ability of large firms to dictate terms so thoroughly to SMEs, but this is a case where technological knowledge and organisational power are highly correlated. Until SMEs are independently motivated to undertake EDI, hub-spoke systems are liable to prevail.

Dynamic change is underway, as we have seen. Arguably, a new paradigm for ecommerce is being created around the Internet and WWW. More SMEs may be attracted to EDI through these media, not least because of outreach to consumers and firms who are not integrated into existing EDI networks. This offers more opportunities for SMEs to liberate themselves from the constraints imposed by large actors. But certain large firms (including those in IT services!) have a considerable stake in the future of Web ecommerce, as witnessed by current efforts to create ecommerce shopping malls, and so on. Whether many SMEs can follow the few that have dramatically expanded their outreach through use of new media remains to be seen. What can be confidently predicted is that there will continue to be demand for a wide and expanding array of supporting services, and that the rate and sophistication of their use will remain very uneven across sectors, regions and applications.

NOTES

1. This work was in part funded by a Marie Curie scholarship to Bolisani, and from the SI4S project of the European Commission's TSER Programme.
2. Explicit knowledge, that can be codified in form of formulae, technical specifications, or embedded in equipment, computer programmes, and so on, is relatively easy to transfer and store.   On the contrary, tacit knowledge (comprising ideas, experience, perceptions, and so on) is highly 'personal' and difficult to transfer; it can only be gained through personal experience, observed through application, and acquired through practice.
3. Bolisani et al. (1999).

7   Environmental Services: Sustaining Knowledge

Ian Miles[1]

7.1   INTRODUCTION

The contributions of services to economic growth, innovation and competitiveness are currently subject to much attention. The role of services in moving business toward more sustainable patterns of development has received much less attention. This chapter considers business services that assist firms confronting environmental problems associated with their activities. Such services are prominent in the exhibitions and directories of the burgeoning 'environment industry', but little is known about their structure, origin, or contributions to innovation. The quotation below illustrates one example of such a service firm:

Industry is under ever-increasing pressure to minimise its impact on the environment. Current and proposed legislation from the UK government and Brussels reveals an array of statutory compliances and heavy financial penalties. ... However these regulations affect you, AES exists to provide the analysis and assessment to help you meet your environmental responsibilities, and to keep on achieving compliance into the future ... AES can offer a skilled staff of over one hundred, operating from four NAMAS accredited laboratories. We ... make a heavy investment in the latest analytical equipment and state of the art computer software and hardware. ... Water Quality ... Air Quality ... Contaminated Land ... Coal & Fuel testing ... (source: brochure from Analytical and Environmental Services, part of Entec Europe Limited, distributed at the trade show *Environment Technology*, 1994, Birmingham)

Defining the environmental services sector is a complex affair. This is not a set of firms readily distinguishable in official statistical classifications.[2] However, the industry may be mapped from environmental directories and the specialist trade press.   These, together with signs of increasing professional and industrial organisation in the area, indicate the emergence of a community of industrial actors. Firms invest in their membership of this community – for example, by advertising, by providing details of their capabilities (not only in directories, but also in exhibitions and other showcases for the environment industry).

The use of environmental services is in part the result of regulatory pressures. Study after study has shown these to be the predominant (if not the only) driver for environmental concerns on the part of business. In the UK, and presumably several other industrial countries, there is continuing criticism of the policy environment for not 'forcing' environmental innovation sufficiently. Environmental service firms and their industry bodies argue that the lack of regulatory pressures is the main reason for markets for their services not taking off in the UK. (They go on to suggest that this threatens the future of the UK environment industry, which faces competition for overseas markets in particular from Germany, Japan and the USA.) At the time of writing, a version of this argument has been deployed in connection with photovoltaic technology, where the UK lacks a domestic industry of anything like the scale of more environmentally active economies. As markets do not grow as rapidly as was expected and/or promoted, some environmental services find themselves operating in a fiercely competitive environment. In the areas of energy- and materials-efficiency, where cost drivers operate as well as regulatory pressures, such service firms are often 'paid by results', charging a proportion of the savings achieved through their intervention for a certain time-period.

Other factors contribute to the use of these services. One is litigation, another external threat drive environmental concerns – in this case the worry that courts may award large damages against offenders – perhaps several orders of magnitude greater than those demanded by regulators. This motivation is prominent in chemicals and several other sectors. But litigation and regulation could in principle be responded to on an in-house basis. What accounts for the use of external services?

A general issue in opting for externalisation is *lack of relevant skills* in-house. Such skill shortages may be temporary, reflecting especially the rise of new demands whose future evolution is uncertain (are they one-off changes, are they liable to intensify?) at a time when taking on new employees is a difficult option for managers (for example, tight budgetary restrictions, corporate stress on downsizing). Other factors can apply, perhaps especially in the case of environmental services. In some instances there may be deliberate strategies of keeping environmentalists at bay (or co-opting them!), or of outsourcing a wide range of 'peripheral' services. Some environmental activities are contracted out for reasons of public relations and credibility. (One interviewee claimed that an environmental audit coming from a consultant would be more acceptable to public opinion, and that this was precisely the reason for commissioning one.[3] The same informant was scathing about the quality of the report thus obtained, while not regretting having used the service. Lacking familiarity with the client industry in question, the consultants preparing the environmental audit had failed to identify the most important problems, coming up mechanically with a diagnosis based on an over-generic checklist.[4])

Such criticisms are easy to find, as is a more widespread sense that the environmental service sector contains more than its share of "cowboy consultants". But it is also conceded that there are many more systematic and serious service firms. This study examines their roles. Are these services involved in developing new knowledge? Or do they just act as a route for transmission of knowledge from other innovators?

7.2 A SURVEY OF THE ENVIRONMENT BUSINESS

A survey of 101 firms, believed to be representative of those parts of the UK environmental industry who sell services to other firms, was undertaken on the basis of a sample from the major trade fair and directory in 1995. These firms can be differentiated according to various dimensions. One of these is the area of environmental concern on which they focus their efforts. In our survey, we asked firms to indicate, using a scale ranging from 0 = not at all, through 3 = moderately, to 6 = to a great extent, how far their activities address: Noise pollution; Air pollution; Water pollution; Soil pollution; Solid waste; Workplace health; Energy efficiency; Efficient material use; Land management/Remediation; Global issues; and Other environmental issues (which they were allowed to specify). Figure 7.1 displays the results of this enquiry.

Putting to one side the 33 responses indicating a wide range of 'other issues', we see that water, soil, air pollution and land management appear to be the services most frequently offered. Some firms specialise in one sort of problem, others cover a range of problems. There are tendencies to focus on specific ranges of problems – factor analysis (Table 7.1) suggests that there are effectively three groups of problem that may be dealt with:

- Heavy waste (soil, land, water, solid waste)
- Economic drivers (energy and materials efficiency – global problems features to some extent here and on the first factor)
- Local problems (air, noise and health issues).

In addition to mapping the sector in terms of the type of environmental problem addressed, our research suggests a further mapping in terms of functions (see Kastrinos and Miles 1996). We asked the firms how much of their output by value fell into each of six groups of activities[5]:

- **Financial and Information Services** *(for example, Insurance, Legal, Financial, Publishing, Awareness, Training)* These services form an infrastructure for environmental technology, without being directly involved in innovation processes.
- **Professional Services** *(for example, Environmental management consulting, Environmental audits, Environmental reports, Environmental Impact Assessment, Risk assessment, Remote sensing data, Equipment testing/certification, Emissions monitoring, Materials testing/ certification, Toxicity testing)* These services play an active role in defining problems in the relations between their clients and the environment, but have very little role in developing solutions to those problems: their role is largely *diagnostic*.
- **Software** *(for example, Control systems software, GIS, Management decision aids, Analysis tools)* Relatively few firms are involved in generating such specialised tools, though such new technical tools are increasingly underpinning the environment sector.
- **Developing and/or Supplying Hardware** *(for example, 'End of pipe' components (for example, filters, scrubbers), Other specialised components (for example, pumps), 'End of pipe' systems: standard/ customised, Control systems: standard/customised, Control system components, Monitoring Instruments)* Many of these firms would normally be regarded as manufacturing firms, though they often perform associated services such as leasing, after-sales, and so on.
- **Technical Consultancy Services** *(for example, Waste management consulting, Recycling systems design, Monitoring systems design, Eco-design, Waste treatment plant design, Remediation consultancy, Remote product support)* These services provide their clients with technical problem solving knowledge and capabilities.
- **Physical Technical Services** *(for example, Waste management, Remediation, Clean-up, Recycling, Re-use of products)* Such services undertake physical tasks involved in solving or at least alleviating problems in the relations between their clients and the environment.

Respondents were asked to indicate how far their firms were involved in each of the six groups of activity. While many firms provide more than one type of service, analysis of the data shows a strong tendency to focus on one or more of the activity areas. Five clusters of services emerged (Table 7.2), with the small set of software and information services combined together (this set was least heavily focused on specific activities). The employment shares of each set of firms displayed in Table 7.2 does not follow the number of firms precisely, since average size varies across the groups.

Figure 7.1 Activities of environmental firms, 1995 UK questionnaire survey
(scores range from 0 = 'not at all' to 6 = 'to a great extent')

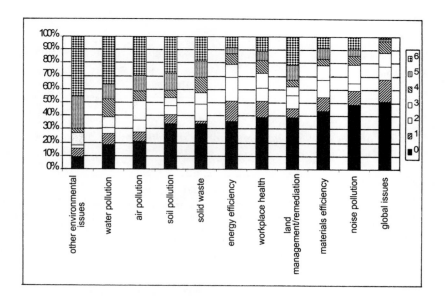

These categories have a clear bearing on the production, coproduction, and use of knowledge related to sustainable economic activity. Let us examine how these services (by their own account) use and share in the development of knowledge.

Table 7.1   Groups of environmental problems addressed by firms (factor loadings)

Topic	Factors		
	1	2	3
Soil pollution	**0.906**	0.141	0.174
Land management/remediation	**0.847**	0.131	0.057
Water pollution	**0.775**	0.000	0.023
Solid waste	**0.638**	**0.544**	0.157
Energy efficiency	-0.151	**0.811**	0.217
Materials efficiency	0.191	**0.799**	0.154
Global issues	0.393	**0.597**	-0.065
Workplace health	0.079	0.044	**0.835**
Air pollution	-0.023	0.084	**0.776**
Noise pollution	0.342	0.346	**0.663**

Table 7.2   Shares of output accounted for by six Activities, for five clusters of Environmental Firms.

Cluster	No. of cases	Mean % of output					
		Info-services	Prof. Diag. services	Soft-ware	Hard-ware	Tech. consult-ancy	Physical services
1 (mainly software)	8	17.75	12.88	31.25	0.00	3.75	1.25
2 (technical services)	21	3.67	27.52	0.57	2.10	56.14	10.00
3 (hardware)	30	0.23	5.00	0.97	88.93	3.50	1.37
4 (physical services)	16	0.47	7.00	0.53	2.33	3.67	86.00
5 (Prof. services)	27	3.59	82.93	1.48	1.30	8.11	2.59
Total	101	3.27	31.44	3.36	27.54	15.72	16.05

7.3 KNOWLEDGE AND ENVIRONMENTAL SERVICES

We asked above whether these services are really involved in developing new knowledge, rather than just acting as a route for transmission of knowledge from other innovators? Our case study work suggests that they often are, and some light can also be shed from the survey analysis. Thus Figure 7.2 presents data on the R&D activities of the firms in the 1995 survey. While a number engage in no R&D, or very little of it, the modal figure is at 2–5 per cent of turnover (generally regarded as quite a reasonable performance for manufacturing firms), while a proportion are much more R&D-intensive.

Figure 3 displays the activities with which these firms report themselves to be involved. They were asked how far the activities involved develop technologies for clients, develop their own technologies for themselves, helping clients develop technologies, or helping clients choose among technologies, using 7-point rating scales.

Figure 7.2 R&D as a proportion of turnover

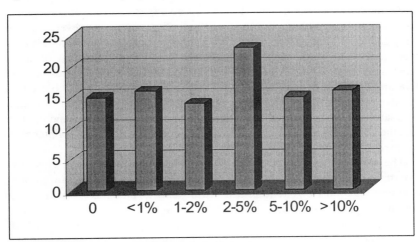

Note: Vertical axis: proportion of firms in each size band.

Source: ES survey.

The results cast light on the direction of their technology efforts. It is apparent that the preponderant effort lies in helping clients choose technologies – this may involve simple off-the-shelf solutions, more complex negotiations between client technological requirements and alternative solutions, or even a challenging of current client practices with novel solutions.   Case study work suggests that the role of services as 'straightforward' agents of transfer of technology is rather important here (though its significance for innovation in clients should not be discounted). Developing technologies for clients is the second most important function (we will not consider development of technologies for own use here). Coproduction of technologies with clients is at least moderately important in quite a few cases.

Of the 101 firms, scores *above* level 3 (which was defined as 'moderately') are obtained as follows:

- 62 (more than moderately) help clients choose which technologies to use;
- 40 develop new technologies to use themselves in the production or delivery of services;
- 37 develop new technologies (including software) for clients to use;
- 32 help clients develop new technologies to use in their products or processes.

So most of the sample report being involved, at least to some extent, in their clients' technology development activities. Some, however, are not. Only four companies score zero on *all four* of these 7-point rating scales, but there are twenty companies who scored 3 ('moderately') or less on all of these activities. Thirteen of these are highly professional services, another five are physical services. This suggests that those companies who are little involved in their clients' technological choice and development are a mixture of (mainly) those providing legal advice, monitoring regulations, and the like, together with those performing service operations (clean-up, maintenance) for their clients.

The range of interactions with clients, and of ways of fusing client and external knowledge to form new solutions, is rather large. We can go on to examine what sort of environmental firm tends to undertake which sort of activity. Again cluster analysis is helpful.

Table 7.3 indicates that six clusters of firms can usefully be distinguished.[6] These range from those whose role in technology choice and development is rather low (the most substantial activity is helping in technology choice, but the score for this is much lower than for the other groups), to those active in all forms of technology development (mean scores well above 'moderately' on all of these).   Three of the 'intermediate' group have significant roles in helping clients choose among technologies – their differentiating feature is where their development efforts are centred. One group is active *both* in developing technologies for themselves and for their clients.

Table 7.3 also indicates the mean scores obtained by each of the sets of firms defined by the clusters of service types defined above. The results are striking. First, *none* of the service function groups display a high average level of codevelopment of technology with their clients. Codevelopment is not the *speciality* of any of these groups. (If we had just isolated software developers in the first cluster, this would have shown a more striking level of such activity.) Software-type services are most prominent in developing technologies for clients, professional services in helping clients choose. Technical services are very much involved with technology choice; hardware services purport to support choice too, but also develop for themselves and for their clients. Physical services, as might be expected given their roles in carrying out waste-related functions for their clients, are most active in development for their own uses, followed by helping their clients' choices.

This analysis makes a good deal of sense, and suggests that the survey questions are answered in a meaningful way. However, statistical data are rarely neat, and simple questionnaire measures are typically 'noisy'. Thus, there is not a neat mapping between the two cluster analyses – Figure 7.4 demonstrates a remarkable variety of one cluster type within the other. Key results are:

- Only technical services to show a strong concentration on one of the technology roles – almost half of them are strong mainly in facilitating clients' choice.
- Another large group of technical service firms are 'active in all'.
- A substantial proportion of software firms are 'low technology' companies. This is a puzzling result, suggesting that this cluster captures some firms involved in information provision, training support, or other activities. A somewhat larger number of software firms are developing technologies for clients, as we would expect, which can be seen by considering the three final rows.
- Professional services were, as expected, also prominent in the cluster of non-technological firms. However, as with software, more of them overall were involved in developing technologies for clients.
- Very few of the hardware and technical service firms were non-technological.
- None of the physical services reported developing technologies for their clients' use.

Figure 7.3 Focus of activities of environmental services firms

☐ developing new technologies (inc. software) for clients to use

■ developing new technologies to use yourself in the production or delivery of services

☒ helping clients develop new technologies to use in their products or processes

▨ helping clients choose which technologies to use

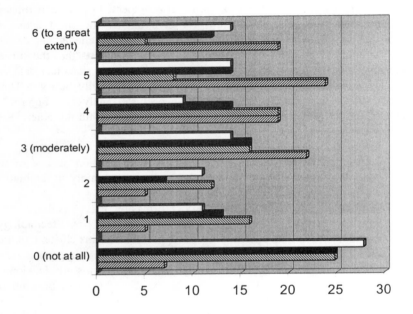

Source: ES survey 1995.

We must, then, be cautious about asserting that one or other type of service firm will be confined to a specific range of knowledge activities with its clients. For example, professional and, especially, technical services firms provide 'strategic' inputs, directing or informing their clients' innovative efforts, rather than substituting for them. These environmental service firms often see their major role as helping clients choose which technologies to use, rather than as being involved in the development of technology *per se.* But there are many exceptions. Our classification is only a step towards more useful ways of distinguishing among and classifying these services.

Our case study work also uncovered cases where contract R&D in the service firm led to a patented process for its client. And among service sectors, environmental engineering services are unusually involved in patenting (see Chapter 10).

Table 7.3 Clusters of environmental firms in terms of technology efforts

	No.	Help clients choose	Help clients develop	Develop your own	Develop for clients
Technology Effort Clusters					
Non-technology firms	14	1.14	0.50	0.64	0.21
Facilitate choice (with some codevelopment)	23	**4.78**	2.39	1.00	1.00
Facilitate and develop own	11	**4.18**	0.64	**4.55**	0.45
Develop for self and client	13	2.77	1.38	**5.23**	**5.54**
Develop for client – and facilitate choice	12	**3.75**	1.92	0.83	**3.92**
Active in all	28	**4.93**	**4.43**	**4.04**	**4.11**
Total	101	**3.87**	2.32	2.70	2.62
Service Activity Clusters					
Mainly software	8	1.75	2.88	2.50	**3.25**
Technical services	21	**5.00**	2.86	2.29	2.43
Hardware	30	**4.27**	2.27	**3.00**	**3.20**
Physical services	16	**3.67**	1.87	**3.73**	2.47
Professional services	27	**3.30**	2.04	2.19	2.04

Note: mean scores – scores greater than 3 – "moderate" – bold.

Case studies identified a second type of technological innovation process involving environmental services – often, in this case, physical environmental services. Here technological innovation is pursued by the service firms in order to expand markets and/or improve (quality or costs of) their processes. This technology development for own use, may involve strategic long-term links (such as equity relations) with clients (for example, with engineering firms and utilities, or as in one case, water utilities). Environmental service arms of the engineering firms provide environmental specifications for engineering works; in water utilities, environmental services are often offered by the corporate laboratory. Such collaborations harness to mutual advantage the functional overlap between environmental services, and the processes the partners use to pursue their business.[7]

Table 7.4 Membership of two types of cluster compared

Clusters by Type of Service	No. in each Service Type cluster	Proportion belonging to each technology development cluster					
		Non-tech. Firms (%)	Facilitate choice (%)	Facilitate & dev. Own (%)	Develop for self & client (%)	Develop for client & fac. choice (%)	Active in all (%)
Mainly software	8	**37.50**	12.50	0.00	**25.00**	12.50	12.50
Technical services	21	0.00	**47.62**	4.76	9.52	0.00	**38.10**
Hardware	30	3.33	**23.33**	13.33	13.33	16.67	**30.00**
Physical services	15	20.00	6.67	**26.67**	20.00	0.00	**26.67**
Professional services	27	**25.93**	14.81	7.41	7.41	22.22	22.22

Note: cells more than 25% bold.

7.4   ENVIRONMENTAL SERVICES, INNOVATION AND REGULATION

Business services can act as carriers of knowledge resources – information on problems and solutions. Environmental service firms can, in principle, enlighten clients as to problems that have not been faced and opportunities that have not so far been grasped. (Examples might include the identification of waste disposal problems through monitoring systems or environmental audits; pointing out gaps in the product portfolio; bringing the practice of competitors or firms faced with similar problems overseas to the attention of clients; providing design consultancy services; facilities management; and so on.) These functions can help stimulate use of 'clean' technologies.

However, the contributions to the development of 'clean' technologies from the proliferation of environmental services are not necessarily all positive. Service firms may not be really familiar with their clients' businesses, nor with the technological capabilities that they possess on an in-house basis. They may, accordingly, fail to stimulate the sort of shift in technological trajectories needed for continued improvement in environmental performance – from end of pipe ('clean up more waste') to more integrated solutions ('create less waste'). Related to this, some environmental services may foster, on the part of their clients, an orientation to compliance, rather than more proactive environmental awareness. Some environmental services do push for more advanced regulations and longer-term perspectives on the part of business. Others are liable to promote end-of-pipe rather than integrated solutions, with little analysis of the potentials for new business opportunities around environmental issues. They may raise the bottom of the firm's *corridor of technological opportunity*, but not otherwise alter the direction in which it is leading.

The emergence of a high industrial division of labour provides opportunities for specialised 'carriers' of innovation to emerge external to the firms whose adoption of 'clean' technology is crucial. But specialisation need not always be overwhelmingly beneficial, since there may be mismatches between different understandings of the regulatory context, the technical environmental issues, and the strategic business needs. Even if it speeds the adoption of specific technological solutions, such specialisation and externalisation may affect, and perhaps even retard or limit, the trajectories along which 'clean' technology evolves in the long term.

All of these possibilities are liable to be influenced by the regulatory context. Regulations, or less formal standards, may even place quality conditions on the activity of services themselves (for example, by specifying the content of an environmental audit, and the best practice for carrying it out; or by regulating waste disposal practices). Less directly, but probably more frequently, the types of regulation which are imposed upon clients will affect the way in which services address their problems – and this in turn may affect the dynamics of the service firm.[8]   For example, different types of emission regulation may lead to different strategies for emission monitoring – for example, is any trace at all of a pollutant to be recorded, or just concentrations above a specified level? Different types of regulatory climate may also impact upon service activities in other ways. Fast-changing legislation, for instance, may be more likely to encourage clients to seek external services than a slower pace of change.

Thus, environmental services are important parts of the environmental innovation system, who should be taken into account when policies are being framed. Unfortunately, as is the case with services' role in innovation more generally, this attention is rarely forthcoming.

The recent KIBS survey (see Chapter 10) confirms the view that professional and trade associations are less well developed for environmental service firms than for other KIBS. Specifically, a question was posed in connection with how firms used various means of protecting the knowledge inputs/core competencies embodied in their *key* business activities. These ranged from formal IPR methods like copyright and patents to informal means like internal working practices and membership of professional associations. Accountants and architects, with well-established professional associations (which input into, and provide information about, regulatory developments) were prone to cite membership of such associations as extremely important. Environmental engineers were much less likely to do so – for example, only 5 per cent of respondents from the larger environmental establishments reported that this method was 'always' used, as opposed to more than half of the corresponding respondents from accountancy and architecture services (see Miles et al. forthcoming).

This raises the possibility that the technology-intensive environmental services sector may be relatively well-linked into *innovation systems*, but poorly linked into *regulatory systems*. Further evidence for this is forthcoming from the KIBS survey results, where we enquired as to which organisations firms interact with to gain knowledge (Table 7.5). The environmental services are most likely to be linked to HEIs, other firms or government programmes – but less likely to deal with professional or trade associations, either as a source of knowledge or a route to contacts. The sector is less professionalised, as we also concluded from the case study work. While it conveys technical knowledge to its clients and is linked into sources of innovative knowledge resources, it appears to lack institutionalised access to regulatory or organisational knowledge resources itself.

We should not overstate this. Some of the knowledge developed by the environmental industry does find its way into the regulatory process. In the case of environmental software, for example, several companies studied did have staff members sitting on industry association committees which propose guidelines, while others are regularly consulted on drafts of regulations. Some of these firms are international players with contacts with both the EU and the US regulatory systems.

Table 7.5 Organisational contacts used to gain information for three KIBS (percentage reporting such contacts)

Source of Knowledge	No. of employees in branch	Sector Accountants	Architects	Engineers
University	1–14	20.0	42.3	78.7
	15–49	11.5	42.1	81.3
	50+	33.3	66.7	95.0
Similar company	1–14	60.0	53.8	71.4
	15–49	34.6	36.8	68.8
	50+	33.3	50.0	65.0
Trade association/ professional body	1–14	80.0	96.2	50.0
↓	15–49	100.0	100.0	87.5
↓	50+	100.0	100.0	95.0
Of those saying yes:				
for technical/ professional guidance	**1–14**	**70.0**	**92.3**	**42.9**
	15–49	**96.2**	**84.2**	**75.0**
	50+	**93.3**	**83.3**	**65.0**
To facilitate links with Other organisations	**1–14**	**70.0**	**7.7**	**14.3**
	15–49	**80.8**	**47.4**	**56.3**
	50+	**66.7**	**33.3**	**60.0**
Government programmes	1–14	30.0	34.6	50.0
	15–49	38.5	52.6	68.8
	50+	46.7	66.7	75.0
Consultants	1–14	60.0	84.6	64.3
	15–49	80.8	94.7	75.0
	50+	66.7	100.0	80.0

Note: Source: KIBS survey

More generally, expert groups involved in framing regulations may contain individuals from the environmental services sectors. (These individuals will typically have been approached as eminent individuals, rather than as representatives of particular firms or sectors. There is some evidence indeed that when recruits are drawn from Southern Europe it is more often the case that private consultancies supply expertise,[9] whereas academics are more likely to be recruited in Northern Europe and the UK.) When major studies intended to inform the regulatory process are being commissioned by the EC – studies, say, of the economic impact of regulations, or the scale of the environment sector – the tendency, however, seems to be to go for big name generalist consultants rather than specialist environmental companies. (An example is the use of Touche Ross for assessment of the Auto Oil programme.) The environmental sector does not seem to be viewed as a repository or original source of key knowledge. There is obviously some loss of expert knowledge here, though on the plus side the large consultancies may be forced to take the environmental business and the issues its raises more seriously than otherwise, and perhaps these are efficient carriers of information to their wider client base.

7.5   CONCLUSION

While their roles are diverse, some environmental services clearly play important roles in the development and, especially, the diffusion of environmental technologies. This conclusion is supported by the responses provided to our survey by environmental firms themselves – there is a clear need for research on the perceptions of their industrial clients.

Services' role in innovation is generally overlooked. In the case of sustainable development, we confront the extra complexities of innovative responses to regulatory drivers. With the increasing division of labour, the technical and other developments involved in meeting changing regulations are distributed widely. Numerous actors – including environmental services – are involved. Their knowledge and strategies affect the way in which the regulatory process unfolds and impacts the performance of industry.

Dutch colleagues suggest (Vlaar et al. 1998) that a trend in the focus of regulation, shifting from end-of-pipe solutions towards the implementation of process-integrated technologies, is liable to prompt clients to demand more and more of environmental service inputs. A highly qualified and internationally competitive environmental sector may thus emerge in response to new environmental requirements. Environmental services will be expected to be more innovative – which should improve their capability to compete on foreign markets. However, the Dutch team also see a problem in the short-term orientation of many clients. This may lead to service firms colluding with them in the search for short-term, often sub-optimal (from an environmental point of view) and less innovative solutions. This would suggest that a strong role remains for public support for basic research and innovation in HEIs and government laboratories, with the service firms playing more of a role of diffusing these innovations.[10]   However, our view is that it is unlikely that public agencies and HEIs can function across the scale and range of service activities that are required. The scale of environmental service firms' R&D, as indicated in this study, suggests that they can make important contributions beyond being mere carriers of innovation. There is thus scope for their more active and widespread participation in problem-solving.

The issues of corporate strategies and innovation processes, and environment industry representation in regulatory processes also require more attention. It would be valuable to locate key individuals who are active in representation of environmental services in regulatory considerations and committees. It would also be important to examine the situation in other countries – is the UK experience here unusual compared to other European policy arenas? Is the environmental services sector developed to an equal extent in countries with 'stronger' or at least different regulatory regimes? Is it incorporated into the policy and industrial knowledge systems in different ways?

But the most crucial questions concern both trends and potentials. What are the trends in the role of environmental services in the 'greening of industry'? And how can sustainable development be facilitated by policy interventions and industrial strategies that fully recognise both the potential and the constraints of firms in this emerging sector?

NOTES

1. Thanks to the Economics and Social Research Council, who funded the project on which this work was based through the *European Context of UK Science* Programme, co-ordinated by the Science Policy Support Group; thanks also to the SPSG and in particular Peter Healey. Nikos Kastrinos was centrally involved in conceptualising and implementing this study, but cannot take what otherwise would be acclaimed authorial credit, due to his current employment status.
2. See OECD (1996b) for various discussions of the issues of classification of this sector.
3. This can be contrasted with the often-cited use of outside consultants to influence opinion *within* the firm.
4. 'They paid a lot of attentions to the lightbulbs which were left turned on, and failed to notice the leaking skip outside the door.' While we treat such criticisms with caution, it is apparent that there is much expression of distrust with 'cowboy consultants' within industry.
5. They were asked to check which of the specific services, given as examples above, they provided. We do not examine this detailed data here.
6. Here, as before, K-means cluster on SPSS was used; lacking an automatic statistical choice algorithm, runs were repeated with different numbers of clusters until diminishing returns set in.

7. It should be noted here that almost half the respondents in our sample either were departments of larger firms or affiliated organisations. About 30 per cent of our respondents had their partners as clients, while for more than half of those their partners were important sources of technological knowledge. For further information see Kastrinos and Miles (1996).
8. One environmental software firm complained that regulations specified the goal to be achieved but not the means whereby this was to be done! Whereas evolutionary economists would generally regard such regulations as providing a positive spur to exploring technological alternatives, for the software company it created a problem in that they did not know precisely what information ought to be included in their product.
9. This is not a universal rule – the Auto Oil programme involved Greek academics.
10. Their emphasis may reflect their research focus on water and waste management services, relatively 'traditional' environmental services.

8 Computer Services: The Dynamics of a Knowledge-Intensive Sector

Jeremy Howells

8.1 INTRODUCTION

As a service activity, the computer service industry still continues to be considered as a passive and reactive form of economic activity. Until recently, it was not seen as an 'industry' at all and was conveniently left off statements about 'industrial policy', or left as an aside from serious initiatives and programmes aimed at manufacturing. The case for computer services, in terms of its economic significance and growth prospects, however, should not be understated. Much has been made of the information technology (IT) 'revolution' over the last two decades or so being the key technological paradigm of the late twentieth century (Hall and Preston 1988). Computer software and services have, in turn, been seen as being at the core of this revolution, radically reshaping the routines and structures of individuals, businesses and government (Alic 1997, p. 9).

The computer service industry *per se* is only part of the economy's total of computer service[1] activity. It is estimated that more than half of all people employed in computer services are working for enterprises not in the industry itself, but in what has been referred to as 'user industries'. These include not only what may be termed immediate industries such as computer hardware manufacturers and telecommunication equipment manufacturers, but also large engineering, aerospace and defence companies as well as from other parts of the service sector such as banks and saving institutions. Almost by definition trying to accurately quantify such workers and activities is difficult. This hidden element of computer services is generally neglected although it still probably forms the largest part of computer services; as such it remains the hidden, but larger part of the iceberg. Even firms traditionally seen as IT manufacturing companies should in reality be seen as IT system integrators, with substantial computer service revenues. Thus nearly half (44 per cent) of all IBM's revenue comes from computer services and DEC and Unisys have even higher proportions coming from software, services and support activities (Howells 1996, p. 26).

Although the growth of computer services in its own right is significant and worthy of interest, the development of the industry more specifically is influenced by a number of key processes which centre on technological innovation, 'externalisation' and the restructuring and rationalisation of the industry. The specific nature and impact of technological innovation and externalisation, in particular, needs to be fully understood in relation to the industry, as these represent critical factors that are helping to shape the industry. For this reason a substantial part of this chapter will be devoted to exploring the nature and role of these key 'drivers' of the computer services and software industry, before a more general analysis of the organisational and locational development of the sector is undertaken.

8.2 TECHNOLOGICAL INNOVATION AND BARRIERS TO GROWTH

Ever since the 1960s there has been the spectre of the 'software crisis' and the 'software bottleneck'. Put simply these arguments suggest that, although there have been astounding advances in the performance, size and cost of much computer hardware, most spectacularly in the case of microchips, the computer software industry has not paralleled this success. Software costs in many application areas have continued to spiral, error rates are still high, whilst delivery dates have rarely been met. As productivity improvements have failed to materialise the industry has continued to suffer from shortages of skilled software engineers. Technology has been seen as the saviour of the industry in terms of bringing about solutions to all these problems, but for the last thirty years they have been slow in coming and many of the pundits that heralded new eras of cheap, reliable software delivered on time have been proved wrong (Brooks 1987). However these problems, and the new technologies that have been introduced to provide solutions to them, have proved critical in terms of how the industry has been shaped. Five main recurring themes are associated centrally with the 'software crisis', namely: (i) poor productivity; (ii) high levels of error; (iii) poor user requirements specification and customer satisfaction; (iv) high maintenance costs; and (v) time overruns. Each of these problems will be discussed briefly below.

1. *Productivity and costs:* Software generation remains a highly labour-intensive activity, and has lagged behind labour productivity improvements in the rest of the IT industry. Thus, although price/performance ratios for hardware have been declining steeply for years, costs per line of software code remain about the same as they did two decades ago (Alic et al. 1991, p. 179).

2. *Error rates:* Related to this, most software that has been written remains error prone. How error prone remains open to question. Some estimates in the US suggest that *detected* error rates in delivered software average between 8–10 errors per thousand lines of code. A study by Myers (1986) has similarly estimated that there are approximately 3.3 errors per thousand lines of code in large software systems. There have been many apocryphal stories of failures in software leading to widespread death and destruction, but even in financial terms poor software quality is costing many billions of dollars every year. It has been estimated that the average cost of software defects is $10,000 per corrected defect.

3. *Requirements specification:* Perhaps the most neglected aspect of problems with the industry is that many customers do not get software which actually meets their specified requirements or more fundamentally is what they actually want. Even today most commentators neglect the vital area of user requirement in the software 'life cycle' (see below). This is associated with poor training and support for personnel in supplier firms, and above all poor management in not allowing more time and resources to be devoted to this area and more structured methods to be imposed, even though it has been shown that a modification in service can cost up to 1000 times more than a modification at the requirements stage (see Bowen and Stavridou 1993, p. 198). In some large systems up to 95 per cent of the code has to be rewritten in order to meet user requirements (Quintas 1991, p. 364). However, user companies are also to blame, again not spending enough time and resources in analysing what they really want and equally changing their requirements throughout the software cycle.

4. *Maintenance:* The maintenance issue is in many ways a reflection of the above problems. Some estimates indicate that as much as 80 per cent of maintenance costs go towards adapting software to customer needs that were not fully understood when the development process began or that changed later (Martin and McClure 1983). Maintenance (which includes upgrades as well as debugging) typically accounts for well over half of life cycle software costs. The cost of maintenance reflect the fact that software maintenance engineers find it difficult to fully understand a software system they did not design or implement; or they have forgotten

the details of the design or code especially if there has been no documentation; whilst any change in part of the software must take into consideration the complex inter-relationship between the change and the rest of the system (Ajila 1995, p. 1155). Not surprisingly in many software companies, over half the employees are involved in maintenance activities.

5. *Time overruns:* Equally time overruns are reflection of all the above problems. Thus in a survey of 288 UK firms only 37 per cent expected their IT systems to be delivered on time and within budget (Quintas 1991, p. 363).

A number of experts see the 'software crisis' as being overstated as it was based on misunderstood and misused statistics. Data collected by van Genchten (1991) indicates that the typical software overruns were only 33–36 per cent over budget and 22 per cent behind schedule. In noting this, Glass (1994, p. 43) describes this as 'clearly a problem but hardly a crisis'. An historical perspective also provides a backdrop to the discussion. In the nineteenth century the scientific community was facing a 'tables crisis' caused by the problem of errors in numerical tables, such as logarithms and navigation tables (Swade 1991). Even the references to the crash of two A320 Airbuses caused by supposed software error associated with their fly-by-wire technology, have echoes in the nineteenth century with the rumour that ships had been wrecked as a result of errors in the navigational tables (Bowen and Stavridou 1993, p. 189). Nevertheless whether all these difficulties can be summed up as a crisis or merely a problem, they still represents an ongoing concern in the industry.[2]

The software process technologies that have been offered as solutions cover fourth generation languages (4GLs), computer-aided software engineering (CASE) tools, structured methodologies, formal methods and object-orientation (OO) and reusability. 4GLs allow software engineers to programme using high level languages without requiring the knowledge of low level languages and enabling programmers to substantially reduce the quantity of program code in software applications. Although 4GLs have been around since the late 1960s it was not until the early 1980s that a new breed of production 4GLs allowed them to be more widely taken up and challenge the use of third generation languages, such as COBOL. CASE tools are computer-based tools which support software development throughout the software life cycle, and cover support in software design and analysis ('Upper CASE') and through to code generation ('Lower CASE'). The trend now is for individual CASE tools to be integrated together to provide 'integrated CASE' technologies (Griffiths 1994; King et al. 1994).

Structured methodologies sought to improve more rigorous procedures to eliciting user requirements and representing candidate designs and they first appeared in the mid 1970s to replace the informal analysis and design practices of the day. The use of formal methods (a more rigorous, mathematical procedure to write software ensuring fewer errors and better productivity) in software generation date back to the 1960s and sought to 'prove' by means of a logical step that a function or component is demonstrably correct with respect to its specification (Tierney 1992, p. 248). In relation to computer software generation, adoption of formal methods in the development process allows proofs to be set up that confirm the properties of the system that are required or assumed to be true, whilst by generating a set of rules or design calculus it allows stepwise refinement of the specification to an executable program (Bowen and Stavridou 1993, pp. 191–2). As such formal methods can permit fewer errors and be more efficient, a key advantage in safety-critical areas. Object-orientation is associated with two principles for structuring systems: via the process of 'encapsulation' it allows storage of data and related operations together within objects, and via 'inheritance' shares commonalities between classes of objects. Both these principles advance software engineering goals of abstraction, modularity and reuse (Fichman and Kemerer 1993, pp. 16–18) which allows both simplification and improved reliability and efficiency in software writing. More specific reuse strategies have been adopted by companies like Hewlett Packard which purposely develops software code and programs that can be reused multiple times, again leading to savings, fewer errors and faster time to market (Lim 1994).

However, although many of the technologies described above have indeed shown superior performance to the prior technologies and methods they sought to supersede, they have faced considerable barriers and opposition. Thus even though formal methods have considerable advantages, particularly in the area of safety critical applications (Bowen and Stavridou 1993), it still has been resisted by many within the industry (Hall 1990). These barriers have tended to be centred on the organisations and individuals themselves rather than technological ones. Thus one of the key barriers to the adoption of formal methods in software production was the fact that software writers and programmers were concerned their jobs would become more routine, less creative and as a consequence would also have less status. Many of the new process technologies required adopters to learn extensive new skill sets, be involved in considerable retraining and to significantly change their working practices. Likewise 4GLs and structured methodologies have not become dominant in their own technological domains. Fichman and Kemerer (1993, p. 13) highlight that one of the key barriers restricting the adoption of structured methodologies was that it threatened the idiosyncratic and 'creative' nature of software generation that still dominates the practices of most development groups. These new methods and technologies may also simply not work in situations of interdependence under uncertainty, where many subtle and tacit elements in the work process are lost (Kiesler et al. 1994, p. 224).

Indeed, although some of these software process technologies, such as CASE tools, can form specific products, others are essentially disembodied innovations associated with new ways of organising and managing the software process, seen in, for example, structured methodologies and formal methods. The most prominent and all-embracing of these has been the development of the 'Software Factory' concept. The original idea of the software factory system was reportedly first employed by General Electric in 1968. The basis of the concept is to place software generation within a software model which would allow substantial economies of scope through specialisation. However, the concept was refined and developed by the Japanese with Toshiba and Hitachi setting up their factories in the mid 1970s. These companies established large factories focused on generating similar products, use of standardised software tools and techniques, with careful monitoring of data throughout the software development process and the institution of appropriate goals and controls. Japanese firms therefore sought to implement the strategic management and integration of software generation with a raft of concomitant procedures, including commitment to process improvement; product-process focus and segmentation; process/quality analysis and control; tailored and centralised process R&D; skills standardisation and leverage; dynamic standardisation system and reusability; computer-aided tools and integration; and incremental product and variety improvement (Cusumano 1991, pp. 9–13). Reusability was also seen as a key factor in making the software factory concept work, hence a focus on standardised structured practices throughout the development and good documentation.

The software factory concept therefore aims to treat software development not as an intellectual, craft-based activity but as an 'industrial' process. 'High-value' activities, such as analysis, would be performed by a few software engineers at the customer's site whilst 'low-value', repetitive activities, such as coding, would be performed by low-paid, lesser-skilled workers in the software factory (Nairn 1992, 22). As such, the Japanese software factories subscribe to a single methodology and work routines which are well documented and subscribed to by all their software programmers and workers. Thus, Cusumano found that out of a sample of 40 large US and Japanese computer systems companies, Japanese companies averaged 50–70 per cent higher output per programmer and a third to a half the level of errors (Cusumano 1991, 1992).   In addition, by using unskilled workers of average capability, Japanese companies have been able to avoid the severe shortages of skilled software programmers that is found in Japan (Yamamoto 1989, pp. 9–11) and elsewhere in the world. Others have seen the concept of the software factory developing still further. Thus the 'older' types of Japanese software factories may be seen as 'component' factories developing and packaging pieces of code which are then supplied as reusable software components to the project teams. 'Domain' factories are seen as a further intermediate level between 'component' and 'experience' factories, with domain factories processing experiences for a specific domain of applications (Nairn 1992, p. 23).

The software factory approach, therefore, adopted many disembodied work practices and work organisation methods (such as structured methods) which offered more structured and effective forms of writing software and integrated this with new tools and languages into a more integrated whole. These are not necessarily leading edge technologies, but the key is that they are integrated in a more effective way. The concept also moved away from the constant battles that exist between software disciplines, in particular the software engineering approach and the more mathematical approaches of formal methods (Bowen and Stavridou 1993, p. 191) that exist in the West. Nevertheless the potential of the 'software factory' remains to be fulfilled, with Kim and Choi (1997, p. 402) stressing that the software factory approach is still limited even in Japan.

8.3   OUTSOURCING, EXTERNALISATION AND DELOCATION

'Externalisation' is a key process in the evolution and growth of the computer services industry. Externalisation at its broadest level refers to 'the shift of a particular set of goods or services from being generated within a firm to outside it' (Howells and Green 1986, p. 120: see also Perry 1990, 1992; Wood 1991; Elfring and Baven 1994; O'Farrell 1995; Lundmark 1995). The process of externalisation can be associated with three key phenomena: (1) the growth of 'outsourcing' in terms of the contracting out of activities formerly undertaken in-house; (2) the continued emergence and spinning out of externalised computer service enterprises that were formerly part of larger industrial corporations; and (3) the geographical dispersal of computer service 'producers' formerly co-located with the user. The externalisation process is important to understand since it represents a crucial dynamic within the European industry in terms of its growth and change and has key implications for the spatial development of the computer services sector. Each of these externalisation processes will now be considered in turn.

8.3.1 Outsourcing

Outsourcing has continued to be a major force reshaping the computer service industry throughout the 1980s and 1990s. Outsourcing, that is the use of third parties to deliver computer services, includes three aspects:

1. delivery of IT and information system (IS) services;
2. management of assets, such as data centres and networks; and
3. the development of a long-term relationship between vendor and corporate customer.

In turn, the major factor encouraging the use of outsourcing by firms has been associated with the following needs to reduce costs, increase efficiency, increase speed of response and create greater flexibility in the organisation (see, for example, Buck Lee 1992; Altinkemer et al. 1994).

In terms of this last aspect outsourcing allows firms to free up key management time and resources to focus on their 'core competences' so that they can adjust more to changing patterns of demand for their products and services. The potential for market growth in outsourcing is seen as considerable. Thus the emergence and growth of the company, EDS, is evidence of the strength of the growth in outsourcing. EDS, founded in 1962 in Dallas, Texas, had by 1994 become the second largest computer service company in the world, second only to IBM and twice as large as Microsoft. The company, which was acquired by General Motors in 1984 and then subsequently spun-off by General Motors in 1996, has built on the provision of computer services to business and government and has been described as 'the outsourcing pioneer' (Moad 1991, p. 65). In Europe it has used the UK as the main bridgehead both acquiring companies, most notably SD-Scicon in 1991, and in capturing key markets. By 1996 it employed over 16,000 workers in Europe, half of them in the UK. EDS has, however, targeted other European countries and indeed one of its earliest acquisitions was Societe Pour l'Informatique (SPI), the computer service operations of Pechiney, the French aluminium and metals group, in 1987.

The merit of computer service outsourcing by firms still remains open to debate. Some companies have had bad experiences with outsourcing and have decided to reverse the trend by becoming 'insourcers' by bringing back their computer service operations in-house. Dissatisfaction of outsourcing has come from various factors. One of the chief causes was that apparent cost savings were disappointingly low (PA Consulting 1995). Other problems associated with outsourcing have been:

- Lack of supplier flexibility
- Supplier unfamiliarity of the business
- Damage to staff morale
- Loss of control over IT within the firm
- Cost escalation
- Time/effort needed to build partnerships with outsourcers
- Over-dependence on the supplier
- Loss of control of core business competence

Many companies assume that having outsourced their computer service operations they can forget about it. However, they still need a team of knowledgeable in-house computer experts to sit between the end-users within the firm and the outsourcer, to manage and monitor the service level agreement and the supplier's capabilities and to assess the impact of new technologies on the IT strategy of the firm (Bragg 1998, p. 129).

Work for 'traditional' outsourcers have become much harder during the 1990s (Rothery and Robertson 1995, p. 117) and companies like EDS will have to offer more than just simple cost savings (still seen as the main factor encouraging outsourcing) and will have to overcome the feelings of loss of control over IT by corporate customers. Many companies now have come to realise that information and IT are central to, or indeed part of, their core competencies in whatever industry they operate in. Outsourcing, therefore, rather than enabling firms to focus on their core competencies, may actually lead to a potential loss of a firm's core competence. Outsourcers are now seeking to provide such additionality. EDS is seeking to offer more value-added services, such as 'data mining' (Maid 1995) which aims to provide a firm with more detailed information about their manufacturing processes, costs and the nature of their operations. Similarly GSI, a large facilities management operator recently taken over in 1995 by ADP, a US computer services company, has sought to focus on providing a more complete service by concentrating on operating and providing solutions for the whole distribution and logistics chains of companies.

8.3.2 Externalisation of Enterprises and New Firms

Whilst externalisation in the form of outsourcing has represented a source of growth for the industry, externalisation in its other main form, the externalisation of enterprises, has led to the emergence of key actors in the industry. Thus a significant number of major computer service operations in the European market have arisen out of in-house computing service departments with large, often multinational business corporations (Howells 1987; defined more recently as 'user spin-off firms' by Baba et al. 1995). Table 8.1 provides details of these externalised operations from across Europe and North America. Significant new industrial operations can be created and developed within existing companies[3]. At a later stage such operations may then become externalised. This may be done via a number of ways. It may be done via partial disposal, in terms of the firm turning the operation into a subsidiary or associate company, where it still retains partial ownership and control and continues to use (but now, in terms of 'open' market, purchasing) the goods and services of the externalised operation. But the firm may also completely dispose of the operation via a management buyout, or support some kind of venture funding which leads to the setting up of a new firm. Alternatively, the firm may sell its operations to another company who specialises in that particular activity. This happened in the case of UCSL and SPI which were both sold by their parent companies to EDS, whilst British Steel sold CMS to Cap Gemini Sogeti. In most cases the existing firm will continue to use (that is, purchase in) the goods or services from the remodelled operation. However, more drastically the company may close down the operation completely and buy-in the services or products from another specialist company.

However, although the externalisation of enterprises is important in the formation and continued restructuring (as spun out firms are reabsorbed by large, dedicated computer software companies such as EDS) of the computer services and other industry sectors (Elfring and Baven 1994) in Europe,[4] more straightforward new firm formation processes also remain significant. The service sector as a whole has been an extremely buoyant section of the economy in terms of new firm formation and the computer service industry is no exception. Although European-wide data are not available, detailed analysis by Keeble et al. (1991, p. 444) of VAT registrations in the UK indicate the strength of the sector in Britain. Thus the total stock of computer service businesses in the UK grew by 89 per cent between 1985–89, yielding some 13,132 new businesses, whilst 93 per cent of the total stock of computer service businesses were small (that is, with turnover of less than £0.1 million).

The computer service sector is not only buoyant in terms of new firm formation, a few new computer service firms can also grow extremely rapidly. Although Microsoft in the US readily comes to mind, two German software companies Software AG and SAP established respectively in 1969 and 1972 have grown at phenomenal rates to become key players in the European software industry.

8.3.3   Geographical Externalisation

The last externalisation process, geographical externalisation, may be better seen as a form of quasi externalisation and is simply associated with the relocation and new investment in computer services in low cost, mainly developing countries, which nonetheless represent significant repositories of scientific and technical capabilities (Howells 1999d). Such moves have long been heralded, however, they are now starting to take effect and may be seen as reflecting the 'hollowing out' of a service (rather than manufacturing) activity by redirecting key research, design, programming and maintenance work overseas whilst retaining customer liaison and general head office and administrative functions.

The most cited example of a developing country that has expanded its software industry is that of India, one of the most impoverished developing countries, but with a substantial scientific and technical base (Balasubramanyam and Balasubramanyam 1997), amounting to some 170,000 scientists, technicians and engineers. India is seeking to expand as a major software centre. India's software explosion, centred on Bangalore (known as India's 'Silicon Plateau' and 'Surf City') has occurred via three main routes. First, by computer companies forming joint ventures (although sometimes running independent operations) with local Indian software companies, such as Tata Consultancy Services (TCS) and Wipro, to run software design centre; examples here include Mahindra–British Telecom (employing 500 staff), Tata-Unisys and IBM-Tata. The second element of growth has come from major industrial corporations which have set up sophisticated offshore development operations and to generate software either for their own use (examples here include Citicorp, General Electric, Intel, Lucent Technologies, Motorola, Siemens, and Texas Instruments), or for resale, such as operations run by Microsoft, Novell and Oracle. Lastly, there are the indigenous companies themselves. Thus CMC has won contracts in overseas countries providing software for London Underground and La Suisse Insurance.

Table 8.1 Corporate spin-offs: examples of externalisation from the computer services

Parent Company	Spin-Off Company	Spin-Off Year	Country/ Turnover	Comments	Acquiring Company	Country/ Turnover	Comments
Banque Societé Generale	SG2	–	France	Founded 1970	–	–	–
BP (Amoco)	Scicon International	1988	UK; £252m; 5,000 staff (1988; post merger)	Merged with Systems Designers (SD; 26% owned by BAe from 1986 purchase) to form SD- Scicon in 1988 (see below)	EDS	US	EDS acquired SD Scicon in 1991
British Steel	Central Management Services (CMS)	1996	UK; £25m (1995)	Sold to CGS; 300 employees	CGS	France	Acquired by Hoskyns, UK subsidiary of CGS
Cadbury Schweppes	ITNet	1995	UK	MBO	–	–	Sold for £32.5m; Cadbury retaining 12.5% stake
Commissariat à l'Energie Atomique (CEA)	CiSi	1996	France	Founded 1972; Failed sell-off to Sema	–	–	–
Compagnie d' Generale Electricité (CGE)/	GSI	1995	France	Founded 1971; Sold to ADP	Automatic Data Processing (ADP)	US	–
Alcatel Alsthom Crédit du Nord (Paribus)	Segin	1990	France; c. FFr2.3bn (1991)	Sold off and merged with FITB and Sodinforg to form Axime	–	–	Crédit du Nord retained 20.5% stake

Table 8.1 (continued)

Parent Company	Spin-Off Company	Spin-Off Year	Country/ Turnover	Comments	Acquiring Company	Country/ Turnover	Comments
1. Eni 2. Fiat 3. Finmeccanica	1. Enidata 2. ITS Information Technology Services 3. Elsag Bailey Informatica 4. Cedacrinord	1996	Italy, L600bn	The first 3 units with Cedacrinord form new firm: Arancia	–	–	–
Heron International	First Computer	1988	UK	MBO	–	–	–
ICL	Workplace Technologies	1995	UK, c.£70m (1998)	MBO from ICL in 1995 for £12m	–	–	–
McDonnell Douglas	McDonnell Information Systems (MDIS)	1992 Founded in 1969	US	MBO	Founded in 1969	UK	McDonnell Douglas spun-off its largely UK based information systems unit
National Westminster Bank	Centrefile	–	UK	–	–	–	–
Neurodynamics	Autonomy	1996	UK	MBO	–	–	–
Olivetti	Olsy	1998	Italy, L42,00bn	Sold to Wang	Wang	US	Sold for $391m; Olivetti takes 18.6% stake in Wang

Table 8.1 (continued)

Parent Company	Spin-Off Company/	Spin-Off Year	Country/ Turnover	Comments	Acquiring Company	Country/ Turnover	Comments
P&O	P&O Computer Services	–	UK	–	–	–	–
Pechiney	Societe Pour l'Informatique (SPI)	1987	France $50m (1987)	Sold to EDS; 600 employees, 1987	EDS	US	–
Pirelli	Pirelli Informatica	–	Italy	–	–	–	–
Rover	Istel	1987; Founded 1978	UK	MBO in 1987	AT&T	US	MBO followed by acquisition by AT&T in 1991.
SD Scicon	Integral Solutions (ISL)	1989	UK; £0.5m (1989)	MBO	–	–	–
Texas Instruments	Texas Instruments Software	1997	US, $250m (1996)	Founded 1984; 1,300 employees	Stirling Software	US, $439m (1996)	Acquired 1997 for $165m
Unilever	UCSL	–	Neth./UK	Sold to EDS in 1984	EDS	US	–

As such, less-developed economies are aiming to establish themselves as low-cost 'research factories' (with wages 90–99 per cent lower than in Europe and North America; Crabb 1995). In addition, eastern Europe, China and parts of the former Soviet Union are also seeking to exploit their low-cost, but under-utilised, software skills to form collaborative links with western companies seeking cheap, 'offshore' software expertise. This should not be seen as an irrelevance to Europe. Thus ICL (taken over by Fujitsu in 1990) which has cut back much of its research, design and engineering functions in software development within Britain, now has some 1700 employees working in Fujitsu-ICIM (which used to be part of ICL before its takeover by Fujitsu and which ICL still has a 36 per cent holding) in India. Similarly two other European companies, Bull and BT with their separate ventures with Mahindra are using India as a low cost base to serve European and US markets (Martin 1992; Ramachaudran 1992).

Moreover the computer service industries in India and other developing countries are not standing still. India, for example, has now moved from virtually no computer service and software industry in the mid 1980s to being the second largest software exporter behind the US in 1999 (Howells 1999d, p. 19). The Indian computer service industry is seen as going through a series of stages of offshore development from:

1. sending Indian software workers to work on turnkey projects at client sites overseas;
2. to provide 'bodyshop' services in the home country writing software or providing emergency backup services via satellite communication;
3. producing definable software products for overseas markets; and
4. further developing indigenous expertise and competitive advantage in specific application areas.

Although cost may be an initial factor in basing operations in such countries[5], these countries are seeking to upgrade and develop their skills and move into more sophisticated high value areas of software generation and development.

8.4 NEW LOCATIONAL AND ORGANISATIONAL FORMS

As the computer services industry has matured as an industrial activity it has gradually loosened its ties from being a largely nationally-oriented industry. As such, unlike much of manufacturing industry and indeed other parts of business services, computer services have arguably been more national in focus and more resistant to pressures of 'globalisation'. It has been noted elsewhere (Gentle and Howells 1993) that there have been five factors sustaining a national orientation in software production and have acted as strong barriers to its wider internationalisation, namely: (1) public procurement; (2) language; (3) dominance of national hardware suppliers with the peculiarities of their own operating systems; (4) national standards, certification, intellectual property rights and regulation; and (5) limited scale and geographical scope benefits.

These factors which previously allowed considerable advantages to domestic computer services are now increasingly being eroded. In terms of public procurement it is now harder for governments to show favouritism in handing out contracts to indigenous software suppliers (Sandholtz 1992; Cooke et al. 1992). The language barrier in the past has been a key factor sustaining national market segmentation within Europe especially in terms of software and programming difficulties. However, as key multinationals both as consumers, such as Electrolux, and producers, such as Cap Gemini Sogeti, have adopted English as the corporate language and more and more executives and middle managers become bilingual this is also becoming a less significant barrier over time. The move to open systems, together with the gradual abandonment of the policy of supporting 'national champions' within the IT industry, has also meant that national markets are tending to lose their technical identity and differentiation.

The adoption of more widespread, international software standards and certification procedures, often in safety-critical areas and associated with formal methods (Tierney 1992; Bowen and Stavridou 1993) has encouraged software producers to standardise their software writing and products for a wider world market, whilst it has also allowed users to feel more comfortable about using non-indigenous suppliers. A number of these standards have indeed specifically been formulated at a European level by bodies, such as the European Space Agency. The emergence of wider process standards, such as the ISO 9000 quality standard, has also led corporate customers to feel more comfortable about choosing overseas suppliers. The formation of European-wide legislation and controls covering such key areas as intellectual property rights is also beginning to have an effect on broadening the horizons of the industry. Thus the lack of Europe-wide data protection and copyright controls as a key factor holding back consumer confidence in the wider information industry in Europe (Torrisi 1998, p. 80).

Furthermore, it has only been recently that major multinational customers have encouraged computer service providers to provide global service and support networks (Roberts 1998, p. 240). However, these major corporate customers are pushing hard for a global seamless solution to their computing and software needs.   Much of this pressure has come from the need to win lucrative facilities management and software sales to multinational companies who want to have a European-wide solution rather than having to deal with a series of indigenous firms in each of separate national territories. The computer services industry has therefore been responding to the emergence of a wider pan-national and indeed international markets.   Key players, such as EDS, have been expanding aggressively across Europe and North America (Gentle and Howells 1994, pp. 316–7), infilling their national networks through acquisition of smaller indigenous firms such as the acquisition by Cap Gemini Sogeti of the UK services group, Hoskyns. Larger multinational computer service firms are also allowing specialisation between national centres in terms of their software development and generation, rather than seeking to maintain a whole set of software specialisms in each individual country.

The emergence of major international players in the computer service industry is also continuing the evolution of a 'dualistic' structure of the sector (Howells 1987, p. 498).   The continued buoyant generation of new firms and their rapid growth within many advanced industrial economies, such as the UK (Keeble et al. 1991, p. 446), does not mask the fact that major computer service companies are also growing rapidly both through above average indigenous growth rates, but also through acquisition activity.   Such acquisition, not only covers the takeover of firms that have always been independent but it also includes those operations that have been spun-off by industrial corporations or through the direct purchase of in-house operations which have not yet been externalised.   There appears to be still a strong process of fragmentation, externalisation and reabsorption in the industry, as the sector spins out computer service activities from largely 'hidden', non-market (and hierarchical) activities within major industrial corporations, towards more open, specialist market operations, either that remain independent concerns or that are acquired by the major multinational computer service firms in the industry.

Lastly here is the issue of co-location, relocation and concentration or decentralisation trends within the industry.   In terms of new firm formation and headquarters location it is possible to discern a concentrated pattern of new firms in the industry and the concentration of headquarters control in the major urban centres and their attractive environs (Keeble et al. 1991).   The computer service industry has always been fairly dispersed (or at least evenly located in relation to population and industry patterns) as much facilities management, turnkey and bespoke software development had by its nature to be located (or co-located) at or near the consumer.   Indeed much of the computer service sector was 'hidden' as operations within the manufacturing firms or banks themselves. However, there have been shifts towards a more decentralised or at least delocated pattern of computer service and software 'production'. Hall et al. (1985, p. 37) in the US context noted a number of major factors encouraging decentralisation. In the US there was a continued need to decentralise activities to build up and maintain customer contact, and it also related to relocating certain activities to retain key clients, such as the shift to Texas for those software firms serving airlines whose companies headquarters had shifted there. There was also some evidence of decentralisation to avoid high cost of living areas in California facilitated by improvements in telecommunications technology and provision.

A key factor in computer service and software location in the past has certainly been the need to be co-located at or near prime users. However, Howells (1987, p. 500) noted that this locational factor may now be decreasing in importance. [6] This is associated with the growth in packaged software, improvements in software generation requiring reduced maintenance activity needing close ongoing contact with the user, and by disembodied improvements, such as structured methodologies, in the organisation of software program generation throughout the software 'life cycle' (see Andriole and Freeman 1993, pp. 167–170, for a critique of the life cycle concept and the 'waterfall model'). As a consequence stages 2–6 of program generation (Table 8.2) need no longer be in such close proximity to the customer and can be located elsewhere (Howells 1987, p. 500). This has been evident with the rise of distance working by such companies as FI Group in the UK. Jones (1994, pp. 238-9) has highlighted the general increase in distance from the customer base with: commercial software packages (such as Lotus and MS-DOS) – average distance now 3,000 miles; systems software (such as PBX telephone systems) – with distances of several thousand miles; and military software (such as for the Patriot and Tomahawk missiles) – approaching 6,000 miles. In other software applications, though, such as management information systems where customer contact is still important, distance between customer and provider can remain a few thousand yards.

The rise of the 'software factory' phenomenon also has implications for the location of the computer service industry. The factory phenomenon already creates a spatial division of labour by the fact that the 'orientation' and 'planned' workers (Thorngren 1970) are the ones who maintain customer contact, whilst the 'programmed' workers remain in the factory writing code. However, many of the concepts are being applied to less-developed countries in combination with improvements in terrestrial and satellite-based telecommunication systems. The diffusion of such telecommunication systems in combination with the disembodied innovations in software development and generation (achieving reusability and reducing the need for so much on-site maintenance work through reduced error rates and better user requirement proving) have meant that computer service companies in less-developed countries can maintain contact with lucrative client bases in more-developed countries. Thus CMC, based in India, undertook its work for the London Underground supported by its connection with the Indonet network and its link to an international satellite system. Similarly software engineers at the BT–Mahindra joint venture in Bombay developed software for a customer service information system for Singapore Telecom linked by satellite to other BT–Mahrindra software engineers working on-site in Singapore.

Table 8.2 Stages of program generation

Main Stages		Specific Elements
Systems definition	1.	User requirements (involves salesmen/systems and requirements analysts)
Functional design and	2.	Functional requirements/specification specification
	3.	How to achieve requirements
	4.	Requirements organization
Development:		
Design and coding	5.	Design specification
Test and validation	6.	Probing/coding specification
	7.	Program proving
Operation and maintenance	8.	Installation, take-up and operation

Source: Howells and Green (1986, p. 189).

Although some computer service companies remain sceptical to how far this delinking can go and whether it is effective, certainly the locational delocation and segmentation of the industry could mean substantial threats for computer service firms in North America and Europe. Even so, it does offer opportunities for disadvantaged regions, such as Northern Ireland and southern Italy, in terms of seeking higher-value industry into their areas. For instance, Nestel (controlled by Finsiel a major Italian computer service company, in turn controlled by the STET holding company), has established a software factory in Bari in southern Italy. Nestel produces software for other companies within the Finsiel group. These affiliated companies undertake project analysis and design at the customer's site, and the resulting specifications are then sent over the telecommunications network to Nestel in Bari. Nestel then generates the code and undertakes the unit testing before sending back the components over the network to the affiliate company so that it can be integrated into an information system and finally delivered to the customer. Nestel employs around 250 staff, who previously had little software experience, writing primarily COBOL code. Another Italian software company, Data Base Informatica, centred in Rome and Milan has also set up a software factory in Naples employing some 400 people.

8.5   CONCLUSIONS

The computer service industry represents a key exemplar of the knowledge-based economy (Alic 1997, p. 8). It is exhibiting high rates of growth in terms of both output and employment and it is highly dynamic. In turn this analysis has indicated that the way that computer services are generated and organised and used is undergoing fundamental shifts, and this could have important ramifications for how the industry is structured and which 'actors' within it will have the greatest influence and advantage. In all these respects the computer services industry remains a 'sleeping giant'. Paradoxically much of the rapid growth in the industry has been characterised by shortage and constraints in terms of labour shortages and technological constraints centred around the ongoing problem of the software crisis. Thus, developments within the industry have been shaped by attempts to get away from, or resolve, these constraints and shortages whether by adopting new methods or by moving into new geographical areas (Howells 1999).

However, the industry's time has now surely come. It shows remarkable economic, employment and new firm growth and this in a period of economic uncertainty cannot be ignored forever. What this growth means for specific nations and regions in the world economy is much harder to determine, given the complex interplay of service-supply structures and market evolution (Cooke et al. 1992, p. 196), although there may be potential for at least some geographical decentralisation within the industry on an international scale. The example of the Indian software industry is a remarkable example of this process. Against this are still strong centralising tendencies in terms of computer service activities within countries, the relatively concentrated nature of new firm formation rates being a significant factor in centralisation of the industry. Undoubtedly the economic impact of computer services will be increasingly felt across the globe.

NOTES

1. For the purposes of analysis, computer services are defined here as composing of two core activities (OECD 1989).
   Computer Software: provision of stored programs for computer operating systems or for applications, either customised for individual clients or packaged to suit multiple clients. Software may be transmitted to the customer via a telecommunications network, via a transportable media, such as a computer tape, disc or CD-ROM, or as part of a complete hardware and software system (turnkey system).
   Computer Services and Consultancy: provision of services from suppliers to customers which may involve the supplier carryout out data processing activities using the supplier's own facilities (bureaux services) or using a customer's facilities (facilities management; FM). Alternatively the supplier may assist the customer to carry out his/her own data processing by aiding system design (system analysis and consultancy), by providing staff to work on the consumer's site ('bodyshopping'), or by providing training and education services.
2. What might be described as a subset of the 'software crisis' was the Y2k problem, where similarly there has been a divergence of opinion over whether it was really such a major problem as was made out by many experts.
3. See Howells (1989b) and Elfring and Baven (1994) for an evaluation of this argument presented by a model.
4. Although the presence of 'maker spin-off' firms (Baba et al. 1995) in Europe appear very limited.
5. Delivered cost of Indian software per thousand lines of code is typically half the cost of producing it in Europe or North America.
6. It should be noted that in other producer services the importance of 'co-location' may indeed be increasing; see Quinn and Dickson (1995) for an interesting analysis of this issue.

9 Knowledge Management Practices and Innovation[1]

Richard Hull

9.1 INTRODUCTION

This chapter discusses the relations between knowledge and innovation *within* the firm. It complements other chapters in this book, whose focus is more on relations *between* firms, and between firms and other organisations, and on the various strategies deployed by firms. As is consistently argued throughout this book, the new service economy is characterised by the intensified mobilisation of knowledge for the pursuit of innovation, and yet the precise ways in which such mobilisation actually improves the potential for innovation remains relatively unexplored, and not just within this book. This chapter describes in detail some of those emerging activities, and discusses their potential for improving the capabilities for innovation. For instance, many firms are now explicitly deploying new information technologies, such as corporate Intranets, for the purpose of improving innovation. Optimistic projections of the benefits of such new technologies needs to be tempered by attention to the finer details of the ways they are actually implemented and put to use. Attention to the extra demands placed on personnel as a result of such new technologies is also required. The strategies of firms in mobilising knowledge, and the actual implementation of those strategies, may be quite different things.

One of the key concepts for investigating and understanding activities within firms and organisations is the concept of 'routines'. This is a central element of many of the various theoretical perspectives on innovation which have developed over the last decades. Routines are regular activities and ways of doing things, whether these are formally specified procedures such as writing a report evaluating a completed R&D project, or informally acknowledged ways of 'getting the work done', such as chatting in the coffee area to keep up to date with other R&D projects.

In this chapter this focus on routines is developed as a method for discovering the various forms of knowledge management actually used within firms, and hence as a way of developing forms of evaluation of those knowledge management activities. Whilst this is clearly of particular interest to organisations developing their knowledge management strategies, it has a wider set of implications in the context of this book for understanding the relations between innovation in general (whether in manufacturing or service firms) and the intensified mobilisation of knowledge. In particular, the theoretical arguments and the empirical material presented here both suggest that attention to routines, what actually happens in organisations, provides much richer perspectives on those relations than attention to the different types of knowledge, such as tacit and codified. Attention to what actually happens can, for instance, highlight the importance of policies and practices for the career progression of key knowledge workers in any organisation, as we illustrate towards the end of the chapter, and also temper the optimistic assertions of the many consultancy firms promoting particular knowledge management techniques and technologies.

We draw upon such observations, gained from case-study research in five large companies, in this chapter. The focus in each case was upon the 'innovation process' – the R&D department or unit, and the various connections between R&D and rest of the firm, such as marketing, customer support and production. The firms were Hewlett-Packard Laboratories, Bristol; Amersham International, Life Sciences division; Ove Arup R&D department (the sole non-manufacturing firm); British Aerospace R&D; and ICI Polymers. Each study included extensive interviews with around a dozen people, drawn equally from senior management, R&D scientists and engineers, and supporting personnel such as IT specialists and librarians (see Coombs and Hull 1998, for a full description). For each firm a list of the specific observed knowledge management activities was then presented and verified. Over the five firms, a total of over 80 different activities were described. The range and diversity of these activities, and specifically the range of distinct forms of 'knowledge processing', can also be seen as a contribution to the discussions elsewhere in this book of the different activities pursued by the various types of knowledge-intensive business services currently emerging.

9.2   KNOWLEDGE MANAGEMENT – BACKGROUND

Knowledge management has quickly come to mean many things to different people, which is one of the reasons why it has often been dubbed as merely a 'new management fad', encouraged by consultants seeking a new label under which to sell much the same services and systems. There is undoubtedly an element of truth to this. However, there is also no doubt that many firms are adopting significant new practices, altering existing operations, appointing specific knowledge management personnel, and installing new systems. These are all intended to improve the various ways in which they manage and 'leverage' knowledge. There has also been a proliferation of academic and practitioner journals and newsletters centred on knowledge management, the establishment of many academic research centres, the development of postgraduate courses, the appointment of academics with the title of 'Professor of Knowledge Management', and the establishment of government units focused on disseminating best practice to firms. Clearly then, the phenomenon is not merely some passing fad, but is in the process of establishing itself as a new aspect of management and organisation.

One of the key reference points on knowledge management is the work of Nonaka.[2]   He has developed a model of the various ways in which organisations create knowledge and suggested a style of management and an organisational structure for best managing the knowledge creation process, namely the 'hypertext organisation'. Central to the model (as indeed to much other work on knowledge management) is Michael Polanyi's distinction between tacit and explicit knowledge. Nonaka argues that tacit and explicit knowledge can be converted from one to the other, and his main focus is managing the interactions between the various modes of conversion. Another major contributor, Dorothy Leonard-Barton (1995), bases her discussion more firmly on the 'core competence' literature of strategic management. She focuses on 'the *whole system* of knowledge management' (ibid. pp. 271–2, original emphasis), which is seen to be an integral element of competitive advantage, or 'core technological capability'. Her specific interest is in the 'key knowledge-building' activities – shared problem solving, implementing and integrating new technical processes and tools, experimenting and prototyping, and importing and absorbing technological and market knowledge.

In addition there have been numerous offerings by the large management and IT consultancies. These were initially focused on IT applications, such as 'intranets' (internal internet – organisational information systems accessed internally with a web-browser and organised on a distributed and hypertext basis), 'extranets' (parts of an intranet which are made available to an organisation's collaborators, customers or suppliers), 'groupware' (software which enables groups of people who are separated by distance or time to collaborate on electronic documents, drawings, and so on), data mining applications (software which 'drills down' into all the data held within an organisation and returns new forms of aggregation), decision support tools, mobile computing and communications systems, and video-conferencing.

More recently, however, their focus has been more on 'the people side', developing schemas and methods for assessing and improving the 'organisational culture', especially as many knowledge management initiatives have been seen to have failed through lack of commitment and supportive action from employees and senior management. This shift mirrors the previous experience of business process re-engineering, where again new IT was claimed by consultants to achieve dramatic improvements in firm performance, only to fail through lack of attention to the 'people side', and often resulting in large-scale losses of middle managers whose experience and knowledge of the firm was then also lost (Coombs and Hull 1995).

Finally, there is the focus on 'intellectual capital', 'intellectual assets' or 'knowledge assets', where the treatment is primarily from an accounting perspective and advice is from those same management consultancies. The emphasis is on developing methods for measuring and auditing the sub-set of a firm's intangible assets (other intangibles include customer loyalty and brand image) such as the number of patents, copyrights or licenses it owns, the numbers of personnel with degrees, and so on. Whilst one can consider this as an aspect of knowledge management, the moves to account for intellectual capital are also clearly driven by the dramatic rise, over the last 20 years, of the value placed on intangibles relative to a firms' tangible assets of capital and labour, whether by stock market analysts or more concretely during valuations conducted for mergers and acquisitions (Yakhlef and Salzer-Mörling 2000).

There are many broad debates about knowledge management – its extent and relative importance; whether it should be confined to 'knowledge-intensive' or 'technology-intensive' firms, or has wider applicability; whether it is primarily a matter of better IT, better human resource management, or driven by accounting standards (see for instance Pritchard et al. 2000, forthcoming). Many of these debates refer to broader discussions about global changes in competitive environments, the shift of emphasis in Western industrialised countries towards the service sector, and global shifts arising from the diffusion and proliferation of new ICTs. Some of these issues are addressed elsewhere in this book. In this chapter, we consider how can we best understand the potential effect of knowledge management upon the innovation processes within a firm.

In asking this question, then, we are firstly focusing on one element of firm performance – innovation – that is currently seen as central to that performance. But we are also approaching knowledge management from the perspective of what is currently known about innovation, and hence treating knowledge management as one of the many aspects of the firm that has some effect on the success of its innovation processes. In other words we are *not* approaching knowledge management primarily from the perspectives of those who advocate particular forms of knowledge management, particular understandings of what is and is not 'correct' knowledge management, or particular methods for knowledge management. Instead we are approaching knowledge management in the same way one would treat other organisational phenomena, with the additional feature that it is a newly emergent phenomenon with unclear boundaries and a variety of manifestations.

9.3   THEORETICAL APPROACHES

Over the last 30 years, studies of technological change have increasingly moved away from their earlier concentration on the 'heroic inventor', and now focus their attention more on the firm and its competitive environment (see Freeman and Soete 1997, Part Two). There have been two significant consequences of this broad group of 'Innovation Studies' (which we take to include historical, sociological, organisational and economic studies). First, there has been a significant challenge to the traditional idea, held by neo-classical economists, that the firm is merely a 'black box' with inputs and outputs. Detailed studies of what happens in firms during technological change has shown that the 'innovation processes' – the operation and financing of R&D departments, the implementation of new technologies, and the marketing of new products – is central to the relative success and very survival of the firm (Nelson 1991). Secondly, the economic growth of any particular nation or region is also now seen to be heavily dependant on its innovation system, and it is at this aggregated level that problematics of 'knowledge in the economy' have arisen (OECD 1996c). However, just as with knowledge management and innovation, descriptions and consequent strategies for improving the leverage of knowledge for economic growth must clearly start with understanding the role of knowledge management within innovation processes.[3]

A variety of perspectives have 'opened the black box' of the firm: social-psychological approaches such as 'bounded rationality' (Cyert and March 1963); business histories of corporate strategy (Chandler 1977); and studies of patterns of technological change (Utterback 1993). One of the central underpinning notions is that, to put it bluntly, history matters: previous decisions and actions, whether in developing new products or implementing new production technologies, have a significant influence on the range of possible options for the future (Nelson and Winter 1982; Coombs et al. 1992). The more formalised way of stating this is the concept of 'path dependency' (Arthur 1989). This is potentially 'located' in three domains within the firm.[4] The first is the specific artefacts such as products, machinery, equipment, software, and so on, which bear the impression of previous choices and chance events, and shape future possibilities. The second is the 'knowledge base' of the firm, either narrowly defined by the specific technologies and markets of which it has experience (Metcalfe and de Liso 1998), or more broadly as the 'culture' of the organisation, the 'shared information ... and habits of thought' (Hodgson 1994). The third location is the collection of 'routines' within the firm, the activities which are repeatedly carried out in order for the firm to conduct its business. These may be repeated daily or monthly, or in response to particular events, and they may range from mundane activities such as filling in a particular form every month to routine visits to customers to assess and discuss their requirements.

We focus on the domain of 'routines', and concentrate on specific 'knowledge management practices' (KMPs), for two reasons. First, the particular ways in which knowledge management will be put into operation in any specific firm is precisely through a new set of routines – some may be specific to new IT (which will in turn require new routines) – but many will instead be paper-based or face-to-face activities. Further, many changes in organisational practice actually start life as informal 'bottom-up' activities rather than 'top-down' directives, developed on the initiative of people who get the work done, and only later officially sanctioned and formalised. The second reason is that empirical case-study investigation of the role of knowledge management within the three possible locations of path-dependency lends itself most clearly to study of the routines within a firm, rather than the other two potential domains – if only because these are tangible phenomena for discussion and debate.[5] Our focus, in other words, is upon the routines which are explicitly intended, or believed, to involve 'knowledge management' within innovation processes, and we call these 'knowledge management practices' (KMPs). They are central to shaping the knowledge base of the firm and making it available in the innovation process; they are central to the styles and 'culture' of innovation processes, and putting into operation new IT and other new productions and operations technologies.

9.4   KNOWLEDGE MANAGEMENT PRACTICES

9.4.1   Definition

In general, 'practices' encompass the variety of ways in which labour is regularised and routinised, whether formally in recognised tasks, techniques and processes – which are sequences of tasks; or informally in acknowledged ways of 'getting by' and 'getting the work done'. KMPs are thus those practices which are either explicitly intended to perform some knowledge management function, or, in the case of some practices which also have other functions such as writing a report for one's line manager, those practices which are believed to additionally have knowledge management dimensions.

9.4.2   The Attributes of Knowledge Management Practices[6]

1.   The character of the practice in terms of what *process* the knowledge is subjected to – or at least, the intended process.
2.   The knowledge *domains* or topics addressed by the practice.
3.   The *format* of the knowledge management practice – its degree of formality.
4.   The part of the organisation's *performance* which is most impacted by the KMP – or at least, what people think is the impact, or the rationale.

Thus a typical KMP may or may not usually be carried out by a particular person, but it will certainly relate to a specific knowledge domain. It will perform some action on the knowledge in a particular way, be conducted within a format which can be identified, and it will be understood to have effects on the organisation, either broadly or highly specified. For example: the manager of a pilot plant for the manufacture of a polymer may prepare a technical report which captures operating data (the process) on the efficiency of a new catalyst (the domain). The report may be rapidly available through Lotus Notes (the format) to R&D personnel working on optimising the catalyst and may therefore improve the efficiency of the R&D process (the performance parameter).

The processing characteristics of the KMP
In addition to the 'traditional' distinction between generation, transfer and utilisation of knowledge, there are *at least* the following additional characteristics: identification of knowledge that may be useful; capture or retrieval of knowledge; altering the format (for instance, codifying knowledge by transferring it onto paper or IT systems); validation of

knowledge (for instance, through discussions with peers); contextualising and re-contextualising (for instance, looking for common aspects between the original context of the knowledge and the intended context); and achieving 'closure' (for instance, the processes of agreeing common definitions). Thus the essential feature of a KMP can range from relatively 'routine' activities such as recording data, through to more judgement-based and potentially contestable activities involving selection and contextualisation of knowledge.

The domain
There is often a specific knowledge focus for KMPs, involving a delimited area of knowledge targeted by that practice. Such areas may include: highly specified areas of scientific and/or technical knowledge, often related to particular journals, conferences, or professional associations; knowledge of particular products or processes; knowledge of particular markets and customer bases; knowledge of particular features of the organisation; and knowledge of projects, project processes and project management. There may also be a more general focus for a KMP, which may include: knowledge that may arise unpredictably, for instance through synergy or co-location; knowledge that is needed by new or younger personnel from time to time, for example, during personnel induction and continuing mentoring practices; and knowledge that others may find useful, as for instance with the practice of publishing material on internal Web pages on an 'intranet'.

The format
As already suggested above, particular KMPs may vary between 'formal' and 'informal'; from a highly specified and standardised job-role of specific individuals, through to a general expectation that people will carry out the practice (for instance, passing on useful knowledge). Any KMP may also be expected to take place at specific times or locations, for instance during particular meetings, or during the 'demand analysis' phase of projects, or within the space where project teams are clustered together; it may be directed at enabling ad-hoc, temporary or rapid arrangements, for instance by establishing links and contacts between people with shared expertise or interests. Alternatively a particular KMP may be set up within or around MIS or ICT systems, and hence be specified and constrained to varying degrees, so that for instance email discussion lists may be seen to be far less formal than a shared database or groupware system with strictly delimited field attributes. This aspect is of particular importance, as it is often IT or 'information management' experts who now advise and set up new KMPs and arrangements.

The organisational performance variable(s) impacted by the KMP
This is the most problematic of the four elements, in that it is less obviously an 'attribute' of a practice. It is more often a question of strategic intent, rather than definitely observable effect. However, it is useful to ask why this KMP is maintained and what are its intended benefits?, questions which will sometimes elicit interesting responses. For example, interpretation of competitors' patents and patent applications, and the communication of that knowledge to an R&D team, can identify the degree of 'design freedom' available to that team and result in a better targeting of their effort.

9.4.3   The Groups of KMPs

Group A: KMPs and R&D management
These are KMPs which are found to varying degrees in all R&D and innovation environments, and which often have other primary purposes. These KMPs grow directly out of the performance of the R&D work itself, and are typically embodied in the R&D scientists and their formal and informal communication patterns within and beyond the lab. The importance of such knowledge-centred activities has been recognised for many years, going back to the work of Thomas Allen[7] on 'gatekeepers'. Some aspects of this set of KMPs have not changed fundamentally since then. Other aspects are changing rapidly as a result of the greater formality of R&D planning processes, and the opportunities to use information technology to change the range of options for the storage and dissemination of documents and data. Examples:

- One company has established technical, customer and competitor stewards to act as 'gatekeepers' to update databases, answer queries and generate and disseminate topic-based analyses, summary reports and other information relevant to their specific cross-boundary responsibilities.
- Personnel from different departments working on an R&D project are located in the same physical area to help develop new domains of expertise, as well as to implement projects more efficiently.

Group B: KMPs and 'mapping' knowledge relationships
R&D organisations are typically organised around project teams and around departments with specific technical expertise. Often these two reference points for organisation form the two sides of the matrix in a matrix management structure. However, even with this type of structure, emergent nodes of technical expertise which develop around particular categories of problem can often be relatively 'invisible' and not formally located within

one of the strong cells in the matrix. Similarly, emergent bodies of knowledge and experience about customers, competitors and market segments can arise in parts of the R&D organisation, but not be formally 'owned' by anyone in the management system. These 'orphan' fragments of knowledge can be even more numerous and difficult to locate if there are multiple R&D centres in a corporate structure, and multiple networks of contacts with business units, and with their customers. In many firms – especially large divisionalised corporations – a group of KMPs have emerged which are concerned with mapping these fields of knowledge and person-embodied skill, and making the resulting maps available to managers to provide new perspectives on the firm's innovation activities. Examples:

- A picture of the technology portfolio of an R&D lab is mapped onto the requirements of the internal divisions who are its potential customers. Similarly, the company's product portfolio is routinely mapped onto end-user market trends.
- Monthly discussion groups are organised through what a company calls 'formalised informality'. These groups share and translate knowledge between participants from different domains with the aim of generating new ideas, solutions and approaches.

Group C: KMPs and R&D human resource management
This set of KMPs are concerned with motivating and rewarding R&D personnel. These are closely tied, to quite varying degrees, to the broader corporate human resource management (HRM) policies such as training and career development activities. R&D HRM will in many cases be confined to simple 'dual-ladder' policies, with procedures for enabling personnel to pursue either 'technical' or 'commercial' careers, but some R&D units have a particular focus on activities designed to encourage knowledge sharing and the development of inter- disciplinary expertise and cross-boundary working, and indeed there may often be conflicts between corporate and R&D HRM. Examples:

- In one case secondments are made routinely between staff in a company's R&D Lab and Product Divisions, typically lasting about six months. These are seen as aspects of career development, as well as seeking to achieve productive exchanges between different knowledge domains and to identify new areas of activity for R&D. In other cases, secondments will be made between R&D and Marketing, or between broadly defined project themes.
- R&D personnel in one company are encouraged to offer consultancy to the company's business units and to answer queries over the phone or

face-to-face. They keep a 'day book' when doing this to help identify emerging themes and issues.

Group D: KMPs for managing intellectual property positions

There are a number of KMPs in the field of intellectual property rights which reflect the fact that in-house IPR experts in R&D labs are becoming more pro-active. Instead of principally providing a service to formulate patent applications and maintain patents, it is now more common to find them actively distributing information about competitors' patent activity to R&D teams, with commentary on its implications for the strategic direction and detail of the company's own R&D. In some cases this activity is conducted jointly with library staff to provide an electronically delivered 'Patent Watch' service available to the desktop of individual scientists.

A second major KMP in this group is the early involvement of IPR staff with R&D teams to formulate the IPR dimensions of emergent instances of novel technology. The distinguishing feature of this practice is that IPR expertise is being brought to bear on the direction of R&D technical activity in mid-project. In addition, there are often issues around the translation between the legal basis of IPR expertise, and the varieties of backgrounds to R&D expertise.

Group E: KMPs and R&D information technology management

As has already been mentioned, information technology applications can be a significant enabler of the emergence of new KMPs. Examples are the electronic archiving of technical documents which emerge from R&D work (Group A above); electronic 'Patent Watch' bulletins (Group D above), and Intranet approaches to the facilitation of clusters of R&D expertise making their skills available to previously unknown collaborators elsewhere in the corporate structure (Group B above).

There is a distinction to be made between those cases where IT *supports* a KMP which has a strong independent existence, and those cases where IT provides the trigger or enabler to create or change a KMP.[8] New 'virtual R&D clusters' have been enabled by the combination of email and the 'bottom up' activity of R&D personnel; similarly with experiments in knowledge-sharing within project teams and the availability of groupware such as Lotus Notes; and the rapidly diffusing experience of individuals using the world-wide-web has raised expectations and interest concerning the potential of its corporate equivalent: the 'intranet'. On a different note however, R&D centres are attracting the attention of information management and IT specialists from the corporate centre who ask 'what is the strategic role of IT in R&D?', and they have varying relevant expertise and patterns of working to actually implement such projects.

9.5 OBSERVATIONS AND ISSUES

9.5.1 Variety

One of the key observations is the sheer variety of the KMPs, across a number of dimensions. From just five R&D settings we identified a total of 132 KMPs which we were able to aggregate into over 80 distinct KMPs – in other words, there was very little duplication, with on average any particular KMP appearing less than twice. However, there was a distinct spread around that average, with some formal KMPs linked to R&D management most likely to occur across all firms; formal KMPs for managing IPR most likely to be duplicated in those firms where IPR was an issue; and KMPs for 'mapping knowledge relationships' most likely to be highly firm-specific and hence yielding the greatest variety.

As mentioned above, although there has traditionally been a broad classification of 'knowledge processing' into just three forms – creation, dissemination and utilisation – we identified a number of different and finer-grained characteristics. This variety, which is rarely if ever detailed in the standard texts on knowledge management, illustrates the utility of focussing on the activities, the things that people actually 'do' with knowledge, rather than attempting to derive those activities from pre-conceived notions of the types and nature of knowledge. It also illustrates that one of the key aspects of knowledge-processing activities, and hence of knowledge management, centres around the problems and difficulties of working across various types of boundary: contextualising and re-contextualising is required for project boundaries, which may be spatial or temporal; and 'achieving closure' is required for working across disciplinary boundaries. Many of these types of activity may thus also occur in other situations entailing the mobilisation of knowledge across boundaries, in particular between different organisations or firms. There are indeed some similarities between the range of activities listed above, and the types of knowledge-intensive business services currently emerging, many of which are precisely positioned at the boundaries between firms, supplying specialised knowledge processing services in new ways.

In terms of the format of the KMPs, approximately 50 per cent of the distinct KMPs were what one might call 'informal' – that is, they were ad-hoc, reliant on initiative rather than being directed, or possessed a low degree of specification, standardisation or specialisation. Interestingly, in two of the case studies the importance of these 'informal' practices was, as it were, 'formally recognised'. Thus, in one unit the phrase 'we're very informal here' was repeated so often and in the same way that it began to seem that it was more of a mantra than a shared perception of the unit. In another unit, there was an explicit attempt to encourage 'formalised informality' whereby bottom-up initiatives from R&D practitioners became sanctioned by senior management, but without attempts by them to formalise or direct those activities.

In terms of the overall aims of the KMPs the greatest variety came, not surprisingly, with those 'informal' or initiative-based practices, where there was clearly a complex mixture of post-hoc rationalisations of the practice, to justify it in terms of 'unit performance', together with clear attempts to advance the relative profile or position of particular groups or individuals. Thus, in one case the library and information support specialists were taking a number of initiatives designed to counter the tendency of R&D practitioners to gather information directly from the Internet. This was seen to bypass the professional expertise of those information specialists, and hence placing the position of the library/information unit in danger. The initiatives were, however, rationalised in terms of attempts to counter the danger of R&D staff 're-inventing the wheel' in painfully learning lessons about information gathering and sifting that the information specialists already knew. In another case, a unit that had previously focused on market research was in the process of re-positioning itself by widening its remit, with the clear intention (expressed in interviews, at least) to just 'survive' – the continued existence of the unit was seen to be in danger unless they could demonstrate their indispensability.

9.5.2   Knowledge Management and ICTs

We have mentioned above the number and variety of significant new KMPs that had been enabled through ICTs. However, in one of the cases the role of ICTs was minimal, and it was not intended that ICTs would play a significantly greater part in KMPs, because of the importance for them of contextualising and re-contextualising, and the importance of relations between experts based on confidence, reputation and reliability. In addition, across all the case studies the role of ICTs was significant for only about 20 per cent of the total KMPs, and 30 per cent of the distinct KMPs. This is despite the fact that knowledge management is often most promoted by those with a handy system to sell (usually some combination of ICTs and consultancy expertise to be used to change procedures and expectations, or rather 'culture'). Many R&D centres are currently under this sort of pressure, and indeed in one of the cases our 'host' had previously worked for a large management/IT consultancy, and was highly focused on that sort of 'solution'; but during the course of our study his orientation shifted dramatically towards the 'people aspects'.

In a number of other cases we heard about disasters with new electronic document management systems, problems with implementing intranets (see below) and in general a high degree of scepticism for 'technical fixes' to knowledge management issues. In other words the trend, mentioned in Section 9.2 above, for the large consultancies to focus more on the 'people side' of knowledge management is justified and hardly surprising – all the experience of problems in developing and implementing large IT systems is that, whatever the scale of the intended benefits, those benefits can only possibly be finally realised through those people who have to work with such systems.

9.5.3   KMPs and the Question of Context

One of the most unexpected outcomes, and a key observation, was the extent of two groups of KMPs that together highlight the emphasis placed, by practitioners, on the relationships and contexts of knowledge. First, there was a large group of KMPs that were directed at what we have labelled 'mapping knowledge relationships'. Second, there was a small number of KMPs directed at 'contextualising and decontextualising' – attempting to come to an understanding of the original context of a body of knowledge, how that relates to that body of knowledge, and how those relations bear on the application of that knowledge in another context.

Both these groups of KMPs are explicitly operationalising an understanding that there are highly complex interactions and interdependencies between 'types' of knowledge (for example, explicit/tacit), domains of knowledge (of technologies, of customers, of competitors, etc.), and the sources of the knowledge. They felt they had learnt, often painfully, that there were severe shortcomings in the simplistic descriptions and prescriptions of those who would paint easy pictures about knowledge – descriptions and prescriptions from knowledge management, or information management, or management studies, or operations research, or organisational analysis. They were, in a sense, putting into operation various self-taught versions of the sociology of knowledge. At the most basic level, this was expressed as, to paraphrase, 'of course we recognise that knowledge and power are connected – that's why simple ideas about knowledge management, intranets and so on, are insufficient.

Two points follow from this. First, these practitioners are clearly attempting to accomplish a very difficult balancing act between 'recognising the partiality of knowledge', and 'knowing the truth of a situation'. Secondly, discussion and debate about 'the social construction of skill and knowledge' is not reserved for academics, and is instead diffused through organisations in complex ways. This would seem to pose some problems for those academics who would presume to have specialised or privileged access to understanding 'the social construction of skill and knowledge'.[9]

9.5.4   Knowledge Management and Career Development

Leading on from the last point, one of the key issues to emerge from the case studies, especially where intranets were being actively developed, was the relationship between KMPs and career development. Put simply: on the one hand many R&D practitioners saw their promotion prospects depending, in large part, on the specialised knowledge they 'held', or 'owned'; on the other hand, there were various initiatives, ICT developments such as intranets, and indeed pronouncements from senior management, to the effect that 'sharing knowledge' was a 'good thing' and sometimes a 'necessity' for the health and development of the unit as a whole. In one case this dilemma had reached such 'serious' proportions – in the sense that 'knowledge hoarding' was seen to be a resistance and an impedance to the health of the unit – that there were at the time moves to radically restructure the 'reward and recognition' (R&R) systems. Interestingly, though, these moves were in combination with moves to build in to the R&R systems a greater degree of equal opportunities (although not phrased that way), with the connection being that the tendency to 'hoard' knowledge reinforced the privilege of those already privileged, through gender or race, whilst the initiatives in 'sharing knowledge' generally came from those attempting to 'level the playing field'. In this case, then, the emergence, development and debates about knowledge management within the unit had to some extent altered the parameters of internal power struggles, to the benefit of those who saw themselves as marginalised in some way, who had been able to rhetorically combine their interests with those of the unit as a whole.

9.6   CONCLUSIONS

In terms of knowledge management and innovation, it is clear that there is now a significant range and variety of KMPs available to companies. Some of these KMPs are having significant effects upon the routines within innovation processes, and hence have the potential at least to significantly affect company performance. We could also suggest there is some evidence that KMPs are enabling those innovation processes to generate a greater *variety* of options for innovation from which to choose. On the other hand, however, there is also evidence of some unresolved tensions involved in the implementation of knowledge management strategies. First, there is a tension between IT enabling an opening up of new practices and routines, and hence increasing variety generation within innovation, and those cases where IT instead hardens existing routines. This tension requires closer attention to the people aspects and also justifies our focus on specific knowledge management *practices*. Secondly, there is a tension between the advice and prescriptions passed down through formal knowledge management strategies, and the actual and emerging practices of practitioners – in our case, the R&D scientists and engineers and their various support staff, such as library and information specialists. One specific aspect of this tension is that practitioners are more likely to have a nuanced understanding of both the 'slipperiness' of knowledge, and its subtle and not-so-subtle linkages with issues such as career development.

This range of available KMPs, and especially the diversity of knowledge-processing activities noted in Section 9.5.1, also suggests a broader conclusion in the context of relations between knowledge, innovation and services. Whilst much of the analytical and policy-oriented research has focussed on the three main types of knowledge processing, and especially the production of new knowledge, it is clear from this chapter that such production is only one small aspect. It is clear first of all that there is a great variety of different aspects to the mobilisation of knowledge in support of the innovation, many of which may be equally as important as the generation of new knowledge. This in turn implies that there are potentially a large number of quite specific knowledge-processing activities which are currently, or could be, carried out by new service functions of firms. In particular, such activities are likely to concentrate on improving the mobilisation of knowledge across a number of boundaries – between firms, between firms and non-market organisations, and between different discipline-bases either within or between organisations. In this context, the characterisation of knowledge-intensive business services as 'intermediary actors', suggested in Chapter 2, can be seen to echo the requirements of knowledge management within firms. Further empirical study of knowledge management within organisations is thus likely to enhance understanding of the characteristics of emergent business service firms.

NOTES

1. Case study research for this chapter was enabled through the support of ESRC Grant No. L125251008, and has been constantly supported by my collaborator Rod Coombs.
2. Nonaka (1991, 1994); Nonaka and Takeuchi (1995).
3. For an even more sceptical appraisal of these approaches to the 'knowledge

economy', see Hull (1999).

4. This is not to deny that path dependency – the importance of historical events – is not also located outside the firm, but for this chapter we are interested in activities internal to the firm.

5. For a more detailed justification for this, see Coombs and Hull (1998).

6. These attributes could be regarded as an instantiation of three general attributes to practices: immediate aim, long-term goal, and format. See Coombs and Hull (1998) for a brief discussion of how these relate to previous work, such as the Aston Studies.

7. Allen and Cohen (1969); Allen (1977). See also Macdonald and Williams (1994).

8. This raises the question of whether it would be possible to distinguish the differential 'effects' of ICTs on specific practices within organisations. This would seem difficult, bearing in mind the degree of 'situated' and 'negotiated' usage and implementation of ICTs (Suchman 1987). However, one approach could entail the classification of ICTs according to their mix of the different 'frameworks of computing', each of which has different perspectives on the nature, role and context of knowledge and communication.

9. A similar observation – of the sophistication with which defence lawyers in the O.J. Simpson trial deconstructed 'forensic knowledge' in ways that were often more finely tuned than the most sophisticated sociological techniques – has recently been made by Lynch (1998).

10 Services, Knowledge and Intellectual Property

Ian Miles and Mark Boden[1]

10.1 INTRODUCTION

Various studies in this book discuss the growing importance of knowledge-based activities and of service firms. This chapter examines a set of issues confronting knowledge-intensive business services (KIBS), as they seek to make use of their knowledge – often in innovative ways. Research relating innovation to the intellectual property right (IPR) system has been almost exclusively centred on the patent system (for more analysis of IPR systems see Chapter 14). The emphasis of patents is on protecting physical artefacts, its focus on tangible products and processes.

There are many cases of services firms employing patents. Typically this has involved firms in sectors like transport, telecommunication and information services, seeking to protect their process innovations. Service processes can often involve highly tangible technology – consider the computer and telecommunications systems in banks, the vehicle fleets and warehouses of supermarkets, the infrastructure of airports and hotels, and so on. Process innovations in services may often involve such technologies. Thus we see large and technology-intensive services actively patenting their innovations – examples in the UK include BT and Reuters.

Service product innovations may also be tangible. A familiar example is the fillings and false teeth that dental surgeries provide. Another case is the 'hushkitting' of aircraft by a rapid mail company: this is performed as a commercial service that enables clients to extend the hours in which freight aircraft can use airports staying within noise regulations. But service product innovations are more often intangible. This must be a major reason why the propensity to patent is much lower in services than in manufacturing sectors.

159

There has been very little attention to what patenting does emerge from services; but also there has been little analysis of the propensity to use other IPR mechanisms – like copyright – among service firms. Application of the copyright system to technological innovation (such as software) is much more recent, and less well defined, than patenting, even though copyright actually has a longer history than the patent system.

Creative content can be protected by copyright rules, and services (and indeed all sectors) may use the copyright system rather than patents, to provide a formal means of protection of their product innovations. A crucial point, though, is that the copyright system does not differentiate technological innovation from other forms of creativity. A new cartoon character, popular song or training video is as much subject to copyright as is a new version of a software package or a new Web service.

10.2 INTELLECTUAL PROPERTY AND SERVICES

It is commonly argued that service companies have adapted to a culture where copying is commonplace and innovation poorly protected and rewarded. This lack of protection has frequently been noted in the case of traditional services – for instance, if a new pizza topping proves a market success, competing restaurants can immediately imitate it with no threat of sanctions. This is an example where there is very little need to apply specialised knowledge or to invest in training and equipment to produce the service – a new service bundle is typically being constructed. But the copying issue is a widespread one in high-tech activities too. It is now very much an issue in the case of new IT-based or IT-delivered services, where the copying may involve imitation of design features, reverse engineering of rules and procedures (and implementing them in a different computer language, for instance), or direct reproduction of code and content. IT innovations, furthermore, have made the copying of many information service products virtually costless. The view that IPR protection was weak for software led to many firms protecting their software in the 1980s by embedding it in microchips as 'firmware'. Other approaches include bundling the software with something that is itself troublesome to reproduce (for example, glossy user manuals), or requiring that users apply a 'key' to be able to use it (for example, special discs, hardware 'dongles', regularly changing passwords, codes, license numbers); and customer helplines that check user status before providing support. The software industry, along with audio-visual publishers, has put much effort into policing copyright law.

Case studies have led Sundbo to conclude that weak IP protection may reduce services' innovation. In a wide range of Danish firms he studied, imitation was seen as a major deterrent to attempting to 'do new things' (Sundbo 1997, 1998).[2] This supports the conventional wisdom. In contrast, results from several large-scale surveys downplay the importance of intellectual property issues.

- A German study (Licht et al. 1997 – especially pp. 75-78) compares service and manufacturing firms' perceived barriers to innovation, finding that service firms saw 'ease of imitation' as a barrier *less* often than manufacturing firms (around 35 per cent of service firms, around 45 per cent of manufacturing firms citing it). Software resembled manufacturing (and high-tech manufacturing in particular) more closely in several respects than did most other services. (Over 40 per cent of the software firms sampled saw see 'ease of imitation' as a barrier.) There were no obvious differences between large and small firms in respect of this problem, though firms in the former West Germany did consider copying see more of a problem than did those in the former East. (Perhaps the latter are less innovative, less entrepreneurial – or more inclined to see innovations as public goods?)
- An Italian study (Sirilli and Evangelista 1998) reported a rather similar result. Of a list of fifteen factors hampering innovation, 'risk of imitation by competitors' was ranked fifth by manufacturing firms. In this study the questions addressed to the service and manufacturing samples varied slightly. Service firms were asked how important they found various barriers, and imitation received *lowest* endorsements as being 'very important', only 2.2 per cent of the sample citing it.[3]
- A Canadian survey also found risks of imitation to be placed low in the rank order of impediments to innovation cited by service firms – a whole range of impediments scored higher, though these varied across service subsectors (Baldwin et al. 1998). Looking at innovators among three KIBS – communications (telecoms and broadcasting), financial services, and technical business services (including IT services) – fewer than half of these were found to use *any* formal IPR arrangements (copyrights, trademarks, trade secrets, patents). However, use of trademarks and patents was higher than in manufacturing (and patents less important). While many innovators did not feel IPR methods to be effective, they nevertheless did innovate. Their means of protecting these innovations involved methods such as complex product design or early entry to the market. For communications imitation was seen as a risk by 19 per cent of respondents (as opposed to 31 per cent citing lack of equity capital, 30 per cent citing legal restrictions, and so on); in financial services 28 per cent cited imitation (as opposed to 45 per cent high costs and 35 per cent risks related to market success, and so on); and for technical services

imitation was seen as a problem by a relatively high 33 per cent (but high costs were identified by 45 per cent, lack of equity capital by 40 per cent, and so on).

These results from surveys of firms in advanced industrial economies tend to undermine the view that (product) innovation in services is being substantially deterred by the ease of imitation. But it might be argued that the firms see copying as less of a problem simply because they are resigned to it; or that they are less innovative and thus face fewer problems (but why does copying then appear lower down the list?); or they have responded by innovating faster so as to stay ahead of competitors. There is no reason why more than one of these explanations can apply in different cases. More detailed analysis of the variations within services in the surveys, and relations between reported barriers and reported innovation effort and objectives, would help to resolve these issues.

At the very least, the results confirm the conclusion of studies of patenting in manufacturing – that there are different IP strategies across firms and sectors. But they also reinforce the point that we are fairly ignorant about the situation and strategies of services. In addition to the use of such systems for protection of their knowledge as patent, copyright, design right, and trademark protection, firms can use methods that step outside of the IPR system. Knowledge may be kept confidential – for example through contracts with clients, suppliers and collaborators, and rules restricting employees' use of confidential information. While too much secrecy can be counterproductive – it can disempower and demotivate employees, limit the scope for collaboration, and so on – many professional services are privy to confidential information about their clients, which necessarily means putting procedures in place to prevent its misuse.

Two other common approaches involve 'lock-in' and entry barriers. A range of strategies are employed to 'lock-in' users and business partners. Some of these involve the use of specific standards and protocols – important in the case of software and IT services. Such standards may allow for easy interoperability of products, to the extent that a software producer may be prepared to give away copies of a basic version of its product. The aim is to create a large enough user base to make it worthwhile for others to invest in the more advanced versions of the software. (For example, Adobe sets the standard with its Acrobat reader, so that authors wishing to publish on the web will pay to acquire the professional software to do this.) Standards can also reduce user learning time and discourage use of products that are not easily compatible with these standards. But there are many other methods of 'lock-in'. Thus, a service supplier may offer a set of related services, in bundles that offer most value to the client who uses several of these from the same supplier. Or there may be ploys like customer loyalty cards (as employed by organisations ranging from supermarkets to airlines) and reward systems.

Entry barriers may not prevent competition from other people in one's profession, but do limit the scope for outsiders to move in. They take various forms, of which the most prominent is the institution of professional qualifications, accreditation and self-regulatory systems. This approach is widely adopted in professional and other business services – and some personal services, such as complementary and alternative medicine. International trade in many of these services is rendered difficult by national variations in these barriers. Many of these methods of protecting knowledge apply to more forms of knowledge than that used in product and process innovation, of course, and we need to examine intellectual property strategies as a whole, since the methods used to protect innovations may well be shaped by the general portfolio of protective activities in the firm. However, one technique that is specific to innovative knowledge is seeking to diminish the impact of copying by staying ahead of imitators, producing innovations that keep them at the forefront. This strategy is widely used in IT services – for example, innovation cycles in the software industry are often less than six months.

In practice, firms in all sectors typically adopt *combinations* of IPR protection methods. Little is known about the strategies taken by different services. We shall examine some results from a recent (1997) UK study, oriented to examining the management of IPR in three types of knowledge-intensive business service (KIBS), demonstrates that very different strategies are adopted for managing their intellectual property.[4] These seem to be associated with the very different types of knowledge associated with different services.

10.3 THREE KNOWLEDGE-INTENSIVE BUSINESS SERVICES

Three KIBS were examined in this study – accountancy, architecture and environmental engineering. These three were expected to vary markedly in their relation to technology:

- Environmental engineering (EE) is in large part supplying technological knowledge, to help clients' diagnose their environmental problems, and identify and implement solutions – in some cases in a very hands-on way.
- Accountancy (ACC) is mainly concerned with processing organisational

data in terms of administrative categories. Though IT is extensively applied in this process, the key to the service is professional knowledge, used, within a range of corporate routines and practices, to process information and produce information products – mostly of a fairly standard sort.

- Architecture (ARC) combines knowledge of materials and building regulations with creative flair and aesthetic sensibility. Typical products are diagrams and specifications; often a good deal of networking is required with other firms involved in construction, as well with clients.[5]

Several further factors differentiate the sectors, however, and these should be taken into account in examining IP strategies. Table 10.1 contrasts the three sectors, though we should not forget their commonalities. Thus, in all three sectors, as with most services, there is a J-shaped size distribution of firms. In other words, there are a few very large players and a large number of very small ones – this is particularly marked in ACC, which has extremes at both ends. There may well be differences in the type of product generated by establishments of different sizes. Often the smaller KIBS are serving local markets only, and may be providing quite routine products for them. Large firms may produce much more diverse and innovative services. But sometimes small firms can be specialised and innovative, providing original products with a wide market base.

The study of these KIBS combined case studies in each of these three sectors with a telephone-assisted mail survey of 50 or more establishments in each.[6] This is a relatively small-scale survey – though an unusually detailed one for KIBS of any sort – but it also did not rely on a completely representative sampling. This reflects the J-shaped size distribution of firms. Though ARC and EE firms were randomly sampled from relevant directories, pilot interviews indicated that this would have led to an ACC sample dominated by very small, often one-person, firms. (These were typically reporting low levels of innovation, and little interest in and awareness of IP issues). Thus, the ACC sample was biased toward larger firms.

In consequence, simple comparison of averages across sectors is not valid. Comparison across sectors within size categories is more meaningful, and here we differentiate between smaller (1–14 employees) and larger establishments (with 15 or more employees). Comparisons between large and small establishments may reflect not only the organisational distinctions between these groups of respondents, but also differences in the types of product and activity they engage in. The small numbers in the cells mean that caution should be used in assessing the results. Ten accountancy firms (just under 20 per cent of the total), 14 environmental engineers (just under

30 per cent of the total), and in contrast 26 architects (just over 50 per cent of the total) are in the smaller group.

Table 10.1 Comparison of the three KIBS

Sector: Features:	Accountancy (core service)	Architecture	Environmental Engineering
Structure of sector	Highly professionalised.	Highly professionalised.	Hardly professionalised.
	Many small and microbusinesses, often serving local and/or specialised markets. A small number of major international firms.	Fewer very small businesses than accountancy.	With few exceptions, a much newer sector than the other two. Nevertheless, some international firms
	Many medium and large-sized firms have sought to branch out from the core service, using knowledge of clients and regulatory issues to offer management consultancy, IT support, and other services.	More emphasis on core services in medium and large-sized firms than accountancy. High division of labour among companies in sector, frequent collaborations with related firms, building engineers, and others.	Very small firms tend to offer information services and consultancy; others may provide physical services (transport, disposal, etc.) as well as more informational ones (monitoring, design, auditing, etc.)
Technology-intensity of service product	Very low. Some delivery of documentation in electronic form.	Moderate. Technical specifications in product. Some delivery of designs and documentation in electronic form.	Heterogeneous. Some services simply apply technology to meet a clients' needs (e.g. waste disposal), some have outputs more like that of architecture (designs and specifications), and some have tangible products like software, modifications to equipment, etc.
Representation of technological knowledge in service product	Very low. Some large firms (and academic accountancy groups) exploring ways of accounting for intangibles like R&D and innovation, and new means of accounting for IT investments, but this not integrated into core product.	Often high, though extensive division of labour in architecture and construction more generally may mean that some outputs are more aesthetic. Documents often deal extensively with materials, physical properties of buildings, environmental variables, and anticipated end-uses.	High, though in cases of facilities management and similar services the client may not be delivered the sorts of manuals, specifications, etc. that are provided in other cases.

Table 10.1 Continued

Sector: Features:	Accountancy (core service)	Architecture	Environmental Engineering
Use of technology in service pProduction.	Has moved to use of IT extensively in recent years. Many packages available for SMEs to use in their operations. Large firms are major users of computer networks and advanced means of co-ordinating work across sites.	Extensive use of IT with some calculation, graphics and CAD packages extremely important. Manual methods still applied frequently du to limitations of technology in many specific cases.	Practically all varieties of EE use technology intensively. IT is pervasive, and monitoring and test equipment, sensors, and transport technologies are among others widely used.
Role of regulations	Underpins rationale for sector. Nature of service product largely determined by regulations (thus little scope for innovation). Regulatory change major source of change in product; relatively infrequent.	Important constraint on products formed by building regulations in particular. Frequent revisions mean attention to detail important.	Underpins rationale for sector. Frequently changing, with rapid pace of development.

Table 10.2 presents data on the sources of competitive advantage perceived by firms in the different sector/size groups. There are many interesting features of these results, but perhaps most striking is the repeated emphasis on various dimensions of client relations. Service quality, and cost competitiveness, are extremely salient to all groups, as is being up to date, while innovative products and services are less so. Environmental engineers are the group most concerned with innovativeness, and large firms are also most likely to endorse this.

What sorts of knowledge do these KIBS consider important? We requested ratings of various types of knowledge as 'Very Important', 'Important' or 'Not Important'. These were:

a. Knowledge of markets
1. evolving client needs and preferences
2. practical experience
3. trials and client/user feedback
4. marketing and market research
5. after-sales and support services

Table 10.2 Sources of competitive advantage

Source		Accountants 1–14	Accountants 15+	Architects 1–14	Architects 15+	Env. Engineers 1–14	Env. Engineers 15+
Speed of response	C	*80.00*	*61.54*	42.31	48.00	21.43	*50.00*
	I	**20.00**	**38.46**	57.69	52.00	71.43	46.88
Innovative prod/serv	C	20.00	15.38	34.62	20.00	14.29	21.88
	I	40.00	46.15	23.08	60.00	50.00	65.63
Work with broad organisations	C	30.00	23.08	26.92	**40.00**	21.43	12.50
	I	50.00	64.10	61.54	**56.00**	35.71	75.00
up-to-date practices	C	*60.00*	28.21	15.38	**40.00**	35.71	**18.75**
	I	**40.00**	**71.79**	69.23	**56.00**	50.00	**78.13**
Advanced organisational structures	C	0.00	2.56	3.85	0.00	0.00	0.00
	I	50.00	46.15	30.77	64.00	14.29	31.25
Contracts with foreign companies	C	0.00	0.00	0.00	0.00	0.00	0.00
	I	0.00	2.56	0.00	8.00	14.29	28.13
International scope	C	0.00	0.00	0.00	0.00	7.14	12.50
	I	30.00	28.21	3.85	32.00	42.86	59.38
Competitive prices	C	**30.00**	**30.77**	**23.08**	**28.00**	35.71	*59.38*
	I	**70.00**	**69.23**	**76.92**	**72.00**	57.14	34.38
Respected name	C	*50.00*	38.46	42.31	*60.00*	7.14	40.63
	I	**50.00**	**61.54**	57.69	40.00	85.71	59.38
Quality of core service	C	*70.00*	*64.10*	*53.85*	*84.00*	35.71	*78.13*
	I	**30.00**	**35.90**	46.15	16.00	64.29	21.88
Adaptability to client	C	*50.00*	*64.10*	*53.85*	**56.00**	*50.00*	46.88
	I	**50.00**	**35.90**	42.31	44.00	50.00	53.13
Offer related services	C	10.00	20.51	7.69	4.00	21.43	15.63
	I	70.00	69.23	50.00	72.00	35.71	68.75
Broad range of Services	C	**10.00**	**23.08**	15.38	4.00	7.14	9.38
	I	**80.00**	**71.79**	38.46	68.00	28.57	62.50
Provide back-up	C	**10.00**	20.51	3.85	8.00	21.43	12.50
	I	**80.00**	69.23	61.54	76.00	35.71	65.63

Notes: Importance: C= critical, I= important; 'Critical' cells with more than 50 per cent italicised; cells where 'critical' + 'important' total more than 90 per cent emboldened).

b. Knowledge of products and processes
1. design criteria and specifications
2. design concepts
3. IT applications
4. quality control processes
5. service production capabilities

c. Knowledge of science and technology
1. knowledge of environment and ecosystems
2. scientific and engineering theory
3. properties of materials and technologies
4. ability to utilise ongoing academic research
5. technical standards

d. Knowledge of activities and competencies of other organisations
1. partners and/or collaborators
2. suppliers
3. practical experience (drawn from outside the company)

e. Knowledge of changing standards and regulatory conditions
1. legally binding UK standards and regulations
2. legally binding EU standards and regulations
3. variations between different countries/regions
4. changes in national govt. policy (UK)
5. changes in EU policy
6. other standards or codes of practice

Table 10.3 provides results concerning these queries.   Customer requirements, standards, regulatory and policy issues are widely seen as very important. EE require relatively more knowledge of science and technology, and of ecosystems, as we would expect; they are also more interested in utilising research.   Such issues, together with knowledge of materials and design characteristics, are of markedly little concern to accountants – who are, however, most interested in the use of IT (though we would guess that the sophistication of IT applications among all but the largest ACC firms is well below that employed in the other two KIBS).

Turning to intellectual property issues, the respondents were asked how they protected the knowledge inputs/core competencies that were embodied in their *key* business activities.[7]   The following eleven mechanisms were rated in terms of 'always', 'sometimes' and 'never' (the option to add an 'other' category was almost never used.):

Table 10.3 Proportions declaring each form of knowledge to be 'very important'

Sector:	Accountants		Architects		Env. Engineers	
No. of employees	1–14	15 +	1–14	15 +	1–14	15 +
Knowledge:						
of customer needs	**70.00**	**74.36**	**80.77**	**64.00**	**64.29**	**81.25**
of practical experience	40.00	**56.41**	**76.92**	**68.00**	**57.14**	**50.00**
From feedback	30.00	7.69	19.23	28.00	28.57	28.13
of market	20.00	5.13	7.69	28.00	21.43	15.63
of after-sales	30.00	30.77	15.38	20.00	28.57	15.63
of design specs.	0.00	5.13	**76.92**	**80.00**	42.86	**56.25**
of design concepts	10.00	5.13	**69.23**	**84.00**	42.86	40.63
of IT applications	**50.00**	30.77	11.54	28.00	7.14	28.13
of quality control	40.00	46.15	15.38	36.00	28.57	18.75
of service production	30.00	20.51	15.38	28.00	14.29	9.38
of ecosystems	0.00	0.00	11.54	28.00	**50.00**	**59.38**
of science/tech theory	0.00	0.00	11.54	4.00	42.86	**56.25**
of properties	0.00	2.56	34.62	36.00	14.29	37.50
Utilise research	0.00	5.13	7.69	12.00	21.43	28.13
of tech standards	30.00	**58.97**	**57.69**	**64.00**	42.86	46.88
of partners	10.00	28.21	26.92	40.00	21.43	37.50
of suppliers	10.00	7.69	19.23	16.00	7.14	15.63
of external practice	20.00	15.38	23.08	12.00	7.14	12.50
of UK regs.	**60.00**	**84.62**	**96.15**	**84.00**	35.71	**68.75**
of EU regs,	30.00	48.72	34.62	**60.00**	35.71	**56.25**
of regional difference	10.00	5.13	0.00	16.00	7.14	25.00
of UK policy change	40.00	**51.28**	30.77	28.00	21.43	**59.38**
of EU policy change	30.00	20.51	7.69	12.00	21.43	43.75
of codes of practice	30.00	**51.28**	34.62	**52.00**	7.14	31.25

Notes: Percentages: cells with more than 50 per cent in bold.

- Copyright
- Design rights
- Patents
- Trademark or company name
- Agreements with partners/collaborators
- Agreements with suppliers or end-users
- Working with trusted partners

- Internal working practices
- Maintaining a lead-time advantage over competitors
- Embodying knowledge in equipment, software and so on
- Membership of professional associations

Striking differences are apparent among sectors .[8] Among the key results presented in Table 10.4, we draw attention to the following:

- Only EE used *patents* at all. Between a third but less than half of the firms in each size band did so: perhaps surprisingly, the smaller firms report more use. Even for these KIBS, patenting is a fairly minor tool of protecting valued knowledge, as compared to other means: environmental engineers have more recourse to copyright than to patenting, for example.
- Architects do almost universally use *copyright*, protecting the documents that embody their core service. Their designs convey their creative inputs – but this is not untrammelled creativity. They have turned their understanding of client requirements and the ways in which these might be technically satisfied into drawings and technical specifications – that is, into codified information which others could well appropriate. *Design rights* are also important to ARC, though to few others. EE make occasional use of both protection mechanisms.
- Accountants use copyright much less frequently, and design rights not at all. Their reports are unlikely to be copied, being highly client-specific (though they may be confidential, and some aspects of their production and presentation may be guarded). ACC may wish to protect other classes of document – their consultancy reports, their internal operating manuals, and so on. Even here, relatively few of the design elements are original innovations that might be protected as such; the valuable contents are more often diagnoses and data, usually with a short shelf life.
- Direct *social relationships* with staff, partners, suppliers and clients are very important for many KIBS in protecting knowledge. These may be informal relationships, or they may be formally governed – by employee law or by contractual arrangements between collaborating or trading firms. *Internal working practices* are very widely cited as important, especially by larger firms. The threat of losing knowledge embodied in essential members of staff becomes increasingly important, and increasingly the focus of management effort, in larger bodies – though it is among the most common methods of smaller EE firms too.
- *Agreements with partners* are important for ARC[9] and EE (little routine ACC work is performed in collaboration with other services[10]).

Agreement with suppliers and end users is fairly often reported as being of some importance – especially in EE and in larger ACC and ARC firms. These results highlight the need for KIBS to establish reliable and trustful relations.

▪ This was not echoed in the importance placed upon *trademarks* and company names. The Canadian survey had found trademarks very important for financial services, and to a lesser extent for technical services. But here, only environmental engineers rate trademarks highly, though for large architects this also plays a role. Despite the relatively low importance awarded to these formal mechanisms, reputation does provide competitive advantage. Table 10.2 showed that having 'a well-known and respected name' was seen as 'critical' or important in company market success for more than 90 per cent of the firms in all size/sector groups.

▪ *Membership of professional associations* was important to all sectors, but least so for environmental engineers, especially its smaller firms. Professional associations may in part act as entry barriers; their system of accreditation and training is important for sectoral knowledge; and the associations provide means of sharing knowledge resources and contacts). This is an important approach for ACC, coming top for the larger establishments. In contrast, EE, which has not yet forged a strong professional identity, has little recourse to this tool (though some professional associations in related fields or consultancy, engineering, and so on, may be helpful, perhaps especially for individual service professionals).

▪ The question on *lead-time advantage* was intended to give an insight into innovation, but on reflection, answers to this question can also reflect entry into new markets and even speed of response. Whichever the case, it was more frequently cited in EE and in larger firms.

▪ *'Embodying knowledge in products'* is surprisingly widely cited – though minorities report 'always' using it. Again, there is some ambiguity into what knowledge is being embodied here – most commercial accountants do not publish guides to how to prepare your own accounts, rather they apply their knowledge to company data to prepare useful information products. Perhaps because these products are meant to be used to gain (or validate) knowledge, they are more likely to see their services as embodying knowledge than are architects, whose products – the result of application of considerable knowledge – may be viewed as expressing their vision. Environmental engineers may well be involved in creating, configuring, or implementing systems with a high technology content.

Table 10.4 Use of IPR Methods by KIBS

Method		Accountants		Architects		Env. Engineers	
		1–14	15 +	1–14	15 +	1–14	15 +
Copyright	A	0.0	0.0	*65.4*	*68.0*	7.1	21.9
	S	10.0	5.1	*26.9*	*28.0*	21.4	34.4
Design rights	A	0.0	0.0	30.8	**40.0**	0.0	12.5
	S	0.0	0.0	34.6	**36.0**	14.3	43.8
Patents	A	0.0	0.0	0.0	0.0	7.1	6.3
	S	0.0	0.0	0.0	0.0	42.9	28.1
Trademark/co. name	A	0.0	12.8	26.9	36.0	14.3	**25.0**
	S	30.0	20.5	19.2	8.0	28.6	*50.0*
Agreements with partners	A	11.1	12.8	3.8	**16.0**	35.7	21.9
	S	33.3	38.5	*57.7*	*52.0*	42.9	*68.8*
Agreements w. suppliers/end user	A	0.0	2.6	3.8	4.0	7.1	**25.0**
	S	33.3	48.7	30.8	*56.0*	*64.3*	*65.6*
Work with trusted partners	A	44.4	**33.3**	19.2	**16.0**	35.7	**28.1**
	S	11.1	*53.8*	*53.8*	*64.0*	42.9	65.6
Internal working practices	A	**20.0**	**48.7**	11.5	**44.0**	35.7	**28.1**
	S	**70.0**	**46.2**	*50.0*	28.0	14.3	*50.0*
Lead-time advantage	A	10.0	10.3	3.8	4.0	28.6	**18.8**
	S	40.0	46.2	23.1	*52.0*	35.7	*53.1*
Embodying knowledge in products	A	**30.0**	**23.1**	19.2	20.0	28.6	**18.8**
	S	**40.0**	**48.7**	26.9	40.0	35.7	*59.4*
Membership of prof. Assocns.	A	**30.0**	*64.1*	*61.5*	*56.0*	7.1	15.6
	S	*70.0*	**33.3**	**23.1**	20	7.1	*53.1*

Notes: Response to: 'Which of the following mechanisms are used to protect the knowledge inputs/core competencies embodied in your key business activities?' (percentage of each size group responding to items)

(Level of use A = always, S = sometimes; Cells with more than 50 per cent italicised; where 'always' and 'sometimes' > 66.6 per cent, figures emboldened)

One outstanding implication of these results is that the formal instruments of IP regulatory systems are seen as being of limited relevance to most of the KIBS firms in these three sectors. (Compare with the Canadian results of Baldwin et al. 1998.) In response to a question as to whether they have ever experienced difficulties with IP, over 90 per cent of ACC and 70 per cent of ARC say they had *not* done so – for EE the figure was 60 per cent. Where IP problems were reported, about half of them were said to have related to unauthorised copying. In all sector/size groups, majorities thought they had been sufficiently active in protecting their IP in the past. Only in EE were more than half of the sample inclined to think that they might need to be more active in this respect in the future.

We suspect that this relative lack of concern with IP applies to practically all professional services, and to a high share of even the more technology-intensive sectors. There will obviously be exceptions firms engaged directly in technological innovation, such as biotechnology and computer services, R&D companies, and so on.

How do the types of protection pursued relate to the types of knowledge deemed important to the firm? There are a large number of statistically significant correlations between firms' responses to these two sets of questions;[11] so many that we shall not seek to display the detailed tables. Because our sample focuses on three sectors, the correlations reported here reflect the major differences between these sectors in addition to the firm-by-firm variations that would be apparent were we to study either a singe sector or a much wider spectrum of firms. Nevertheless, some interesting patterns do emerge.

Among these results, we draw attention to the following:

- Though there are significant correlations between 'knowledge of customers and markets' questions and IPR strategies, the correlation coefficients are never very high ones – the largest is 0.37 (between knowledge from feedback, and trademarks). 'Knowledge of networks' similarly has low correlations with IPR (the highest being knowledge of suppliers with design rights at 0.34). And in the case of 'knowledge of external factors', the highest correlation is only 0.40 (between knowledge of UKL regulations and membership of professional associations[12]). In contrast to these more social types of knowledge, more technical knowledge does display many higher correlations. Thus where it comes to forms of knowledge associated with the quality of the service, copyright and design rights have high associations (from 0.53 to 0.64) with the importance of design specification and concepts.[13] Where it comes to 'Knowledge of science and technology', knowledge of ecosystems and service design highly correlated with copyright (0.45 and 0.55 respectively), and knowledge of service properties again with design rights.[14]

- The general picture, then, is that the more technical forms of knowledge are more closely related to the formal means of protection of intellectual property. Almost without exception, the use of copyright, design rights, patenting, trademarks, agreements with partners, and agreements with suppliers, are positively associated with the importance of knowledge of ecosystems and S&T theory. These are the domain of ARC and especially EE. Thus, not so surprisingly, utilisation of research and knowledge of service properties are also correlated to these methods.[15]

- Agreements with suppliers and end users, surprisingly, were *not* related to the perceived importance of knowledge of suppliers, though they were linked to knowledge of the market, and to knowledge from feedback and that of customer needs.
- Knowledge from feedback emerges as rather important: the more it is seen as important, the more a range of formal IPR methods (but not copyright) and the embodiment of knowledge in products are used.
- Knowledge of the market is important for use of 'organisational' methods – agreements and working practices, but also copyright and trade marks (which are both important for establishing brand awareness in the market)
- Some of the few negative correlations are found between patenting and knowledge of regulations and of codes of practice. The reason for these is the *relatively* low concern that EE, the only patenting KIBS, have for these topics. Otherwise, regulatory and policy knowledge seem most highly associated with design rights (that is, with ARC): and with stress on internal working practices and professional associations.

10.4 CONCLUSIONS

The survey results were complemented by case studies and interviews with industry sources, which, together with the survey results, allow us to draw a number of conclusions.

First, achieving a reputation and networking are crucial to KIBS. They are ways in which KIBS firms mark out their intellectual territory, within a competitive landscape defined by codified norms of professional practice and tacit cultural traditions; and in some case by rapidly changing technology and regulations. These methods may be seen as being an important part of the knowledge-based economy – they represent knowledge of the KIBS firm being diffused in its market environment.

Related to this, professionalisation is important for well-established services. It provides support networks for individual professionals, and self-regulation and entry barriers, together with a measure of quality assurance for clients. Particular firms (especially small practices) operate in specific niches (closely related to the client base) within which qualifications may play an important role. Professional associations provide a national access to networks for smaller KIBS, who often need to co-operate with erstwhile competitors in local markets – for example, referring clients when there is surplus demand or conflict of interests.

A rather different point is that firms may build on their capabilities and knowledge base to extend their product range, diversifying the services delivered, adding peripheral or complementary services. This strategy is more or less the norm for large companies, who are well aware of the scope for using their knowledge of clients to offer them new services. Such KIBS stamp their identities on a range of services, thus becoming better known. Diversification is particularly important where innovation in the core service is inherently limited. (For example, the core products of accountants are framed by regulations, and offer little scope for novelty. Similar restrictions apply to many other financial services and professional KIBS, and to utilities such as water and gas supply.) It is also important where competition is intense. However, there are also pressures to consolidate around the core business or at least to rationalise the new structure (as in other sectors with perceived over-diversification).

Returning to formal methods of protecting knowledge, while these are seen as irrelevant by many KIBS firms, there are some KIBS in which copyright in particular is an extremely important protection method. This is especially true where the core service involves written documents, diagrams, and so on (and software/multimedia products) which embody aesthetic creativity and/or technical knowledge. In certain cases, specific intellectual products (for example, architectural drawings) are also protected by legal mechanisms like design rights. Internal documentation (for example, published guides to practice in some large ACC firms), may also be protected as part of firm strategy.[16] Contrary to a widespread belief, some services do use patents. Among the KIBS surveyed, this was only a feature of EE. But more generally, we know of IT-intensive services that patent product and, especially, process innovations. As well as the 'usual suspects' of IT services and IT-using information services (such as Reuters), we find supermarkets and other bodies patenting some of the technologies with which they interact with clients.

To an extent, the client-specific nature of much KIBS activity limits the commercial relevance of the IP generated within many service encounters. However, more appropriable knowledge is generated in the management of the encounter itself. The quality of the service delivered is combined with the knowledge dimensions of this relationship management process, and with the firm's participation in wider networks (of suppliers, clients, partners and competitors), to help define reputation (in particular, its intellectual parameters). Understanding of the client base, the associated market(s), personal relationships and patterns of communication, constitutes a firm-specific body of knowledge. In competitive situations (which are becoming the norm in KIBS), this is closely defended. Personnel-related IP problems include the departure of senior staff, and their knowledge of and links with the client base. Employment law and other mechanisms for dealing with such trade secrets are highly significant.

Though patent data are poor indicators of innovative activity in services, it is also apparent that considerable variations exist across sectors and firm sizes in the use of copyright, and in its application to technological innovation. A similar point applies to other formal protection mechanisms. The importance of other approaches – such as management of employees and of relationships with other firms, and participation in professional organisations – suggests that more case study and survey research at the firm level will be required to understand the dynamics here, and develop more robust indicators. Innovation and knowledge management in KIBS is to a very large extent a matter of the management of staff and network relationships. This supports the view that the knowledge activities of KIBS are very much grounded in human resources and interpersonal interactions.

NOTES

1. The research on which this study is based was funded by The Economic and Social Research Council, under its Intellectual Property Initiative.
2. 'Doing new things' was the subject of enquiry, since the term 'innovation' was often not recognised as appropriate by firms in this sample.
3. Both the German and Italian surveys found high variation across different service branches in terms of rates of innovation. Both also confirmed the familiar result that larger firms and establishments are more likely to report innovations than smaller ones.
4. The team at PREST responsible for originating the research project 'Management of IPR in KIBS' included N. Kastrinos and M. Boden; survey design was advanced considerably by P. Windrum, and P. Shearn contributed extensively to data production (telephone interviews and some postal completion of questionnaires) and analysis.
5. In each case we focus on the core services of the KIBS, not including related services – such as IT consultancy – in which many of them engage.
6. A small number of case studies were conducted in each sector, typically with the bias toward firms who appeared to be consciously grappling with IP issues. In addition interviews were held with relevant academics and industry commentators. Related work was also carried out which drew from and input into the project's IP concerns, notably Flanagan and Miles (1999) which looked at alliances and strategies around IP in multimedia, and an MSc dissertation by Sumon (1999).
7. Note that this is not the same thing as asking them how they protect their innovations. While most firms reported undertaking innovations, few of these would be new-to-market innovations, copying of which they might seek to limit.

Majorities of firms in all size groups and sectors report undertaking innovation. In response to the question *'Has the company introduced any new or significantly modified services/products or processes/methods of service production or delivery in the last 2 years?'* most firms replied positively. Two sectors display the usual positive relationship with size; larger ARC and EE respondents overwhelmingly report having undertaken innovation (72 per cent and 94 per cent respectively, as against 62 per cent and 74 per cent of smaller firms in these sectors). This relationship is reversed for ACC, where 80 per cent of the smaller firms, 73 per cent of the larger ones report innovation. Possibly this reflects late uptake of relatively basic IT – in the form of PCs, faxes, and so on – in small ACC firms. A further question, for those that did report innovation, asked *'Are these modifications based on organisational changes and/or the introduction of new technologies?'* Organisational innovation by itself emerged as rare among these KIBS. The smaller establishments report that their innovations are mainly technological, while the larger ones report solely technological, and combined organisational and technological innovation, to almost equal extents.

8. Much the same story would be told were we to examine the approaches that respondents say are 'never' used. In general, those approaches which are most often cited as 'always' used are least often cited as 'never' used. But one interesting feature does emerge from the cases where this is not so. In particular, EE firms seem quite divided about the methods that are 'never' employed. This suggests that this sector may be particularly diverse in the types of product supplied – and the services provided do range from paper-based reports through software to actual physical operations.

9. See also the stress put on knowledge of working with collaborators in Table 10.3.

10. Working with trusted partners is, however, frequently cited as 'always' being used by smaller ACC establishments, and is also among the most often cited approaches by EE firms.

11. Strictly, the non-random nature of the sample limits the meaningfulness of significance tests, originally designed to indicate how generalisable results might be to the wider universe from which a sample was drawn.

12. Accountants place high premium on both.

13. Architects consider these issues and IPR methods important.

14. Architects again, and probably environmental engineers.

15. Perhaps surprisingly, knowledge of technical standards is not related to patents, but does strongly influence copyright and design rights. (Recall that technical standards has been interpreted in very different ways in the different KIBS.)

16. Large accountancy firms publish reports, brochures, and various other materials in paper copies and now increasingly on Websites. Internal rules of practice and guidebooks may also be subject to copyright, as is the computer software that they produce.

11 The Internationalisation of Knowledge-Intensive Business Service Firms

Joanne Roberts[1]

11.1 INTRODUCTION

The providers of knowledge-intensive business services (KIBS) are undoubtedly becoming increasingly international in scope.[2] However, the internationalisation of firms within the sector has yet to be fully explored. As noted in earlier chapters, and elsewhere (Antonelli 1999; Miles et al. 1995), KIBS play a significant role in the creation and transfer of knowledge both within and between firms at the level of the region, the nation and internationally. Consequently, an appreciation of the internationalisation of KIBS firms is desirable if a full understanding of knowledge and innovation in the new service economy is to be achieved. It is then the purpose of this chapter to explore the internationalisation of KIBS firms.

Generally, firms become international when they extend their activities into overseas markets. The more involved they are in such markets the greater the level of internationalisation.[3] The process of internationalisation usually occurs in an evolutionary manner with firms extending their overseas involvement gradually, passing through various stages in the course of entering, and establishing a production facility in, a foreign market. Drawing on evidence from KIBS firms, active in the UK during the 1980s and early 1990s, this chapter demonstrates that such firms pass through a number of stages in the process of internationalisation. Moreover, contrary to the widely held view that the export of services is limited, the findings reported reveal that exports both independent and intra-firm play a significant role in the course of overseas expansion.

The KIBS sector includes a range of activities, however, the focus here is specifically on the four sub-sectors of advertising, accountancy, computer services and management consultancy services. These sub-sectors display high levels of internationalisation and potential for further overseas expansion. They also display a number of common characteristics which act as constraints on the methods of internationalisation utilised, including: the need for personal contact between producer and client; the importance of quality and reputation; a long-term buyer/seller relationship; human capital and knowledge intensiveness; and the need for cultural sensitivity.

The chapter is divided into four sections. First, consideration is given to the internationalisation of business service firms. This is followed by a discussion of the process of internationalisation. The various methods of international service provision will be considered and the argument that the internationalisation of KIBS firms occurs in a number of discrete stages will be elaborated upon. A further section reviews the survey evidence and considers the extent to which it supports a stages approach to internationalisation among KIBS firms. Finally, the wider relevance of the research is considered and suggestions for further research are raised.

11.2 THE INTERNATIONALISATION OF BUSINESS SERVICE FIRMS

The internationalisation of business services has attracted much attention in recent years (O'Farrell and Wood 1998; Bagchi-Sen and Sen 1997; O'Farrell et al. 1995, 1996; Aharoni 1993; *inter alia*). The overseas expansion of business service firms dates from the late nineteenth century and early 1900s, with some of today's large accountancy and advertising firms having become international at the turn of the century (Leyshon et al. 1987; West 1987). This process clearly gained momentum during the 1970s and 1980s. The development of large multinational advertising, accountancy, and consultancy firms such as WPP Group plc, PricewaterhouseCoopers and McKinsey Co. respectively, provide evidence of the increasing levels of international activity in the sector. Moreover, worldwide exports of business service are increasing (GATT 1994m p. 2). European Union credits arising from 'other business services', which include advertising, accountancy and management consulting services, increased from a value of US$30,281 million in 1987 to US$129,535 million in 1996. Whilst for the US, over the same period, credits arising from 'other business services' rose from US$10,635 million to US$32,360 million (OECD/EUROSTAT 1999, pp. 76–77).

According to UNCTC (1990) this international expansion is the result of both demand- and supply-driven forces. With the increasing globalisation of economic activity, business service firms have come under growing pressure to follow their multinational clients; this accounts for the demand-driven internationalisation.   The influence of multinational clients on the internationalisation of service firms has been widely recognised (Weinstein 1974; Dunning 1989; Esperanca 1992; *inter alia*). Furthermore, the general ongoing activity of restructuring production within the manufacturing sector, with firms concentrating their efforts on core activities whilst buying in peripheral intermediate goods and services, is leading to a rising demand for producer services.   This process of externalisation is of particular significance to the growth of business service firms (Martinelli 1991; Perry 1992), which can achieve economies of scale and scope when providing services to a large market (Enderwick 1992). However, in many cases, a market of sufficient size may only be achieved through internationalisation. In this respect the international expansion of business services can be seen as supply-driven, in the sense that firms have sought to reach out to a wider client base.

New information and communication technologies (ICTs) have also enabled business service firms to achieve economies of scale and scope. Being information intensive, they lend themselves to the application of computer and telecommunications technologies that facilitate the rapid collection, analysis and dissemination of information. Indeed, the increased use of ICTs throughout the economy has given rise to a demand for business services concerned with both the implementation and management of technology within firms, and the management of the organisational restructuring that is often essential for technology to be used efficiently. Moreover, as is evident from earlier chapters, technological development like the Internet are providing new channels through which business services may be delivered. Consequently, ICTs are also guiding the level and manner of internationalisation among business service firms.

Additional factors driving the development of major business service firms include, first, the opportunity to leverage further the business name and reputation of the firm by diversifying into new areas; secondly, a search for exclusive access to privileged information, thereby making it costly for clients to change suppliers by increasing the opportunity cost of such changes; and, finally, the desire to raise costs of entry for potential competitors (UNCTC 1990). Together these factors have encouraged the formation of large multinational firms in the sector.

Although foreign direct investment (FDI) in the services sector is dominated by the financial and distributive sectors (Dunning 1993), FDI in the business services sector is increasing. Nevertheless, the impact of this growth measured in terms of FDI flows is limited since firms in this sector tend to be relatively small, when compared to their manufacturing counterparts, and are generally skilled labour-intensive rather than capital-intensive. Further, in certain sub-sectors multinational expansion occurs through mechanisms other than FDI, for example, in the accountancy sector international partnerships are the usual method for the creation of multinational accountancy firms.

Internationalisation appears to be the dominant strategic objective for many large business service firms seeking continued growth. Firms will initially tend to extend their geographical reach in the national market prior to international expansion. However, in some cases firms will become internationally active prior to any extension of national coverage this is particularly the case for those business service firms located in capital cities or in other major areas of agglomeration (Roberts 1998). In such locations, firms are likely to have internationally oriented clients at an early stage in their development encouraging their international rather than inter-regional expansion.

It is clear, then, that business service firms become international in scope for both demand-pull and supply driven reasons. Once the firm has expanded overseas its international activity will be determined by a more complex strategy than simply following multinational clients into foreign markets. The market for its services widens to include a growing number of medium and small-sized business customers. As the firm becomes more international in scope, supply-driven forces will increasingly influence further overseas expansion.

11.3 THE PROCESS OF INTERNATIONALISATION

It has been argued that, in the manufacturing sector, the internationalisation of firms occurs in a number of evolutionary stages (Johanson and Wiedersheim-Paul 1975; Stopford and Wells 1972; Aharoni 1966; *inter alia*). For example, on the basis of their research into the internationalisation of Swedish firms, Johanson and Wiedersheim-Paul (1975, p. 306) argue that internationalisation occurs in four distinct stages:

1. no regular export activity;
2. export via independent representatives (agents);
3. sale subsidiary; and,
4. production/manufacturing.

Such interpretations of the internationalisation process have been criticised (Hood and Young 1983; Hedlund and Kverneland 1984; *inter alia*). Turnbull (1987), for instance, refutes the evolutionary approach to internationalisation, having failed to find supporting evidence in a study of the internationalisation of British manufacturing firms. So the question arises as to whether an evolutionary model of internationalisation can be of value when exploring the overseas expansion of KIBS firms?

It is generally assumed that the majority of services are non-tradable, in the traditional sense they are what Boddewyn et al. (1986) refer to as 'location-bound'. Consequently, it is often proposed that the internationalisation of services occurs through the establishment of a presence in the overseas market, that is through FDI and other related means. A study by the Office of Technology Assessment of the US Congress (1986) suggests that, with the exception of legal services, US business service firms supply foreign markets primarily through foreign affiliates due to a combination of technological, economic and regulatory factors. First, despite the application of new ICTs, much of the process of production in business services remains embedded in the direct relationship between client and producer. Secondly, in a sector in which attention to quality, service and local tastes has become a formidable competitive weapon, to compete effectively business services producers must have personnel deployed in the market place. Thirdly, the desire to protect reputation and intangible assets, together with the necessity of absolute confidentiality, discourage international provision without producer–client contact. Finally, certain forms of international transactions, not only pure cross-border trade, but also transactions based on the temporary movement of professionals, are at times not possible for regulatory reasons. For example, most countries do not allow auditors from other countries to practise locally, unless they have gained relevant local qualifications (UNCTC 1990).

Methods of overseas expansion that minimise costs and risks may well be essential. Knowledge-intensive business service firms may set up a reciprocal arrangement with a firm in the overseas market or participate in a joint venture. Through this type of arrangement the firm can gain experience and knowledge of the foreign market, thereby reducing the risks and uncertainty involved in the process of internationalisation. As the firm becomes more committed to an overseas market it may choose to increase its ownership share in the local presence (Johanson and Vahlne 1977). This may indeed be required if, as commitment increases, intangible assets are shared. Increased ownership will facilitate greater control over the foreign presence and thus ensure the protection of intangible assets. This is particularly notable where the knowledge assets being shared with overseas subsidiaries are non-codifiable (Buckley and Casson 1976), which is often the case for KIBS firms that deliver customised services to their clients.

Furthermore, it has been suggested that some service exports are only possible if the firm has a presence in the overseas market, which can act as a delivery system. For such services internationalisation requires the establishment of an overseas presence, and so producers progress rapidly from a national to an international firm without a period of exportation. This pattern of internationalisation is confirmed by Sharma and Johanson's (1987) study of technical consultancy firms. Although this may be the case in many instances, it is proposed here that the stage of exporting is an important one in the overseas expansion of KIBS firms. The place of exports in the internationalisation process has been neglected, although the exportation of services, both independently traded and intra-firm, are integral to the process of internationalisation among KIBS firms.

To regard all services as non-tradable is misguided. There have been many attempts to classify international service transactions (UNCTAD 1983; Sampson and Snape 1985; Vandermerwe and Chadwick 1989; Edvardsson et al. 1993; *inter alia*). It is possible to summarise international service transactions into first, those which are traded, and secondly, those which involve factor movements. The international transactions undertaken by KIBS firms are listed in Table 11.1, which illustrates a wide range of activities involving both trade and factor movements. Whether a KIBS firm is involved in exportation prior to establishing a presence overseas will depend largely on the characteristics of the service together with the nature of the firm's clients.

Many KIBS firms follow various stages in the process of internationalisation. As firms grow in size and domestic geographical spread they become international. Internationalisation initially takes the form of exports. If the firm provides services in the domestic market for foreign clients, then clearly, exportation does occur in the form of *domestically-located service exports*. Trade frequently arises when overseas customers enter the domestic market, seeking the services available there. For example, the foreign earnings of UK law firms overwhelmingly accrue to the activity of solicitors and barristers in the City of London, where they carry out an essential back up function to all the main financial service industries (Sowels 1989). Services may be provided to the overseas client in, for example, a letter or report; here exportation occurs in the traditional sense in the form of *embodied service exports*. Personnel travelling may facilitate *people-mediated exports*, and finally, services can be exported through telecommunication networks in the form of *wired exports*. Evidence of exportation in the above forms can be found in the UK balance of payments, where services exports are recorded as provision by UK residents to nonresidents, with no need for services to cross borders.   In addition, data revealing growth in credits and debits for business travel and telecommunications[4] might reflect, to some extent, the growth of services provided by personnel travelling and services exported 'over-the-wire' in all sectors of economic activity, especially in the form of intra-firm service transactions.

Table 11.1 A classification of international activities conducted by KIBS firms

Exports:
- Embodied services e.g. report, letter, video.
- Wired services e.g. telephone conversation, telecommunications data transfer, Internet based service.
- Domestically-located service exports e.g. legal services provided to a foreign client in the home market.
- People-mediated exports e.g. personnel travelling to overseas market to advise foreign client, or present a report.
- Intra-firm exports e.g. services delivered from the home country to foreign clients via a local office in the overseas market.

Overseas presence*:
- Export delivery system.
- Service production facility – producing services for the local market and perhaps geographically proximate foreign markets.
- International production unit – e.g.: involved in collecting data on local markets to be used in other countries - management consultants, market research firms; or, data entry facility or computer programming unit taking advantage of lower labour costs in overseas market and exporting output back to the home country.
- Operations in conjunction with other firms, local or international, to provide services to a particular client e.g. consortia of firms often used in the computer services sector.

Notes: A KIBS firm may be involved in any combination of the above within individual markets and between markets.
*These may include wholly- or majority-owned subsidiaries, joint ventures, franchise or licensing operations, partnerships, associate firms, reciprocal arrangements, together with other methods of local representation.

The competitive advantage of the KIBS firms studied here is rooted in intangible assets such as human capital, firm-specific experience and accumulated technological information, or goodwill.   Thus internationalisation will frequently necessitate the movement (temporary or permanent) of highly-skilled professional staff abroad. Given that the firm's assets are primarily incorporated in personnel, the costs of setting up a presence overseas are relatively low when compared to a firm in the manufacturing sector.   Independent exports are somewhat limited, in the sense that they may not be the most effective long-term method of servicing foreign markets. It is therefore likely that if a firm has clients in an overseas market it will eventually establish a presence in that market in order to ensure optimum service quality, and to fend off local competition. The level of exports necessary to give rise to the consideration of the establishment of an overseas production facility is likely to be much lower for KIBS firms than for manufacturing firms because the costs involved are significantly smaller. All that is required is an office and the appropriate skilled labour, whereas in the manufacturing sector costly plant and equipment will also be required. Moreover, the office equipment utilised by KIBS firms will generally be non-specific and therefore available in competitive markets at relatively low cost, and often through leasing arrangements. Skilled labour may be costly and sector specific, although the high mobility of such labour facilitates its easy transfer between locations and activities. Consequently, the level of market commitment required for a KIBS firm to establish a presence in an overseas location can be expected to be less than that required for a manufacturing firm. KIBS firms may then be expected to set up an overseas presence at an earlier stage in their development than manufacturing firms, or indeed more capital-intensive service sector firms.

A firm may be at different stages of international development within different foreign markets or regions. This, together with different regulatory environments,[5] explains the use of a variety of types of international activity within one firm. As a firm's experience of foreign markets increases, there will be less risk and uncertainty when entering new markets. With increased internationalisation service firms may establish overseas presences more rapidly, with less need for caution, and with higher levels of market commitment from the beginning (Erramilli 1991).

Exports play a crucial role in the internationalisation of KIBS firms. It is through serving overseas clients in the domestic market, together with serving domestic clients in overseas markets through personnel travelling and other forms of exporting, that such firms get their first experience of internationalisation. It is interesting to speculate upon the relative importance of the various types of exportation available to KIBS firms. Since 'face-to-face' contact is necessary in the delivery, if not the production, of many services it can be argued that forms of exportation which incorporate such contact are those which are likely to be used most frequently. Additional factors necessitating client–producer contact include the need for cultural sensitivity and local knowledge, regulatory requirements, the desire to protect intangible assets such as reputation, and the need for absolute confidentiality. Exports of services embodied in goods or exported 'over-the-wire' will be less significant than those involving the movement of the client to the location of the producer, or the movement of personnel to the client's location. With advances in ICTs, embodied service exports and wired exports may become closer substitutes with other forms of service exports and therefore used more widely. Although, it is questionable whether ICTs can facilitate the effective transfer of knowledge, especially tacit knowledge (Roberts 2000), which is central in the provision of KIBS. Non-client contact exports undoubtedly play a valuable supportive role enabling the transfer of data, information and codified knowledge. Such exports, to some extent, facilitate other forms of export and internationalisation through other means. This type of trade is often likely to be intra-firm, rather than direct, and this is an element influencing the international organisation of KIBS firms. Foreign direct investment takes place in certain circumstances to facilitate intra-firm trade.

Internationalisation may occur through a merger or take-over or indeed the firm may start a presence from scratch. Mergers and acquisitions have many advantages. First, there is the speed with which an international network can be established. Secondly, a firm gains access to an established client bank and wealth of local market knowledge. Thirdly, the firm avoids a period of loss making while establishing a new market presence. Fourthly, the difficulties of establishing a new enterprise in a highly developed and competitive market are avoided. For firms seeking rapid international expansion, mergers and acquisitions are utilised, apart from in markets where KIBS are underdeveloped (for example, Eastern Europe and parts of South East Asia), and the establishment of a green-field operation is required.

The manner in which KIBS firms become international will vary considerably from firm to firm. In particular, the age of the firm and the period in which it first embarked upon a strategy of international expansion will be significant factors. Internationalisation through acquisitions and mergers is of particular importance to firms that are latecomers to the international market. As a result, it is a common method of overseas expansion in the computer services sector (Roberts 1998).

To summarise then, internationalisation generally begins with exports and progresses to the establishment of an overseas presence, either through FDI, joint venture, or contractual arrangement with an overseas firm. The establishment of an overseas presence may be accompanied by trade, in particular intra-firm trade in services that merely require delivering to the overseas market through a local presence. Over time the local presence will develop the ability to supply the market independently of the parent firm. At this stage intra-firm trade will continue but consist of intermediary services (that is, service components). Moreover, the flow of intra-firm trade may also become two-way. Clearly, many KIBS firms follow an evolutionary path in the development of their international capabilities; it should, though, be noted that firms may progress gradually or rapidly through this process.

Indeed, some firms may skip the process completely by gaining extensive international capabilities through a merger or acquisition.

11.4 EVIDENCE FOR A STAGES APPROACH TO INTERNATIONALISATION

To explore the internationalisation of KIBS, and to substantiate the argument forwarded here, evidence was collected through a postal survey of UK KIBS firms conducted between May and September 1990. The survey sample was selected from four sub-sectors; advertising, accountancy, computer services and management consultancy. Given resource restrictions, the survey was targeted at the large firms. It was essential to ensure that a significant portion of the firms surveyed was of a certain size because internationalisation is generally associated with the larger firms.[6] With the prevalence of small firms in the sector, a totally random sample would undoubtedly have thrown up only a very small number of firms with international activity. The business services sector is one with low barriers to entry and amenable to the self-employed, because of the low start-up costs and high value-added, hence the large number of small firms in the sector (Bryson et al. 1993). Table 11.2 provides details of the sub-sectors surveyed and the response rates achieved. The total usable returns amounted to 279, an overall response rate of 31.2 per cent, providing a useful sample through which to explore the internationalisation of firms within the sector.

Table 11.2 UK business service sub-sectors surveyed and response rates

Sector (SIC 1980)	Number surveyed	Responses		% Responses	
		Total	Usable	Total	Usable
Advertising (8380)	289	99	88	34.3	30.4
Accountancy (8360)	203	78	62	38.4	30.5
Computer services (8394)	205	84	68	41.0	33.2
Management consultants (8395/1)	196	88	61	44.9	31.1
Total	893	349*	279	39.1	31.2

Note:*70 constituted nil returns.

The characteristics of the sample (Table 11.3) indicate that the group of firms surveyed provides an accurate reflection of the wider population of firms in the UK KIBS sector. For example, the concentration of activity in the south of the UK, the high proportion of young firms in the sample, the dominance of small firms measured both in terms of turnover and employment levels, are all features of the sector as a whole. The sample also reflects the polarisation of activities within the sector between a large number of small firms and a small number of large firms.

The survey evidence indicates that KIBS firms use a variety of methods of foreign market servicing. Exports and FDI are important, but firms also use joint ventures, franchise agreements, and reciprocal arrangements, among other means. Respondents were asked a set of questions relating to the nature of their exports, the results are presented in Table 11.4. It can be seen that the most popular ways in which KIBS are exported are through domestically located exports and people mediated exports. This evidence confirms the view that exports that incorporate face-to-face contact will be more popular than those facilitated through embodied service exports or wired exports.

Table 11.3 Sample characteristics

Location		Date of Establishment		Company type	
South	199	<1900	18	Sole proprietor	18
Midlands	33	1900–1950	29	Partnership	52
North	33	1951–1960	11	Limited	95
Scotland	8	1961–1970	41	Public limited company	28
Wales	2	1971–1980	73	Wholly owned subsidiary	72
N.Ireland	1	1981–1990	90	Majority owned subsidiary	8
	N=276			Associate	4
			N=262	Other	2
					N=279

Turnover 1989			Employment 1989		
£	UK	Overseas		UK	Overseas
<0.25 mil	31	158	<10	30	187
0.25–0.5 mil	16	12	10–20	35	12
0.5–1 mil	14	11	21–50	70	8
1–5 mil	73	14	51–100	44	5
5–10 mil	48	6	101–200	43	5
10–25 mil	31	5	201–500	22	5
25–50 mil	15	5	501–1000	10	3
50–100 mil	12	4	1001–2500	9	6
100 mil+	18	19	2501+	8	13
	N=258	N=234		N=271	N=244

Source: Postal survey.

A similar pattern of exports was found among all the sub-sectors, although a few discrepancies are noteworthy. Only the advertising and computer service sectors had any firms which claimed that exports were always carried out in the form of embodied exports, 7.2 per cent and 3.6 per cent respectively, while 90.9 per cent of accountancy firms indicated that they never exported in this manner. This type of export also seemed to be of little significance to management consultancy firms. People-mediated exports appeared to be of particular importance to management consultancy firms with 21.8 per cent always, and 34.5 per cent often, exporting in this way. Again, this method appeared to be less important to accountancy firms with 54.5 per cent saying they never exported through personnel travelling.

With regard to wired exports, 10.9 per cent of computer services firms said they always used this method compared to 3.2 per cent for the whole group. This greater use of a telecommunications network as a means through which services are exported may be accounted for in terms of the nature of computer services, some of which are embodied in codified knowledge (for example, software), and consequently can be easily transmitted 'over-the-wire'. It is clear, though, that computer service firms use a variety of methods of exportation. Although 48.2 per cent of the whole group claim that they never used wired exports, this leaves 51.8 per cent that do use this method at some time. Exports of this sort do occur, and will no doubt increase as ICTs become more integrated into the process of service provision. A factor that may inhibit the rapid growth in the use of ICTs in the exportation of KIBS is the lack of standardisation apparent in much KIBS activity. Where services can be standardised, and their provision is facilitated through the transfer of codified knowledge (for example, access to data banks), there is scope for ICTs to become more important in the internationalisation process. Where there is less scope for such standardisation, and service provision requires the transfer of tacit knowledge, the function of ICTs in terms of internationalisation will be more limited. Nevertheless ICTs may still be significant as a means of supporting other types of exports, such as through personnel travelling. The element of personal contact with clients is of particular significance in many KIBS activities, and client relations ranks high as a source of competitive advantage, with 73.6 per cent (N=269) of firms ranking this as an extremely important source of competitive advantage.

Moreover, ICTs may become of increasing significance as conduits for intra-firm trade. Intermediate services may be provided 'over-the-wire' as inputs into a final service, which is created by personnel located in the overseas market. Skilled personnel can in a sense become the transaction facilitator, providing the interface between the firm in the home market and the client in the overseas location. Personnel located in close proximity to the client can combine their tacit knowledge with codified knowledge delivered 'over-the-wire' to provide a customised service to the client. Additionally, the role of ICTs in promoting the efficient management and organisation of resources on an international basis should be recognised. As

Quinn and Paquette (1990) note, ICTs enable a complex yet flexible organisation of resources that can be used to maximum effect to satisfy the needs of individual clients.

Support for a stages approach to internationalisation is found when examining the 27 firms that attributed all of their overseas revenue to exports, of a total sample of 112 firms that attributed a portion of their overseas revenue to exports. Exploring these 27 firms more closely, it was found that they appeared to be smaller in size, in terms of both UK employment and turnover, compared with the group as a whole (112). These 'export only' firms also had smaller levels of overseas turnover generally, which suggests that they are in the early stages of internationalisation and general development. It is interesting to note that 'export only' firms made greater use of embodied and people-mediated service exports (Table 11.4). In particular, much greater use was made of people-mediated exports with 29.6 per cent of these firms always using this method compared with 10.9 per cent for the whole sample. Exportation as a stage in the internationalisation process cannot be overlooked in the case of KIBS firms. Exportation does occur, although the period during which a service firm only uses exports to service foreign markets may be less prolonged than is the case for manufacturing firms.

Table 11.4 How KIBS are exported

	Embodied service exports %		People-mediated exports %		Domestically located service exports %		Wired exports %	
	All firms	Export only firms	All firms	Export only firms	All firms	Export only firms	All firms	Export only firms
Always	3.2	7.4	10.9	29.6	4.5	3.7	3.2	0.0
Often	10.8	18.5	19.5	33.3	24.3	22.2	10.5	11.5
Sometimes	14.4	29.6	21.7	14.8	32.4	40.7	15.5	15.4
Occasionally	23.4	11.1	17.2	11.1	21.2	14.8	22.7	23.1
Never	48.2	33.3	30.8	11.1	17.6	18.5	48.2	50.0
	(N=222)	(N=27)	(N=221)	(N=27)	(N=222)	(N=27)	(N=220)	(N=26)

Source: Postal survey.

It is clear from the survey evidence that KIBS firms are able to export services prior to setting up a permanent presence in an overseas market. When asked whether they export to countries in which they do not have a presence, of a total sample of 216 firms, 124 (57.4 per cent) said 'yes' whilst 92 (42.6 per cent) said 'no'. This confirms that KIBS firms are able to export services independently of a permanent presence in the export market. Firms were also asked if, when an overseas presence is necessary to provide services to overseas clients, such a presence would initially be used merely as a delivery system for services largely produced elsewhere. Of 143 firms responding to this question 68 (47.6 per cent) said 'yes' whilst 75 (52.4 per cent) said 'no'. Overseas presences are in some cases established in order to facilitate 'exports' from the domestic market. They may be regarded as transaction-specific assets that promote the flow of intra-firm trade in services. It should, though, be noted that in the majority of cases overseas presences are established as more than just a delivery system, and are actively involved in the production and provision of services to the market.

Exploring the sub-sectors the results vary; only 26.7 per cent of accountancy firms indicated that a presence is purely a delivery system. This figure is substantially lower than for the group as a whole and reflects certain characteristics of the sub-sectors. The regulation of accountancy firms, for instance, often requires practising accountants to obtain local qualifications. Thus, if personnel are located in an overseas market they must possess the ability to produce services locally.

Table 11.5 Correlation coefficients

	Date of establishment	UK turnover	UK employment	Overseas turnover	Overseas employment
Date of establishment	1.0000 (262)	-0.2198* (244)	-0.3558** (256)	-0.2444** (221)	-0.2219* (230)
UK Turnover	-0.2198* (244)	1.0000 (244)	0.9158** (228)	0.5416** (231)	0.6092** (241)
UK employment	-0.3558** (256)	0.9158** (228)	1.0000 (234)	0.5102** (231)	0.6037** (230)
Overseas turnover	-0.2444** (221)	0.5416** (231)	0.5102** (231)	1.0000 (258)	0.7473** (252)
Overseas employment	-0.2219* (230)	0.6092** (241)	0.6037** (230)	0.7473** (252)	1.0000 (271)

Note: Coefficient/(cases)/two-tailed significance: * -0.01 ** -0.001.

Source: Postal survey.

The relationships between age, UK turnover and employment, and overseas turnover and employment, were explored through an examination of the correlation coefficients between these variables (Table 11.5). When firm age, (indicated by the date of establishment), and the level of UK turnover were correlated, a negative relationship was found. The older the firm (that is, the lower the date of establishment) the higher the level of UK turnover. Although the correlation coefficient reported does not appear to be strong, the two-tailed significance test shows that the linear association between the variables is statistically significant. The correlation coefficients between the level of UK turnover and employment, and overseas turnover and employment, are higher and statistically significant; indicating a positive and stronger linear association between UK size and the level of internationalisation (measured in terms of both overseas turnover and employment), compared to that between age and level of internationalisation. The rapid growth in the number of business services firms over the past 25 years may account for the weaker correlation between date of establishment and the level of internationalisation. A number of firms have grown rapidly and become international in only a short period of time, primarily through a process of mergers and take-overs.[7] Indeed, the sample surveyed displayed a relatively youthful age profile reflecting the rapid growth of KIBS firms in recent years.

The results reported here add weight to the view that KIBS firms progress through various stages in the process of internationalisation. Specifically, the stage of exporting must be recognised within the course of overseas expansion. From the empirical research five stages in the internationalisation of KIBS firms can be identified:

1.   Provision of services to domestic clients only (no exports).
2.   Provision of services to foreign clients in the domestic market (domestically located exports).
3.   Provision of services to foreign markets through embodied service exports, people-mediated exports and wired exports.
4.   Establishment of a presence through which to deliver a service largely produced in the domestic market (intra-firm exports).
5.   Establishment of service production facility in the overseas market.

The number of stages through which firms pass, and the length of time spent in each one, is variable. Indeed, firms may skip stages, even becoming international in one step through a merger or acquisition. Not only can mergers and acquisitions enable a KIBS firm to enter a particular market rapidly, but they also facilitate the speedy establishment of international networks. International capabilities can also be acquired rapidly through contractual arrangements.[8] Despite this, the significance of stages, and especially the stage of exporting, in the internationalisation of many KIBS firms must be emphasised.

11.5 CONCLUSIONS

This chapter has explored the manner in which KIBS firms are becoming international in scope. The evidence presented supports the argument that KIBS firms progress through various stages in the process of internationalisation. The nature of the stages through which these firms progress may differ from those through which manufacturing firms pass. Furthermore, it is clear that not all KIBS firms progress through all of the stages outlined above. However, it is evident that internationalisation does occur in an incremental manner for many KIBS firms.

The importance of exports in the internationalisation of KIBS firms has been illustrated. The implications of this research will have more relevance for other services with similar characteristics to those of KIBS, for example, other knowledge-intensive services and professional services. Nevertheless, the findings underline the need to reassess the role of exports in the internationalisation of service firms generally. Moreover the significance of intra-firm trade in the early stages of internationalisation among KIBS firms has been highlighted. The role of intra-firm trade in the international development of service firms warrants further attention. Intra-firm trade may act as a substitute for direct trade, and it is also a major influence on the organisational development of international KIBS firms.

A number of factors which direct the nature of internationalisation among service firms have been identified; these include the regulatory characteristics of overseas markets and ICTs. The harmonisation of regulation, through initiatives such as the General Agreement on Trade in Services (Broadman 1994) and the World Trade Organisation Service 2000 negotiations, will undoubtedly have an impact upon the pattern of trade and investment in KIBS. In addition, developments in ICTs are likely to influence the process of internationalisation, since they facilitate internationalisation in a number of ways. First, ICTs make the organisation of an international firm more efficient. Secondly, they provide a means through which services can be exported across borders. Although the survey results show no major shift towards wired exports, technology is advancing rapidly. Indeed, major developments have occurred in the commercial use of the Internet since the date of the survey from which the findings of this study are derived. Nevertheless, the extent to which technology can replace face-to-face contact is still limited, although this will not necessarily remain the case. The client–producer relationship is certainly a constraint upon the use of wired exports. Firms which find ways through which to successfully alleviate this constraint will have a competitive advantage in the supply of services since they will have greater flexibility in their methods of supplying overseas markets compared to those firms which depend heavily upon client–producer contact.

Removal of the client-producer contact constraint would allow KIBS firms to become international in scope purely through the use of ICTs. The relationship between clients and their suppliers in the area of KIBS provision would certainly benefit from further exploration. It may well be useful to analyse such relations in terms of issues such as trust and cultural factors, particularly in terms of how these factors influence the transfer of knowledge that is central in the effective provision of KIBS.

This chapter provides an insight into the internationalisation of a sample of UK KIBS firms active in the 1980s and early 1990s. The role of exports and intra-firm trade in the internationalisation of KIBS firms has been highlighted. Additional research is required to verify and update the results reported here. For instance, an examination of the extent to which new Internet-based mechanisms of supplying services are influencing the internationalisation of KIBS firms would be of particular interest. It is clear, though, from the research reported here that the internationalisation of KIBS and services more generally require further investigation.

NOTES

1. The author would like to acknowledge the support provided by the Economic and Social Research Council (Grant No: A00428722021) for the research project from which the chapter draws.
2. This chapter draws on data presented in an earlier paper entitled 'The Internationalisation of Business Service Firms: A Stages Approach' published in *The Service Industries Journal*, Vol. 19, No.4, 1999.
3. Methods for measuring of the level of a firm's internationalisation include, for instance, the proportion of turnover derived from overseas markets or alternatively, the proportion of the firm's assets located overseas. For KIBS firms many of their most significant assets are difficult to measure because they are intangible or embodied in skilled personnel. Consequently, the measurement of internationalisation in terms of overseas turnover is more appropriate in this sector.
4. For example, between 1986 and 1996 credits on the UK Balance of Payments current account deriving from business travel rose from £1,552 million to £3,364 million, whilst debits increased from £1,131 million to £3,514 million. Over the same period credits from telecommunications and postal services increased from £638 million to £988 million and debits from £721 million to £1,221 million (The UK Balance of Payments 1997, p. 39).
5. Restrictions that impede the international expansion of business service firms include regulations concerning: local ownership and rights of establishment; international payments; mobility of personnel; technology transfer; transborder data flows; procurement policies; restrictions on the business scope of firms; and restrictions on the use of a firm's name (Noyelle and Dutka 1988).
6. The samples were weighted towards firms that ranked among the top 30 of their

particular sub-sector. These were identified from the trade press and directories, such as *Campaign* (1989), *The Accountant* (1989), and *Computing Services Association Official Reference Book* (1989). Having selected the top 30 firms for each sub-sector the remainder of the samples were selected at random.

7. The advertising groups WPP plc and Cordiant plc are examples of this rapid growth among business service firms achieved through mergers and acquisitions.

8. For instance, M&C Saatchi advertising agency's arrangement with Publicis (May, 1995).

12 Outsourcing Novelty: The Externalisation of Innovative Activity

Jeremy Howells[1]

12.1 INTRODUCTION

This chapter examines the process of research and technology outsourcing in relation to the wider innovation process, investigating the growth of the phenomenon within a systems framework. The first section outlines the growth and dynamics of the outsourcing process in relation to research and technological activities using material based on Howells (1999a). Developing some of these findings, the chapter then places the process of research and technology outsourcing within the wider framework of innovation outsourcing and externalisation. The last section reviews the implications of research and technological outsourcing and innovation outsourcing more generally within the wider conceptual and analytical context of systems approaches to innovation. These approaches centre on the 'systems of innovation' model based originally on the 'national systems of innovation' (NSI) studies developed by Freeman (1987, 1988), Lundvall (1988, 1992) and Nelson (1992a, Nelson and Rosenberg 1993), but also includes the 'technology system' approach developed by Carlsson (1995). The term 'innovation system approaches' is used throughout the text to denote both the 'systems of innovation' (both national and sectoral) and the 'technological system' models.

Studies of research collaboration have concentrated upon inter-firm relations between manufacturing companies (manufacturing–manufacturing relations) operating in the same or related sectors. Such analysis has been within the context of long-term dynamic competitive and technological trends. Thus firms, even large multinational corporations, can no longer expect to be totally dependent on their own in-house research and technical resources to maintain their innovative performance. This chapter seeks to outline the implications of these dynamic trends for the conduct of the innovative activity by firms in relation to research and technology outsourcing and place it within the wider context of a systems of innovation framework. Moreover the growth in the external sourcing of R&D and other design and technical activities by firms has played an important role in the creation and development of the research and technology 'market',[2] in terms of the commercial purchasing and trading of research and technology (R&T). Related to this has been the growth of organisations serving this contract research and technical 'market'. This includes Contract Research Organisations (CROs; or increasingly much wider-based Contract Research and Technology Organisations – CRTOs) and Research and Technology Organisations (RTOs)[3] as well as a wider group of companies and organisations with some involvement in the R&T 'market', which has important implications for the development of the innovation support infrastructure in national and local systems of innovation.

The focus of this chapter, therefore, is on the outsourcing of R&D and technical activity formerly undertaken by manufacturing and service firms and now outsourced to firms and organisations which supply the R&T 'market'. These are primarily private CRTOs, but also include a range of private non-profit and related hybrid organisations. The focus is, therefore, not on what has become termed as 'inter-firm' research and technical collaboration, involving both horizontal cooperation, with firms from the same or related manufacturing sector (sometimes direct competitors), and vertical cooperation, associated with collaboration along the supply chain between suppliers and their customers. The analysis did not specifically cover 'university–industry' or 'government–industry' collaborations, although certain hybrid organisations such as university-owned spin-off companies and government laboratories which are trading companies are increasingly important in the research and technical contract market. All these forms of research and technical collaboration form part of the external research and technical profile of the firm, and are of relevance to the wider analysis of R&D outsourcing and externalisation.

12.2 THE DYNAMICS OF RESEARCH AND TECHNOLOGY OUTSOURCING

12.2.1 Growth and Significance

Ringe (1992, p. 2) has defined 'contract research and development' as 'work of an innovatory nature undertaken by one party on behalf of another under conditions laid out in a contract agreed formally beforehand'. The primary focus of this Chapter is on R&D, but it also covers such other technical activity as design, prototyping and specialised engineering services. Indeed many of these non-routine activities are now anyway included under the revised and extended Frascati definition (OECD 1993) of R&D activity. Similarly in the realm of services, the study also includes software design and development (also now included in the revised Frascati definition). The boundaries of what the R&T 'market', and the organisations involved in it, covers are nonetheless never going to be complete. For example, Ringe (1992) excludes 'testing houses' in his definition of contract R&D, stating that testing and accreditation are too routine a set of activities to be included in the process of R&D. However, testing houses do increasingly undertake certain applied development work. There are a wide range of organisations and activities on the fringes of contract research and technical activity where contract work may not represent their central activity but is an important element of their work and should not be excluded from comprehensive study of the R&T 'market'. Individually such organisations may not be key actors in the CRT industry, but cumulatively they can have a significant impact on the whole sector.

There has been significant growth in the amount of extra-mural or contracted out research in advanced industrialised economies since the 1970s (Whittington 1990). Thus, in Canada an estimated 7 per cent of industrial R&D expenditure was extra-mural in 1993 (Rose 1997, pp. 10–11). Similarly in the UK some 10 per cent of Business Expenditure on Research and Development (BERD) was extra-mural in 1995. Veugelers (1997, p. 308) in a study of Flemish companies, also noted that 10 per cent of the total R&D budget of such firms was spent extra-murus. Moreover there has been a substantial growth in external research work. In Germany an increasing proportion of company R&D budgets are spent externally, from a figure of 3.5 per cent in 1969 to 9.8 per cent in 1983 (although levelling off to 9.2 per cent in 1989; Häusler et al. 1994).[4] In the UK there has been a doubling in the amount of extra-mural BERD in the UK between 1985 and 1995, from £450 million (in constant 1995 prices; 5.5 per cent of the total) to some £935 million (10.0 per cent) in 1995. In some sectors this level was even higher, with an estimated 15.5 per cent of UK pharmaceutical R&D being extra-mural in 1995 (Jones 1997, p. 13).

Although this growth in the outsourcing has been rapid in recent years it should not be considered a completely new phenomenon. Thus, as Teece (1987, p. 258) notes in relation to the United States 'During the late nineteenth century and the first half of the twentieth century ... practically all of it [research] had been conducted outside of the firm in stand-alone research organizations.' Up until the inter-war period, in-house R&D

laboratories were considered novel and most firms that needed to undertake research would contract it out to universities or independent research scientists when necessary. Even in sectors with a relatively long scientific tradition, such as the pharmaceutical industry, this was still the most usual method of conducting research up until the First World War (see, for example, Liebenau 1984; Swann 1989). However, during the 1920s, 1930s and 1940s there appears to have been a significant decrease in R&D contracted out to independent research organisations as can be seen in the decline in the proportion of scientific professionals working in such establishments to all scientific professionals working in all (in-house and independent) research laboratories in the US (Table 12.1).

In Britain, the emergence and development of in-house R&D departments came much later and was less complete in important respects when compared to that occurring in the United States (Mowery 1983, 1984; Mowery and Rosenberg 1989) and more especially Germany. Indeed, Germany was more advanced than the United States in terms of not only the formation of industrially-based research (Meyer-Thurow 1982; Homburg 1992; Marsch 1994), but also in relation to the development of industry-academic links (see, for example, comparisons made by Sanderson 1972; Barnett 1986).

It was therefore only effectively after the inter-war period (for the United States) and more especially after the Second World War (for the UK and for most other leading European countries, excluding Germany) that the 'tradition' of large, centralised R&D laboratories became commonplace. Thus, although in one way the comment that 'Many companies are experimenting with multiple new outside sources for technology, and are tapping them through mechanisms and relationships largely unknown to the previous generation' (Graham 1985, p. 87) is true; managers are, in a sense, having to re-learn what the generation before them saw as the 'norm'. However, although there is a relearning process here from previous collaborative practices of the late nineteenth and early twentieth centuries, it is being accompanied, in many cases, by continued growth of in-house research and technical capacity. A new era in terms of research and technical competences and collaborative patterns for firms therefore seems to be emerging[5] as companies now seek a more balanced and mature approach to their research and technical requirements. Firms accept that they need in-house capacity to adequately appraise, select and then use 'brought in' research and technical elements. They also recognise the need to retain certain core technological competences within the firm because it can be more effectively undertaken on a hierarchical, non-contractual basis, including here reasons associated with secrecy, trust and appropriability.

Table 12.1 Employment of scientific professionals in independent research organisations as a fraction of employment of scientific professionals in all in-house and independent research laboratories in the United States, 1921–46

Year	Employment fraction
1921	15.2
1927	12.9
1933	10.9
1940	8.7
1946	6.9

Source: Mowery (1983).

The above analysis has therefore suggested that research and technology outsourcing is not a new phenomenon. It was the main method for companies to have research and technical work undertaken via this route up until the nineteenth and early twentieth centuries, but it then declined throughout the inter-war period before making a comeback in the late 1970s and early 1980s. What were the factors underlying this reversal and then comeback? More specifically, what are the factors behind this more recent growth in contracted out research and technical activity? Much can be gained from recent studies seeking to uncover the motivations encouraging external research and technical links and these will now be discussed below.

12.2.2 Outsourcing Factors

A range of studies has sought to explain the growth in the use of external research and technical resources by firms and why firms should seek to collaborate or contract out their R&D, design and engineering needs (see, for example, Pisano et al. 1988; Thomas 1988; Pisano 1990; Arora and Gambardella 1990; Hagerdoorn and Schakenraad 1990; Charles and Howells 1992; Häusler et al. 1994; Katz and Martin 1997; Chen 1997). Some of these studies highlight the transaction cost model developed by Williamson (1975, 1979; see also Ouchi 1980) as a means of explaining why there may be a shift from an in-house vertical and hierarchical provision of such research needs towards a more market mediated approach. However, although useful as a general guide for such changes, it has a number of problems associated with its use.

First, trying to operationalise transaction-cost theory to specific organisational contexts or more aggregate empirical surveys have largely been abandoned due to serious logical and empirical problems (Robins 1987, p. 68; see also Englander 1988).[6] More problematic, the transaction cost model explains on one level why there should be *no* contracting-out of R&D activities of the firm. This is because of the high degree of complexity and uncertainty associated with R&D which makes contractual relationships difficult or impossible to negotiate. Thus under conditions of bounded rationality, together with a high degree of complexity and uncertainty, bargainers are unable to define complete contractual agreements because neither all alternative features nor their corresponding prices can be determined (Williamson 1975, p. 25). Similarly, Ouchi and Bolton (1988, p. 11) note in relation to R&D projects 'when the task in hand is complex or uncertain, contractual arrangements will be difficult to specify and monitor, and post-contractual opportunism will be common'. Because of these reasons, the transaction cost model foresees that R&D would not be undertaken in a market- mediated system but rather carried out under conditions of internal organisation within the hierarchy of the firm.

There is also a problem with how Williamson uses bounded rationality,[7] a concept developed by Simon (1957). Williamson makes clear the distinction of transaction-cost economics from earlier neo-classical economics, by using the notion of bounded rationality ('the absence of unlimited computational capacity') together with the additional assertion that decision-makers do not seek always to maximise because of 'atmosphere'. Thus 'Individuals are not (all) given to strict maximization of expected pecuniary gain but also consume "atmosphere". ... preferences for atmosphere may induce individuals to forego material gains for nonpecuniary satisfactions ....' (Williamson 1973, p. 317). However, after asserting these maxims he departs from this standpoint in subsequent discussion. Williamson thus often sees conditions of bounded rationality and satisfying (rather than maximising) decision-making as unusual deviations from the norm of more rational and computational ways of thought and decision-making (see Buckley and Chapman 1997, p. 141). However, more particularly, where bounded rationality is apparently maintained in the discussion, it then appears to be encompassed within a much more rational and optimising framework. As such it is set within a 'conditioning environment' approaching optimal decision-making (aimed at maximising or satisficer frameworks) and highly rational decision-making based on high levels of available information. Thus decision-makers undertake 'careful calculations' under highly complex decision sets, making correct decisions of whether to allocate resources under markets and hierarchies based on different conditions of uncertainty, complexity, asset specificity and opportunism.

Of course, Williamson has moved on from his earlier work. He has sought to develop and highlight different contractual arrangements under classical, neo-classical and relational categories of contract law (Williamson 1986; using concepts originally outlined by Macneil 1978) which allow for a wider range of contractual relations. More recently, Williamson (1996) has in turn highlighted hybrid forms of governance structures between markets and hierarchies which can help account for greater complexity in contractual and organisational forms in the real world. Others have also sought to stress networks and other forms of collaborative organisation as governance structures between markets and hierarchies (see, for example, Håkansson 1987; Powell 1990; Croisier 1998).

Moreover, not all R&D has high degrees of uncertainty and complexity attached to it (Freeman and Soete 1997). There are forms of R&D which have low levels of uncertainty and complexity (Table 12.2) where market-mediated contracts can function. By contrast, more complex and uncertain research requirements would preclude market-based contracts. This is emphasised by Mowery (1994, p. 581) who notes 'The effectiveness of contracts in the provision of research is undermined by the uncertain nature of the research enterprise, the imperfect character of knowledge about a given project, and the thin market for spealized research services. These contractual difficulties are likely to be greater for more technically complex, uncertain research projects.' However, this suggests that contracted out research and technology would be restricted to these shorter-term, simpler less uncertain technology activities which does not appear to be the case in reality (see below). It is presented here that the extension by Williamson of his own work and reinterpretation of his work by others, although valuable, can only go so far in helping to explain and understand the phenomenon of technology outsourcing.

A potentially more valuable framework is that provided by Winter (1987) and Prahalad and Hamel (1990) in relation to their respective and related notions of 'strategic assets' and 'core competences' of the firm. Both approaches emphasise that firms have key assets or competencies that have resulted from previous rounds of investment and from learning-by-doing. These core competences can be seen as 'resources' (Hall 1992) as well as capabilities which are accumulated over the long term which firms seek to both develop and deploy to gain competitive advantage (Penrose 1959; Richardson 1972). Coombs (1996) has sought to employ the 'core competence' model as a lens through which to analyse changes in the strategic management of R&D over time. Thus the core competence approach (Coombs 1996, p. 354), suggests why firms may be over-reaching themselves in their desire to decentralise and outsource their R&D portfolios, ultimately weakening their core technological competences.[8] However, such an approach is somewhat at variance with researchers who have sought to highlight the 'virtual organisation' (Chesbrough and Teece 1996) and more especially the virtual organisation of R&D activities (Chiesa and Manzini 1997).

Table 12.2 Degree of uncertainty with various types of innovation

1. True uncertainty	• Fundamental research
	• Fundamental invention
2. Very high degree of uncertainty	• Radical product innovations
	• Radical process innovations outside firm
3. High degree of uncertainty	• Major product innovations
	• Radical process innovations in own establishment or system
4. Moderate uncertainty	• New 'generations' of established products
5. Little uncertainty	• Licensed innovation
	• Imitation of product innovations
	• Modification of products and processes
	• Early adoption of established products
6. Very little uncertainty	• New 'model'
	• Product differentiation
	• Agency for established product innovation
	• Late adoption of established process innovation and franchised operations in own establishment
	• Minor technical improvements

Source: Freeman and Soete (1997, p. 244).

More empirically-driven studies have sought to emphasise both push and pull factors in the desire of firms to externalise at least part of their R&D portfolio.   The most frequently cited push factors are the increasing complexity of the research process and the cost and risks of R&D. As many of the simpler scientific and technical discoveries have now been made, companies are increasingly having to deal with much more difficult and intractable scientific problems.   Products are also becoming more sophisticated catering for these new more complex problems and consumer demands. The number of technologies per product is therefore increasing in many consumer and business products (associated with, for example, the shift from mechanical to electro-mechanical systems in the automobile industry; Miller 1994, p. 30).   Many companies simply do not have the necessary scientific resources to cope with additional burdens and seek outside support to overcome internal technical limitations (Haour 1992). Many of these new (fundamental) research issues cover several scientific and technical disciplines further encouraging collaboration between organisations with strengths in different fields.

The increasing complexity of the R&D process in turn increases the costs of research. Research may therefore become less attractive without partners to share the cost. More simply the firm may lack the financial resources to undertake research even if it remains an attractive proposition. Associated with this, the traditional barriers between scientific and technical disciplines are being broken down, as the interchange between basic research and development work grows. In the field of semiconductors basic research is undertaken with a view to future applications right from the outset. This pressure to improve the interface between basic research on the one hand and applied and developmental work, on the other, also stems from the pressure to reduce innovation cycle times. Scientific and institutional inertia may also play a key role. Pisano et al. (1988, pp. 191–3) have, for example, outlined the defensive response by many major pharmaceutical companies in the 1980s, grounded in chemistry, which sought links with new biotechnology firms and universities to gain research expertise in biotechnology.

In relation to 'pull' factors these cover the relative attractiveness of external sources of expertise over internal firm resources which the firm may not possess, or only very inadequately. They also cover other motives such as the desire to enhance the scope and testing of in-house scientific and technical activities; as a general scanning mechanism of technological opportunities existing outside the company; and as a means to network with other organisations. This latter factor is associated with enabling in-house staff to be part of a wider 'invisible college' within the specific research community and to share information and knowledge more informally. Lastly, there are government policies and incentives to participate in collaborative research and technical projects.

Care must be taken when emphasising both the benefits to firms of such trends towards R&D and technical outsourcing (Coombs 1996) and the implications of such a shift in terms of in-house research and technical effort. In the former context, Häusler et al. (1994) emphasise that the current literature tends to give a rather positive image of external research links, even though there are good reasons against cooperation. MacPherson (1997) in his study of producer service outsourcing more generally (including research and technical services), has noted that the 'necessity effect' (where a firm has an urgent need but no in-house resources to satisfy that requirement) was the most single important factor motivating outsourcing for firms in New York State (see also Oliver and Blakeborough 1998). There may be firm size effects here, with more smaller firms experiencing this problem (see Rothwell 1991, p. 105).

Going further back in time, Mowery (1984, p. 52) highlights the British reliance on the external contracting of R&D and 'market' mechanisms as a key factor hampering innovation and expert performance amongst British firms before 1950. In particular the use of consulting engineers in the British electrical industry in the late nineteenth and early twentieth centuries hindered innovation and the design process in the industry (Byatt 1979). In the latter context, the increase in external outsourcing of research and technical activity does not imply that there is necessarily a contingent decline in-house R&D activity. Indeed, as Arora and Gambardella (1990) have suggested, external collaboration of research is complementary to, rather than a replacement for, in-house research activity. Thus they note in their study of large–small firm links in biotechnology that 'large firms with higher internal knowledge are more actively involved in pursuing strategies of external linkage. .... In sum, internal knowledge also appears to be complementary with the strategies of external linkage of large firms' (Arora and Gambardella 1990, pp. 373–4). This has been echoed earlier by Mowery (1983, p. 369), who in the context of independent research organisations during the period of 1900–1940, noted 'rather than functioning as substitutes, the independent and in-house research laboratories were complements during this period, exhibiting a division of labor in the performance of research tasks'.

Factors associated with using CROs are more likely to focus on cost, speed of delivery and the availability of specialist expertise, although it should be stressed that there are likely to be considerable national differences in terms of motives for research and technical collaboration (Charles and Howells 1992, pp. 148–50). Ringe's (1992, pp. 28–9) survey of selected UK firms found that the desire to gain specialist expertise was the most frequently cited motive for contracting out R&D, together with access to specialist techniques or equipment. The need to tap additional manpower was the third main factor, followed by the ability to gain tight control of R&D timescales and budgets, in order to get the job done.

12.2.3 Research and Technology Outsourcing: Altered Perspectives?

This analysis has outlined some of the key trends and issues occurring in the research and technology outsourcing. Many companies are still reluctant to outsource 'critical' technologies to outside suppliers, but they are increasingly willing to contemplate the sub-contracting of more routine, low value-added research and technical activities. As the R&T 'market' continues to develop, less of this routine R&D and technical work will be undertaken 'in-house' and instead will be the responsibility of CROs and their employees either working on- or off-site. The R&T 'market' appears to be highly dynamic, not only in terms of the appearance of more dedicated CROs, but also of a much wider set of partial players, who may over time become more central participants (Howells 1999a). Research and technology outsourcing is 'coming of age' and should be seen as a major industry in its own right.

However, large parts of the nature and operation of the R&T 'market' remain virtually unknown. Much is made of manufacturing firms as users of CROs, but little is known about how service firms make use of them. Similarly in delimiting the boundaries of the R&T 'market', how far should computer service companies providing bespoke software solutions to companies be seen as a part of the R&T sector? Although mention has been made of CROs capturing foreign markets, not much is know about the internationalisation process of these organisations. There has also been in a number of countries, most notably the UK, a public–private shift in research provision during the 1980s and 1990s which still remains to be assessed.

The study has revealed potentially more fundamental, conceptual issues associated with research and technological outsourcing and externalisation. As noted earlier, explanations presented as to why firms may wish to outsource their research and technical activity have explicitly or implicitly assumed a high degree of rational knowledge and optimal decision-making. However, the assumption of highly systematic decision-making based on hard evidence does not appear to be borne out so far by the case study firms. Decision-making was often undertaken on what can be described as subjective 'hunches' or desires to meet corporate targets, in particular cost-cutting, which had little to do with gaining the best for the firm's long-term research and technological requirements and aspirations.[9] R&D cost and efficiency measurement within even the most advanced firms remains highly partial and incomplete (see, for example, Bergen 1990) and this provides a poor framework for managers to make highly informed decisions about what might be 'best' for the firm. Moreover even under simplified decision contexts, executives only consider a limited amount of information they have available (Tyler and Steensma 1995, p. 61). This overall view is indeed supported by Buckley and Chapman (1997, p. 138) who have studied outsourcing practices in the UK pharmaceutical and scientific instrument sectors and note

.... we have come across no case whatsoever in which managers involved in decisions had access to, or personally generated for their own purposes, anything like a numerically justified assessment of transaction cost issues.

Much of the literature on outsourcing in relation to (manufacturing) firms using contract (service) firms for research and technological inputs has assumed a highly contractual and formalised set of relationships. This is despite recent research on R&D collaboration between manufacturing firms which has shown the strong informal and non-contractual relationship ties existing between firms which are research partners (Dickson et al. 1990).

However, there is an indication from the research to suggest that although contracts were often in place, with much of R&D being an uncertain (and frequently serendipitous) process as strict parameters on the outcomes were not laid down by the parties. Trust (particularly what Sako 1992, p. 39, has termed 'goodwill trust'), sharing and reciprocity were much in evidence, helping to increase certainty (Lane 1997, p. 218). Even where contracts were strictly laid down in more routine technical activities, these were 'put under the table' and were frequently not referred to again. Although the parties involved could therefore, in extremis, refer back to them if serious problems occurred and no agreement could be found, generally they were ignored and more informal discussions and bargaining took place to resolve difficulties. Formal, contractual documents bore very little relation to the usual and day-to-day contacts that were the 'real' research and technical links between parties. In part this misrepresentation may reflect much of the literature which has discussed more routine supply of service activities, where costs and efficiency criteria can be readily assessed under more predictable outcome conditions. It may also reflect the fact that a snapshot, on an individual basis, of a particular research and technical link between a firm and a contract research and technology organisation tends to ignore the wider 'envelope' within which the relationship may be part. The partners may have links stretching back decades, with close personal and informal links between them. The routines of the two organisations may also be very familiar to staff from both sides.

It was discovered that the standard, implicit model of manufacturing firms deciding, a priori, to outsource part of their research or technical activity and then selecting a service firm to deliver the service or 'solution' can often be misplaced. This is associated with the continued perception of service firms being 'passive' or 'reactive' in the innovation process. However, the study has revealed that there are a number of examples of service firms (in this case CRTOs) initiating and developing a new product and only 'putting out' the final more routine stages of the development. This was associated with the tooling up and production of the new product by a single manufacturing firm or set of companies (where independent components or systems were required to be incorporated into the final good). In this context, manufacturing firms are reacting to the initiation of ideas and action by the service firms and supply limited technical capability and manufacturing as their input to the whole process. Here the focus is on the service firm, the CRO or technology intermediary firm, as the key actor in the innovation process and the manufacturing firm undertaking a more peripheral role. Indeed such firms may more centrally move into manufacturing to fully capture the benefits of the innovation process,[10] following the 'soft' model of firm formation.

This particular construct therefore turns 'on its head' the simple linear, uni-directional concept which is typically envisaged in research and the technical outsourcing process. This model sees outsourcing as involving a single manufacturing firm using a single service company (manufacturing$\Rightarrow$service links). Arising from this study, an alternative picture emerges which has at its centre a proactive service firm integrating routine production and technical inputs often from a set of manufacturing firms, sometimes involving a uni-directional linkage (service$\Rightarrow$manufacturing), but more often a two-way or multi-dimensional link (service$\Leftrightarrow$manufacturing). It should be stressed that outsourcing does not only imply manufacturing$\Rightarrow$/$\Leftrightarrow$service or service$\Rightarrow$/$\Leftrightarrow$manufacturing links. An increasing proportion of work for CROs is to provide research and technological inputs and resources to *other service* firms. Service$\Rightarrow$/$\Leftrightarrow$service innovation links need, therefore, to be recognised in the outsourcing and externalisation process.

12.3   OUTSOURCING AND INNOVATION SYSTEMS

The growth of research and technology outsourcing has a number of important issues and implications for innovation systems approaches and the wider understanding of the knowledge economy. The first is whether the whole activity of innovation outsourcing can be treated as a system in itself. On one level, it can be argued that the more restricted research and technological outsourcing 'market' outlined earlier has all the essential attributes of a system that is required by classical systems models (see, for example, Hall and Fagen 1956), with CROs and their 'customer' firms and organisations forming the key *elements* of the system and the collaborative relations between as the *links* combining the different elements in the system.

However, defining the boundaries of such a system is not easy. There are clearly many diverse systems associated with research and technological outsourcing and externalisation, rather than just a single system. These systems (or sub-systems) relate to specific geographical areas (for example, in terms of national (or even regional) research and technological outsourcing systems), as well as more specific sectoral or technological outsourcing systems (for example, those associated with specific technologies or industries, such as pharmaceuticals).

However, innovation outsourcing does not readily fit into either the systems of innovation or technological systems approaches, as the phenomenon cuts across both national and technological boundaries. This is important in itself – but it also highlights inadequacies about the existing approaches, namely that they assume that there are neat systems which have uniform structures and that tightly interlock with each other. The US national system of innovation is separate and different from those of the French or Danish system of innovation; similarly the pharmaceutical technological system is separate and different from that of the energy technological system. In one sense this is true; these systems can be *treated* as separate. But the systems approaches largely ignore the issue of 'nesting' (hierarchies; Blalock and Blalock 1959) of systems, and their overlap with each other.   (See Howells 1999b in relation to the issue of regional innovation systems versus national systems of innovation).[11] A key element in defining a system is being able to draw a boundary around the set of elements (firms and organisations) and their chosen links within it.   In practice, though, few systems have clear and mutually exclusive elements, links and boundaries, particularly when viewed over time (static actors and relationships are extremely unlikely in innovation systems!). Thus there is no ready acceptance that firms or organisations can be members of multiple innovation systems. This represents a key danger of a systems approach in that it encourages the conceptual mindset of having separate and 'closed' (in terms of not having, or rather not considering links and interrelationships external to the system) innovation systems.   This is where considering innovation outsourcing challenges such a notion since research and technology outsourcing are usually involved in multiple sets of innovation and technological systems, both geographically and sectorally.

The effort to define a system around the formal and informal innovation outsourcing market, which includes both service and manufacturing firms and organisations, is also revealing. Delimiting such a system obviously cuts across many technological systems and national systems of innovation as they have been highlighted in earlier studies! The key *elements* in such a system would be both CROs *and* their 'manufacturing' (but also service) customers (forming in turn a wider 'organizational population' of different actors and agencies; Reddy and Rao 1990; see also Phillips 1960).   The *boundary* of the system could be defined in straightforward 'market' terms, but as has been indicated above, there are strong informal and non-traded elements in the R&T 'market' which involve high levels of reciprocity and trust and which parallels much of what Dore (1986) would term as 'relational' networks.   In terms of this wider system, many of the links described would not be based on purely monetary transactions and formal contracts, but involve informal know-how trading and patterns of exchange (see, for example, Von Hippel 1987; Kreiner and Schultz 1993).   A clear *nesting* of the wider system is also apparent hierarchically with *sub-systems* evident in relation to specific technological systems where the research and technology outsourcing market may operate, such as energy or environmental 'services', but also narrowing down to specific national or regional systems of research and technology outsourcing. This has outlined the basic framework of a system, but it has crucially left out the institutional, as well as more general cultural, social and economic, elements in such an innovation system. Without these elements the framework that has been described is more akin to a simplified innovation network (Håkansson 1987) or linkage structure (Andersen and Lundvall 1997, pp. 248–51). Institutions are central to the notion of any kind of system of innovation (Edquist 1997, p. 24). They provide the dynamic context (the routines and 'guide posts'; Lundvall 1992, p. 10) through which systems evolve and change and linked with the notion of technological paradigms and trajectories. This can be seen in the way the institutional frameworks associated with intellectual property can shape the innovation process (Chapter 15).

Although innovation systems literature has so frequently stressed the dynamic qualities of such systems and the approach, it then usually goes on to treat such systems in a static fashion. The wider innovation outsourcing system, or one of its sub-systems, in period $n1$ is going to be different in period $n2$. Key elements or actors will have disappeared between the two periods and have been replaced, leading to new and different linkage patterns and changes in the overall shape and configuration of the system (with some of these changes being measurable and therefore allowing systems to be compared).

Indeed, much of systems theory development has been driven by its ability to describe and map different contexts in a dynamic fashion. What might be considered to be the appropriate 'system' in one time period or for one set of analyses is unlikely to be the same for a different period. Appropriate systems modelling should also allow the ability to move between different hierarchies or 'nests' so that particular phenomena or processes can be focused upon or conversely the analysis can be widened out to allow a broader view. In transport systems modelling the focus can be on the whole transport system covering all transport modes (car, rail, air and sea) on a national perspective, a single transport mode such as car traffic within for example a single urban system, or indeed the car itself can be treated as system (or indeed the electrical 'system' of the car can be viewed as a system). Much is lost from systems analysis by sticking rigidly to viewing and conceptualising one particular system and innovation systems, it is argued here, are no different from other systems. One of the chief merits of systems theory is its hierarchical nature and ability to flexibly move between these hierarchies over time, when conditions allow or when analysis requires this. Our view of what a system is, depends on what phenomenon (or what attribute of a phenomenon) we wish to study. This determines what the 'element' (or basic unit) within the system will be.

Research and technology outsourcing in this way can be treated as a 'phenomenon-based' system of innovation (PBSI) which can be seen as nesting and overlapping with existing geographical and sectoral systems of innovation, but in a more time-specific and dynamic set-up. The transitory and evolutionary nature of such systems in this way is stressed but it accepts that other, more macro national or sectoral systems are operating at the same time and in part provide part of the institutional, economic and social context for these meta systems. Indeed this perspective has parallels with the notion of Lynn et al. (1996, pp. 99–101) on innovation community's which stresses the dynamic elements of change within such communities, such as entry and exits, as well as methodological issues to do with boundary permeability and connectedness of organisations within a group.

The growth of innovation outsourcing and externalisation also has more general implications for innovation and technological systems. In particular, that the growth of external innovation links by firms and organisations will lead to the overall increase in the *connectivity* within and *openness* between innovation systems. On a more abstract level, and in terms of systems theory, this may suggest innovation systems have increased susceptibility to volatility, dislocation and radical change. This, in turn, is related to the major effect such changes will have on the spatial and temporal diffusion processes in relation to innovation. With increased connectivity and interlinkage, innovation waves will diffuse in significantly different ways. Above all, innovations will diffuse more rapidly throughout the system associated with increased and more pervasive information flows between diffusion actors (although major barriers remain; see, for example, Turpin et al. 1996, p. 271). From a policy perspective, Hicks and Katz (1966, pp. 43–5), in relation more specifically to inter-firm collaboration, have reviewed some of the implications of an increasingly collaborative science system in industrialised economies.

The analysis of research and technology innovation in relation to innovation and technological systems also has important implications for how service firms, activities and indeed innovations are viewed in existing literature. Although Carlsson (1995a, p. 444) does place certain service firms in a more central role, within his technological system, as 'bridging organisations', the innovation system literature in general still tends to see service firms and innovators in a passive, peripheral and support role. Manufacturing firms still take the 'centre stage' and the systems are defined around them. Service firms and organisations (including here public agencies and research establishments and Higher Education Institutes) provide the 'supporting cast'. They at best represent what are admittedly seen as key elements in the innovation infrastructure (see, for example, Smith 1997), but their role is still firmly placed as 'supporters' and 'facilitators' rather than those who lead the innovation process. Above all, the innovation and technological systems which have been outlined so far have been based on manufacturing firms and their innovative processes; around them the boundary of the system has been defined and in system terms they have formed the core 'elements'. By contrast, service firms have been viewed as being at the edges of the system and/or operating in a supporting or indirect role (as subsidiary or second tier 'elements') within the innovation system.

It is argued here that such a perspective is at best dated, partial and incomplete and at worst false and misconceived. Many service sectors and technologies now have a lead role in key areas of the modern economies. Service activities and service firms are frequently the 'drivers' in the innovation process, not the other way around. The above analysis of research and technology outsourcing has also indicated that at the very least, 'manufacturing-centred' conceptual frameworks of innovation systems do not readily accommodate the realities of many CROs and the formal and informal R&T 'market'. As has been outlined earlier, CROs frequently take the 'lead' in the innovation process and undertake their own R&D work (see, for example, von Emloh et al. 1994). They commission the research and undertake much of the basic, groundwork R&D *before* then approaching likely manufacturing firms who may participate in delivery *support* manufacturing and technical inputs which can help to produce a final innovation. Manufacturing firms represent the passive elements here, whilst the service firms are the *proactive* elements and represent the 'innovation integrators' and leaders.

12.4 CONCLUSIONS

This research has highlighted a number of issues which have not been adequately captured in previous studies that have explored external research relations and systems of innovation. The decisions-making process surrounding the decision to use external research and technology is much less rational and optimal than frequently assumed, with decisions generally made on an ad hoc, informal basis. The view of contract research and technology activity as being formal, routine, repetitive, cost-based and having short time horizons and levels of uncertainty is being challenged as contract research and technology organisations are moving towards longer, more relational types of research and technology partnerships. Different forms of innovation outsourcing are becoming less distinguishable and increasingly blurred over time.

Research and technology outsourcing and its changing dynamics also more specifically contributes to notions underlying the systems of innovation approach through widening its articulation and conceptualisation. The chapter has suggested that research and technology outsourcing can be treated as a PBSI which can be seen as nesting and overlapping with existing geographical and sectoral systems of innovation. A PBSI is more time-specific and dynamic than previous conceptualisations of systems of innovation and may be more fragile in this sense. These qualities arguably are missing in existing systems of innovations. However, PBSI is not meant to be seen as replacing existing systems of innovation approaches, but rather provides an additional mechanism to view innovation within a systemic way. Indeed many of the interesting facets derived from taking this approach centre on the relation between systems. Thus the research and technology outsourcing (RTO) system will be expected to be different between the UK and Germany because such RTO systems are operating against a different national system of innovation 'backcloth' which will crucially influence the underlying institutional economic arrangements between the UK and German RTO systems.

Finally, this approach challenges the notion of the role of service firms and the support infrastructure in systems of innovation approaches. Service firms and (perceived) innovation intermediaries, such as contract research and technology organisations, should no longer be seen as passive agents or a 'supporting cast' in relation to innovative activity. Increasingly they are taking on more proactive, central and pivotal roles in the innovation process. Indeed the service sector is becoming an important source of demand for external research and technology services in its own right. All these issues suggest that our current view of the innovation system in advanced industrial economies needs to be challenged, if not altered, on the basis of these prospective change elements.

NOTES

1. *Acknowledgements:* This chapter is based on paper published in *Industry and Innovation* (see Howells 1999c) and earlier versions has been presented at the 'Systems and Services Innovation' Workshop at Manchester, 17–18 March 1998 and the Berlin Workshop on 'Innovation Systems and Industrial Performance' at the Wissenschaftszentrum Berlin für Sozialforschung gGmbH (WZB), Berlin, 23–24 October 1998. The research is supported by the UK Economic and Social Research Council.
2. The word 'market' is in quotation markets here, because as will be shown many of the links are not formal, market-based relationships but are informal and involve a high degree of non-monetary reciprocity, that is, what may be generally termed 'non-market' relations.
3. Kluth and Andersen (1997, p. 69) in their analysis of a Research Technology

Organisations (RTO) stress the difference between RTOs and CROs and CRTOs which they specifically excluded.

4. Although Häusler et al. (1994, p. 49) note that according to official statistics of industrial R&D in Germany portray a wide range of R&D resources devoted to external R&D.

5. This is not a novel suggestion. Thus, for example, both Graham (1985) and Coombs (1996) have outlined a set of R&D 'eras' or stages which differ somewhat in their number, duration and key characteristics.

6. However, see Brockhoff's (1992, p. 523) analysis and his suggestions for ways to improve the use of the transaction-cost approach as an analytical tool for R&D cooperation.

7. Defined by Williamson (1973, p. 317) as 'Bounded rationality refers to rate and storage limits on the capacities of individuals to receive, store, retrieve, and process information without error.'

8. Although this still appears to be going on; Bowthorpe, the electrical components manufacturer, announced in 1996 that it was handing over large parts of its product development work to UK and overseas laboratories.

9. This echoes Knight's (1933) thoughts on decisions concerning firm size and efficiency, namely that such decisions are 'largely a matter of personality and historical accident rather than of intelligible general principles' (quoted in Coase 1937, p. 394).

10. Although the importance of this wider process is disputed (see, for example, Cooper 1971, p. 5).

11. Reference to, and analysis of what is meant by, the word 'system' has been strangely muted in innovation systems literature. Lundvall (1992, p. 2) has been most specific here, at least in terms of definition, although still brief. Thus he makes a short reference to Boulding's (1985) definition of a system as 'anything not in chaos' as well as noting that a system 'is constituted by a number of elements and by the relationships between these elements'. Little reference is made to earlier work on systems theory or in terms of how they originally defined, or perceived, a system (see Hall and Fagen 1956 noted earlier).

13 Services and Systems of Innovation

Jeremy Howells

13.1 INTRODUCTION

Most of the debate surrounding the 'systems of innovation' approach has concerned the manufacturing industry. The analysis has proved a rich vein of intellectual questioning, although it has often remained diffuse and ambiguous (Edquist 1997, p. 30). However, the 'systems of innovation' approach has largely ignored the role of services in studies of innovation systems or, at the very least, viewed them from a 'manufacturing-centric' vision of the innovation. Worse than the 'Black Box' of technology in relation to economics highlighted by Rosenberg (1982), where at least inputs and more particularly outputs ('consequences', p. vii) were noted and analysed, services in the innovation process have remained hidden within the context of technology studies.

This chapter seeks to address and analyse some of the issues surrounding the hidden or neglected features of services innovation and aims to provide a more balanced view of the innovation process and systems in the modern knowledge economy. In so doing it is certainly not seeking to abandon results and conclusions arising from earlier 'systems of innovation' studies, but hopefully provide a wider avenue from which the systems of innovation approach can be further developed. Such reflection and repositioning should not be unexpected given that the systems of innovation approach is still a relatively new conceptual framework and such readjustments should not be considered unusual. Moreover the 'manufacturing-centric' view of innovation is not something which is peculiar to the systems of innovation approach but is evident more broadly within the study of technological innovation. As such it is something which has been inherited from earlier studies of innovation and the economics of technological change (Gallouj and Weinstein 1997, p. 537); as conceptual ambiguity about the innovation process has been inherited more generally by system approaches (Edquist 1997, p. 30).

13.2 SERVICES AND SYSTEMS OF INNOVATION: A SECTORAL PERSPECTIVE?

13.2.1   Sectoral Innovation Systems: Emergence of a Concept

The 'systems of innovation' approach has developed and evolved since its initial appearance in the form of the 'national systems of innovation' (NSI) studies presented by Freeman (1987, 1988), Lundvall (1988, 1992) and Nelson (1992a). Freeman (1987) introduced the concept to help interpret the performance of Japan over the post-war period. He identified a number of vital and distinctive elements in the Japanese system of innovation, such as its model of competition (Freeman 1988, p. 338), to which could be attributed its success in terms of innovation and economic growth. It has subsequently been applied to a variety of sales and levels, many of which have been outside the original focus of a national setting. Thus, although the national focus remains strong, and rightly so, it has been accompanied by studies seeking to analyse the notion of systems of innovation at an international (or pan-national) level and at a sub-national scale.

Studies have also sought to examine the systems of innovation approach within the context of a sectoral or technology perspective. Thus Carlsson (1995a) has developed what has become termed the 'technological systems' approach, which indicates that systems can be specific to particular technology fields or sectors. Sectors and technologies do matter and have their own dynamic, but as Nelson (1993, p. 518) still acknowledges 'nationhood matters and has a pervasive influence'. However, it is not an either/or issue. Sectors (and technological systems) within a nation have a powerful shaping influence on the structure and dynamic of a national innovation system. Equally, national contexts have important influences on sectoral performance and conditioning (Howells and Neary 1995, p. 245). The concepts of national (or spatially-bounded) systems of innovation and technology systems (or sectoral innovation systems) should not be seen as alternatives, but rather establishing the interrelationships between the two can yield valuable insights into the wider systems of innovation approach (Archibugi and Michie 1999, p. 13).

The existence of sectoral systems of innovation, which may be stronger and more coherent to participating firms and organisations than national geographical boundaries, has been highlighted by Kitschelt (1991) in his analysis of the Japanese system and Carlsson and Stankiewicz (1991) in relation to their concept of 'technology systems'. Strong sectoral or industrial patterns of technology advantage have also been highlighted by Archibugi and Pianta (1992; see also Pianta 1995; Grupp 1995) and alternatively by Howells and Neary (1995) in an analysis of a weak industrial and innovative sector in Japan, pharmaceuticals. More recently, Breschi and Malerba (1997) have interestingly sought to develop the notion of sectoral innovation systems (SIS) in the context of technology regimes (TRs).

13.2.2 Sectoral Innovation Systems and Services

The existence of sectoral systems of innovation have been recognised and acknowledged by researchers, although little research has been undertaken on their nature and extent (see, though, Carlsson 1995a). What discussion and analysis there has been has centred on the manufacturing industry and the implicit, if not explicit, conceptual frameworks surrounding such analysis has been very much within a manufacturing innovation paradigm (MIP; see below). If we are not careful, analysis of sectoral systems of innovation will be shaped by a latent assumption of manufacturing 'traits' concerning innovation, which ignore many differences that exist between these traits and those of services. Table 13.1 provides a bi-polar delineation of these traits. In some instances they may reflect broad generalisations rather than clear traits, more particularly they may exhibit the historical backgrounds of these two 'grand' sectors in the modern economy: the 'secondary' and 'tertiary' sectors (if we leave aside the 'primary' sector and the 'quaternary' sector; a subsector of the 'tertiary' sector).

Many of these service 'traits' in innovation have been viewed as 'peculiarities' (Miles 1993; Miles and Rush 1997; Sirilli and Evangelista 1995) because of the dominance of the manufacturing innovation paradigm and despite the fact that the service sector is by far the largest sector of the economy. Thus, for example, the intellectual property rights (IPR) regime of services is very different from manufacturing. Intellectual property in services is protected (if it is protected at all) by copyrights and trademarks, compared to primarily patents in manufacturing, as well as short cycle times and secrecy (Howells 1997a; Andersen and Howells, Chapter 14).

Other aspects of the broad manufacturing and services systems split can be seen in terms of technology characteristics and industry characteristics (which have an important bearing on technology). These include technology orientation, research generation and acquisition, the impact of technology on labour productivity and innovation cycle times (Table 13.1). In relation to wider industry or system traits that have a bearing on the innovation profile of each sector, there are product characteristics, related to the 'tangibility' and its 'storability' between manufacturing and service products; the phasing of international market servicing; and the actual geographical scale and reach of manufacturing and service systems. Some of these traits may be debatable and may have never existed to any significant extent, some are undoubtedly

Table 13.1 Sectoral systems of innovation: manufacturing versus services 'system traits'

	System Trait	Status/Significance	Manufacturing	Services
1.	IPR	Current, strong	Strong; patents	Weak; copyright
2.	Technology orientation	Historical, declining	Technology 'push'; science and technology led	Technology 'pull'; Consumer/client led (co-terminality)
3.	Research/innovation generation and supply	Declining significance; manufacturing and services converging	'In-house'	Mainly sourced externally
4.	Technology/labour productivity	Current, but declining significance	High impact	Low impact (until 1980s?)
5.	Innovation cycle times	Declining, weak	Short	Long
6.	Product characteristics	Declining significance; Medium	Tangible, easy to store	Intangible, difficult to store
7.	International 'servicing'	Current, medium	Exports, then FDI	FDI, then exports
8.	Spatial scale of system or 'reach'	Declining significance; services catching up on internationalisation	National $\Rightarrow$ Global	Regional $\Rightarrow$ National $\Rightarrow$ Global

of declining significance and entail that the manufacturing/service divide is disintegrating in terms of that particular trait.

However, the distinction between these two sectors is not the suggested course for analysing services within a systems of innovation framework, rather it is employed here to highlight the trap of trying to assume or apply 'manufacturing' traits to service sectoral systems of innovation analysis. Moreover, one of the most important points here is the range and diversity of different sectors within services (Miles 1994, p. 247) and in manufacturing (see, however, Malerba and Orsenigo 1995). Indeed this is the essential raison d'être of sectoral systems of innovation that there is this difference between sectors; without such variation sectoral analysis would be pointless. Service sectors have very diverse system traits. Some technical knowledge-intensive business services (t-KIBS) sectors are very similar to high technology manufacturing sectors in relation to R&D effort and technological intensity (Hipp et al.1999, Chapter *x*). Other service sectors exhibit the 'supplier-dominated' (Pavitt 1984b) traits associated with the reliance of adoption and implementation of technology developed elsewhere in the economy (Brouwer and Kleinecht 1995, p. 145).

Pavitt (1984b) distinguished between three types of firms and their sectors: (1) *science-based* companies; (2) *production-intensive* companies; and (3) *supplier-dominated* companies. The 'supplier-dominated' classification, characterised by firms within the sector undertaking little or no R&D, and receiving their innovations from outside the sector, has typified the traditional conception of 'laggard' service sectors. Soete and Miozzo (1989) adapted Pavitt's taxonomy more specifically to services. They still retain the supplier-dominated category to cover large sections of the public, personal and distributive services, but include other new categories. The first centres on production or scale-intensive services, a group which includes service activities which depend on large-scale processing (back-office) administrative tasks (such as banking and insurance) and/or physical and information networks, such as transport and telecommunications service sectors. The second main category is specialised technology suppliers and science-based activities which generate and develop their own innovations and new technologies.

A significant proportion of service sectors and firms still do display very low levels of innovative activity, measured via a variety of different indicators, such as R&D intensity and a wide range of tangible and non-tangible investment expenditure related to innovation (see, for example, Young 1996; Sirilli and Evangelista 1995; OECD 1999). More detailed analysis has been hampered, though, by poor data collection and availability on innovative activity within service sectors. R&D expenditure within a number of service sectors has grown sharply over recent years (Young 1996) and this has not been too difficult to track, even though it is still heavily under-recorded (OECD 1999). The real problem is that much innovative expenditure and activity is centred in non-R&D areas (Sirilli and Evangelista 1995) where data availability is even poorer.

The whole issue of data availability in relation to service innovativeness forms another important aspect of the 'hidden box' phenomenon of services in terms of technological innovation. However, it also directly impinges upon potential analysis and application of the study of sectoral systems of innovation to services. Table 13.2 seeks to present a speculative and explorative typology of service sectors based on a range of existing studies (from which it is intended to more rigidly standardise and test the framework using a range of data). However, it seeks to draw out a further issue not adequately discussed by other studies examining service innovation data using more macro data (particularly here from national government sources and the Community Innovation Survey (CIS) within the European Union), most data analysis of services is undertaken and presented at the two-digit level of analysis. Most analysis of innovativeness within manufacturing is undertaken at a four-digit level. Services being constrained to two-digit analysis causes obvious problems and implicitly confirms the low innovation 'tag' of services. Thus at the key two-digit level it is only computer services and R&D services which stand out as high innovativeness sectors (although even within computer services there are arguably less innovation intensive sectors such as training); most of the other areas of innovativeness within services are within smaller industrial pockets at three-digit (notably telecommunications) or more generally four-digit levels. This data, and therefore analytical constraint, however, is undoubtedly heightened because of the sparcity of innovation across the service sector as a whole. There appear to be more prevalent (*vis-à-vis* manufacturing) 'micro-pockets' of service sector innovativeness (at four-digit levels and below) within much larger 'seas' or 'deserts' of low intensity service sector segments (at two-digit levels). This may reflect a number of factors, including the more nascent nature of innovative activity within services, but deserves more attention and research. However, it can be seen as fitting in with the view that clustering and micro-pockets of innovation are to be expected where new knowledge and technology frontiers are merging and beginning to be expanded (see, for example, Ayres 1988).

What can be concluded from this discussion for the sectoral system analysis of services? First, that adopting and applying manufacturing orthodoxies to service sector systems analysis is not going to be particularly successful (Table 13.1). The conventional manufacturing innovation paradigm, at the very least, is going to be less helpful when studying service sectors, but more especially is likely to continue the myopia of viewing all services as lacking innovative capacity. New perspectives and tools need to be developed to overcome this.

Secondly, although service sectors overall have become innovation-intensive and there are some significant service sectors, such as computer and telecommunication services, which are technologically-intensive, there are still large deserts of low innovation-intensity service sectors. Systems of innovation analysis of these sectors, although important in terms of moving back the frontiers of unknown territory in this respect, are likely to reveal low densities of innovative activity and confirming the conventional, laggard and 'import' technological dependence of these sectors, at least using conventional innovation measures. However on closer analysis they may reveal higher levels of disembodied and intangible levels of innovative activity centred on new ways of doing and organising such activities. The more fundamental issue here will be in terms of how valid and robust a systems of innovation approach in relation to these sectors will be when the 'landscape of innovation' is so poor and sparse.

Table 13.2 Classification of service sector technological innovation intensity: provisional synthesis

Level of Technological Innovation Intensity	SIC/NACE/ISIC
High Technological Innovation Intensity:	
Architectural, engineering and related technical	74.2
Computer-related activities	72.0
Research and development	73.1 / 73.2
Technical testing and analysis	74.3
Telecommunications	64.2
Medium Technological Innovation Intensity:	
Air Transport	62.0
Defence	75.22
Education	80.0
Human health	85.1
MotionpPicture and video production	92.11
Sale of pharmaceuticals (dispensing chemists)	52.31
Radio and television	92.2
Retail sale of medical and orthopaedic goods	52.32
Veterinary activities	85.2
Wholesale of pharmaceutical goods	51.46
Wholesale of chemical products	51.55
Wholesale of other intermediate products	51.56

Thirdly, there is the issue of what a sector is and at what level it should be analysed. Leaving aside the computer services industry and the unique and somewhat problematic R&D services sector, *arguably* the innovativeness and the systemic qualities of most service sectors seems to be occurring on a more detailed sectoral (four-digit) and sub-sectoral level (sectoral innovation communities and networks). This may in turn relate to the smaller size and scale of sectoral innovation systems within services and their fragmentation. However, this aspect undoubtedly relates back to their hidden, 'behind-the-scenes' role in many innovation arenas and closeness to their customers, often in manufacturing. Service firms may either not be identified as the source of innovations purchased by their manufacturing customers, or, with the ever closer supplier–buyer relations involved with research and technology, it remains too difficult to unbundle the individual innovation contribution of service and manufacturing firms involved in Distributed Innovation Processes (DIPs; see below).

Table 13.2. Classification of Service Sector Technological Innovation Intensity: Provisional Synthesis (continued)

Level of Technological Innovation Intensity	SIC/NACE/ISIC
Low Technological Innovation Intensity:	
Activities of membership organisations	91.0
Extra-territorial organisations	99.0
Financial intermediation	65.0
Social work	85.3
Hotels and restaurants	55.0
Insurance and pension funding	66.0
Land transport	60.0
Motor vehicles: wholesale, retail and repair	50.0
Other service activities	93.0
Postal and courier services	64.1
Private households	95.0
Public administration	75 (excl. 75.22)
Real estate	70.0
Recreational, cultural and sporting activities	92 (excl. 92.1; 92.2)
Renting of machinery	71.0
Retail trade	52 (excl. 52.31; 52.32)
Sewage and refuse disposal	90.0
Supporting and auxiliary transport activities	63.0
Water transport	61.0
Wholesale trade	51 (excl. 51.46; 51.55; 51.56)

Sources: compiled and revised from: Butchart (1987); Brouwer and Kleinecht (1995); Evangelista and Sirilli (1995); Hipp et al. (2000)

Centrally there remains the issue of when is a sector a sector? As with the issue of moving down from a national to a regional to a local innovation system the 'system' being considered becomes less rich in terms of its scale, diversity and institutional thickness. This equally applies to a sectoral level. How sparse can a sectoral system of innovation become before it loses its systemic qualities and becomes more like a technological system or an innovation network or community? Carlsson and Stankiewicz's (1991, p. 49) technological system can be seen as a more 'stripped down' version of an innovation system, whilst, for example, the 'innovation community' of Lynn et al. (1996, p. 97) provides an even more micro-level framework of organisational interaction surrounding a specific new technology. Obviously institutional presence is important here. Simple size and scale issues are also important. The presence therefore of: an industry body or association; a network of specialist suppliers and consumers; the availability of specialist education and training courses; professional societies who in turn provide a professional qualifications and status for key workers in the industry; and a definable set of industry, technology or trade journals are all qualities that a definable innovation sector would possess. Many of these organisations would form what Lynn et al. (1996, p. 98) would term 'superstructure' organisations which act to provide collective goods to their members and helping to facilitate and coordinate the flow of information to 'substructure' firms (those actually producing the 'innovation' or its technological complementaries). These 'superstructure' organisations closely parallel the 'linking organisations' of Carlsson's conceptual framework.

However, these institutional superstructure or linking organisations and their facilitating mechanisms would not necessarily be all available or present within a national system of innovation. A service sectoral system of innovation may have some components at a national level and others available only on an international basis (such as specialist trade journals or an industry association not on a national level but available on a European wide basis within the European Union). In certain circumstances certain regions may even be able to support all the necessary 'system elements' to form a sectoral innovation system for that industry (see Carlsson and Stankiewicz, 1991, p. 49). This is where local and regional systems collide and cross-cut with sectoral systems and can be considered in certain instances with the industrial district phenomenon.

The nascent qualities of many innovation systems within services is also important here. Institutional and industrial structures necessary for a fully functioning sectoral innovation system may not be in place, or have only been recently started. The hidden dimension of services apparent in academic study is paralleled by their low profile in industry, government and trade circles.

13.3 THE WORLD TURNED UPSIDE DOWN?

Perhaps one of the most significant changes of perspective gained by looking at the service sector in terms of a systems perspective and its implications for how we view the innovation overall is the role of service firms and organisation as agents within the system. Most NSI studies have treated services as largely passive, reactive agents within innovation; namely, innovation 'laggards' (Miles 1993 p. 661). They have primarily been seen as representing as consumers, albeit often significant consumers, of innovations produced by manufacturing firms. Even those services companies, particularly here t-KIBS firms, which have a more research and technically intensive profile, are still viewed as having a supporting role in the innovation system. As such, they represent elements of the innovation (Smith 1995) or technological (Tassey 1991; Carlsson and Stankiewicz 1991; Teubal et al. 1996) infrastructure. This is not meant to suggest that previous researchers have underplayed their role. Lundvall (1992, pp. 14–15) for example highlights the central role of national education and training systems in the national innovation system seen through the lens of the learning economy. Similarly, Shohert and Prevezer (1996, p. 295) have highlighted the crucial and pivotal role that service-based intermediaries have played in the growth and development of the UK biotechnology sectoral system of innovation. However the criticism here is that service firms have been viewed as supporters, or at best reactive agents, which have facilitated the central, proactive players within the system, manufacturing firms.

Evidence is becoming available to suggest that service firms are taking a more central (sometimes a leading) role in the innovation process. Thus studies on the role of consultants (Bessant and Rush 1995; Baark 1999); specialist design and engineering service firms (Elfring and Baven 1994); environmental service companies; software systems designers and integrators (Quintas 1994; Khazam and Mowery 1996); and research contract companies and other technical service organisations (Howells 1999a; Chapter 12) have all highlighted the central role that service companies can play in the innovation process. Software designers through their pivotal role in the development of computer systems and their vertically-integrated links with hardware manufacturers can create de facto standards which have powerful 'bandwagon effects' across the whole computer industry. Applications software libraries could have in the future a more important impact on the enduring 'dominant design' of computer architecture than hardware-embodied technologies (Khazam and Mowery 1994). Thus, the 'software "tail" wags the "dog" that is technology commercialization in hardware' (Khazam and Mowery 1996, p. 97).

This is not to suggest that the roles are now reversed, with services leading manufacturing in the innovation process, or that services have gained 'the upper hand' over manufacturing (the importance of manufacturing to services more generally has been forcefully put recently by Kitson and Michie 1997, for example). Merely the discussion seeks to stress that our perceptions about services should not always be locked into the dominant 'manufacturing innovation paradigm' (MIP) where services are seen as consumers of innovation and passive elements in the innovation system. At best they are perceived as part of a supporting innovation infrastructure 'looking on' to the real innovation performers, manufacturing firms, or occasionally giving them a helping hand. The MIP has focused on physical and tangible aspects of technological innovation, on the manufacturing process, on the consumption of physical goods and artefacts, on patents and R&D as indicators for innovation and for the lone manufacturing firm pioneering innovation in various industrial (read manufacturing) sectors.

The rise of studies investigation networks in the innovation process (see Freeman 1991) and the distributed nature of the innovation process (Coombs and Metcalfe 1998) are also important issues here. These studies have served to highlight that innovation is rarely undertaken in isolation by a single (manufacturing) firm. Innovation more frequently now involves bilateral or multilateral networks of (manufacturing and service) firms working together, in turn often collaborating with HEIs or public research establishments. The focus of attention surrounding innovation moves from a single entity, the (manufacturing) firm, to a distributed innovation process (DIP) of firms and organisations working in partnership to produce an innovation. In this context service firms, organisations and agencies can be seen as more equal partners, mainly following but sometimes leading manufacturing firms in the innovation process.

This study is not seeking to develop what might be termed a separate 'service innovation paradigm' (SIP) which would seek to displace or downplay the role of manufacturing in the wider innovation process, but rather to highlight SIP as a key element within a new, broader paradigm that hitherto has been the neglected contribution of services to innovation. As such SIP should be seen as an element or adjunct onto parts of the former dominant MIP that which still have validity to form a more realistic and holistic view; that of a new 'innovation paradigm' (IP).

The basic tenets of SIP, which should be injected into a more balanced IP, would include:

1. Acknowledgement that services are becoming more research and technologically intensive over time, as reflected by R&D expenditure recorded by OECD and in patenting activity.
2. Some specialist service firms, associated with the t-KIBS sector, can be as R&D-intensive and technologically innovative as high technology manufacturing firms.
3. Service firms are taking a more central role in innovation within national and international innovation systems.
4. Service firms and organisation have a more proactive role in the innovation process than formerly perceived.
5. With the rise of innovation networking and DIPs, service firms and organisations are increasingly being drawn in and becoming partners to manufacturing firms, which in the past undertook innovation on their own.

6. Service firms themselves are becoming important customers of R&D and technical service firms.
7. More exceptionally, certain service are taking the lead role in the innovation process, subsequently subcontracting out production to manufacturing firms.
8. There has been a shift in the innovation balance from artefact to non-tangible innovations. More innovations in their generation, delivery and consumption are involving fewer direct physical products, processes and equipment. This has always been true of disembodied, organisational innovations, but it is increasing in more direct and specific areas of computer services, multimedia and products and services associated with the internet.

These basic tenets remain to be fully tested. And it is stressed that the SIP should not be seen as overthrowing the role of manufacturing industry in the process of technological innovation, but rather seen as acting as a more balanced counterweight to how we should view the innovation process with systems of innovation. The MIP has dominated so long because for the very reason that it was largely an accurate reflection of the innovation system until the 1970s, but the paradigm has also lasted for two other reasons. First, there has been inadequate measurement of service-based innovations in terms of indicators and datasets (Patel and Pavitt 1995). However, secondly, most academics did not consider disembodied, organisational or non-tangible innovations as being of much significance up until the rise of a number of factors in the 1970s; of which two in particular were important. It was based on the growing significance of computer software to the development of the whole information technology (IT) industry in industrialised economies. It was also related to the realisation that the growing importance of the Japanese economy was not simply based on their strong technical, artefact-based innovation process, but subtler disembodied factors ranging across the range of scale from the micro through to the macro, such as the 'ticketing system used in just-in-time procedures, the notion of 'zero defects' shopfloor, firm and inter-firm (supplier) levels and onto institutional arrangements highlighted by Freeman (1987) in his study of the Japanese innovation system.

More recently the growing significance of the role of information (Lamberton 1997), knowledge (Nonaka 1994) and learning (Lundvall and Johnson 1994; Lundvall 1999) have also led a further shift away from the focus on the tangible elements of the innovation to the intangible; what has sometimes been referred to as 'soft technology' (Morgan 1990; Howells 1996) and the 'soft side' of innovation (den Hertog et al. 1997). Undoubtedly there have also been a number of exceptional thinkers who challenged the manufacturing bias in the study of technological innovation, but mainstream interests have still largely centred on manufacturing industry until recently.

13.4 CONCLUSIONS

This analysis and review has attempted to uncover something of the 'hidden box' of service innovation. The systems of innovation approach is a good tool and model to help unpack the complexity of the innovation process within services, particularly in relation to the disembodied, intangible nature of so many service innovations and their more distributed nature. The traditional 'manufacturing innovation paradigm' is not a useful starting point in analysing the innovation process within many services. However, it should be acknowledged that there are differences not only between manufacturing and services in relation to innovation, but also between different services. This is to be expected when services in most advanced knowledge-based economies account for over two-thirds of their employment and output.

Research and development and the technological intensity more generally of services has been increasing over time, although significant sections of service activity do have low rates of innovation and where the 'supplier-dominated' typology still remains applicable. More effective analysis of service innovation is hampered by lack of adequate data, much official statistics are not sufficiently detailed to pick up the emerging, but dispersed, 'micro-pockets' of innovation across the whole of the service sector. However, if we are to accept these altered notions about service innovation from a sectoral systems of innovation analysis of *service* sectors, it also has implications for the way we view services in relation to sectoral systems of innovation analysis of *manufacturing* sectors or more widely applied to the whole industrial sector. Service firms, organisations and institutions may not (arguably increasingly not) always the passive or supportive agents in the innovation process helping the 'lead' innovation agent, the manufacturing firm. Service organisations do not always play such a subservient role, occasionally but increasingly they may take the lead role themselves. More often they play a more equal role, as partners, in the increasingly distributed innovation process of knowledge-based economies. We should be less confident that services are always in the dim backdrop of the innovation process away from the main fire of the innovation. Service firms and organisations are not always the supporting elements in the innovation infrastructure (or technology infrastructure) but do take on more leading roles at the heart of the fire itself. As Khazam and Mowery (1996) note, the service 'tail' starts to wag the manufacturing 'dog'. The service innovation infrastructure can, therefore, become the main agents of innovation and manufacturers become the supporting technology infrastructure; at the very least the 'us' and 'them' of the manufacturing/service divide in innovation has become more blurred; even if the world, as yet, has not altogether turned upside down.

Lastly, if we are to have successful national systems of innovation, we need successful, *dynamic* systems (Patel and Pavitt 1994, p. 91) of both nations *and* sectors. Efforts to study or create policy for such systems, need to recognise the intangible – but crucial – nature of innovation in many service sectors.

NOTES

1. This chapter draws on data presented in an earlier paper entitled 'The Internationalisation of Business Service Firms: A Stages Approach' published in *The Service Industries Journal*, Vol. 19, No .4, 1999.
2. Methods for measuring of the level of a firm's internationalisation include, for instance, the proportion of turnover derived from overseas markets or alternatively, the proportion of the firm's assets located overseas. For KIBS firms many of their most significant assets are difficult to measure because they are intangible or embodied in skilled personnel. Consequently, the measurement of internationalisation in terms of overseas turnover is more appropriate in this sector.
3. For example, between 1986 and 1996 credits on the UK Balance of Payments current account deriving from business travel rose from £1,552 million to £3,364 million, whilst debits increased from £1,131 million to £3,514 million. Over the same period credits from telecommunications and postal services increased from £638 million to £988 million and debits from £721 million to £1,221 million (The UK Balance of Payments 1997, p. 39).
4. Restrictions that impede the international expansion of business service firms include regulations concerning local ownership and rights of establishment; international payments; mobility of personnel; technology transfer; transborder data flows; procurement policies; restrictions on the business scope of firms; and restrictions on the use of a firm's name (Noyelle and Dutka 1988).
5. The samples were weighted towards firms that ranked among the top 30 of their particular sub-sector. These were identified from the trade press and directories, such as, *Campaign* (1989); *The Accountant* (1989); and *Computing Services Association Official Reference Book* (1989). Having selected the top 30 firms for each sub-sector the remainder of the samples were selected at random.
6. The advertising groups WPP plc and Cordiant plc are examples of this rapid growth among business service firms achieved through mergers and acquisitions.
7. For instance, M&C Saatchi advertising agency's arrangement with Publicis (May, 1995).

14 Intellectual Property Rights Shaping Innovation in Services

Birgitte Andersen and Jeremy Howells[1]

14.1 INTRODUCTION: PERSPECTIVES ON IPRs

The exploitation of knowledge embodied in product and process innovations, new ideas, or related to intangible assets and symbolic material, is in most mature economies protected through the use of intellectual property rights (IPRs). Key IPR measures here include patents which protect the inventor for exploitation of his or her knowledge embodied in – mainly industrial – product and process inventions; then there are copyrights which provide rights to the creators of certain kinds of – often symbolic – material to control the various ways in which his or her material may be exploited or to control his or her intangible assets. Lastly, there are trademarks which relate to any word, name, symbol or device which is used in trade with goods to indicate the source or origin of the goods and to distinguish them from the goods of others. The US IPR system is probably the most developed IPR system in the world, and thus the IPR definitions of the US Patent and Trademark Office and the US Library of Congress are presented in Table 14.1.

The study of IPRs covers a diverse range of subjects, disciplines and legal regimes. As such it includes a whole set of different types of legal statute such as property, contract and competition law as well as involving a wide spectrum of economic and social issues relating to, for example, trade, monopoly and competition issues.

Table 14.1 A classification of intellectual property rights: The US context*

IPR	Nature of Protection
What are patents, trademarks, copyrights, and trade secrets?	Patents, trademarks, copyrights, and trade secrets are sometimes referred to as "intellectual property" – referring to products that come from the creative mind. Intellectual property is imagination made real.
Patents ...	provide exclusive rights to make, use, import, sell and offer for sale a product and process invention for up to 20 years.
Utility patents ...	protect useful processes, machines, articles of manufacture, and compositions of matter. Examples: fiber optics, computer hardware, medications.
Design patents ...	guard the unauthorised use of new, original, and ornamental designs for articles of manufacture. The look of an athletic shoe, a bicycle helmet, and the Star Wars characters are all protected by design patents.
Plant patents ...	Are the way we protect invented or discovered, asexually reproduced plant varieties. Hybrid tea roses, Silver Queen corn, Better Boy tomatoes are all types of plant patents.
Trademarks ...	Protect words, names, symbols, sounds, or colours that distinguish goods and services. Trademarks, unlike patents, can be renewed forever as long as they are being used in business. The shape of a Coca-Cola bottle is a familiar trademark.
Copyrights ...	Protect works of authorship, such as writings, music, and works of art that have been tangibly expressed. The Library of Congress registers copyrights which last for the life of the author plus 70 years.
Trade Secrets ...	are information that companies keep secret to give them an advantage over their competitors. The formula for Coca-Cola is the most famous trade secret.

Source: Based upon http://www.uspto.gov/web/offices/ac/ahrpa/opa/kids /kidprimer.html (March 2000).

Although most research on IPRs has been with respect to the possibilities of using them as indicators and specialisation indices or related to their economic value or worth, it is presented here that the IPR system also represents an important institutional and legal framework; one that deserves study in terms of widen our understanding concerning how the IPR system provides a shaping element in innovation dynamics. This is related to the broader institutional framework of the IPR system in relation to the systems of innovation (Lundvall 1999), as well as related to the appropriation of IPR and its involvement with corporate strategy (Davis 1999).

Up until recently, most of the focus of research on innovation and the IPR system has been almost exclusively in relation to the manufacturing sector and the patent system, with its emphasis on protecting physical artefacts centred on new products and processes. Even the valuable work by Foray (1995) on IPR and systems of innovation focuses on the patent system (albeit certain aspects of software development are included in this discussion). By contrast, the nature and needs of the service economy, based on intangible assets and creative expression, has been largely ignored. Hence, a primary focus of the discussion in this chapter surrounds the intangible nature of most (though not all) service innovations, and the various means which have been employed to protect such forms of innovation, with a specific focus on the copyright system.

14.1.1 Chapter Outline

A brief history, and evolution, of IPRs in relation to services is first presented, followed by an analysis of how the evolution and development of IPRs is directly associated with the structural dimensions of technological as well as economic development. A key issue concerning the IPR system is then addressed in terms of what is the rationale of the IPR regime itself. Why is there such a system in the first place? The macro-economic efficiency of the system and the role of some micro aspects of copyrights, concerning IPR incentives and strategies, is then addressed. Some studies on appropriation have already analysed this issue in relation to industrial patenting (Foray 1995; Davis 1999), but little or no research has considered this in relation to the other intellectual rights, despite the increasing importance of knowledge-based service innovations with respect to technological innovation as a whole. It has been highlighted that as technology changes the efficiency of the system changes or perhaps even decreases it (see Dible 1978, p. 114, for example, in relation to the American Copyright Act of 1909[2]).

With the growing recognition of the importance of technological change in the competitiveness and growth of firms and countries there has been an increasing interest in searching for new innovation indicators. Hence the analysis concludes by reviewing the way, and degree to which, intellectual property rights may reflect innovative creativity in the service economy. This is in turn related to the extent and degree to which IPRs, and the related IPR regime, serve as shaping elements for innovation dynamics in services, and vice versa. Lastly, the discussion concludes by outlining the potential use of copyright as a technological indicator, and the possibilities and problems associated with this measure.

It should be stressed that much of the analysis presented here is exploratory in nature and requires further elaboration and more specific testing, nonetheless this study will hopefully open up a dialogue with other researchers interested in this field.

14.2 AN HISTORICAL OUTLOOK ON IPRs

Although property rights relating to intellectual endeavour are not the first official property rights enforced by law (land, capital and labour rights came well before), Bainbridge (1996, p. 17) has argued that intellectual property is nonetheless the most basic form of property right because people employ nothing to produce it other than their own mind. The evolution of the IPR legislation is intertwined with the history of technological opportunities as well as industrial evolution and the outgrowth of the service economy.

Studies in the past have focused on the development of the patent systems, which took off with the rise of corporate capitalism during the Industrial Revolution (see, for example, Noble 1979; Sullivan 1989). The rise of corporate capitalism during the nineteenth and early twentieth centuries, based on the manufacturing system and associated with physical artefacts and processes, helped to shape and push the development and structure of the modern patent system. The more recent growth of the service economy which has resulted in a rapid growth of information infrastructure and information service innovations (and the convergence of computer and communication technologies) has, however, revealed that these more intangible innovations cannot be adequately protected under patent law. This indicates that copyright perhaps only presents one recent aspect of the formal IPR regime and informal IPR mechanisms employed by innovating service firms to protect their intellectual property rights (see below). However, it should be stressed here that any formal means of protecting service innovations is a very recent phenomenon.

Copyright legislation can be traced back to the UK with the establishment by Royal Decree in 1586 to the Stationers Company, more formally incorporated under legislation associated with the Statute of Anne in 1710, and in relation to the United States with the First Federal Copyright Act of 31 May 1790 (Dik 1990). However, the history of what might be termed the application of copyright to protecting advances in science is much more recent, dating back only to the 1960s and 1970s. Indeed, it was only in June 1974 that the Director General of the World Intellectual Property Organization (WIPO) convened an Advisory Group of Experts that looked into the protection of computer programs and found that only in a few countries might computer software be adequately protected without changes to existing laws (WIPO 1987, 21[3]). However, the principal IPR legislation in most European countries today have been amended as a result of European Community Directives in the copyright field. These European Community Directives includes areas of new technological challenges such as, for example.: (i) The legal protection of computer programs (cf. Directive 91/250/EEC implemented by the Copyright (Computer Programs)

Regulations 1992 [Statutory Instrument (SI) 1992 No. 3233], which came into force on 1 January 1993), and (ii) copyright and related rights in relation to cable and satellite broadcasting (cf. Directive 93/83/EEC implemented by the Copyright and Related Rights Regulations 1996 [SI 1996 No. 2967], which came into force on 1 December 1996). Currently being discussed in Council Working Group is a proposal for an EC Directive on the harmonisation of certain aspects of copyright and related rights in the information society.

14.3 RATIONALES, REGIMES AND INSTITUTIONAL STRUCTURES FOR IPRs

It is important not just to assume the existence and nature of an IPR regime, but to ask the question why we have it in the first place. This may help us to understand the heterogeneous attitude to IPR administration at the national level as well as trade-related aspects of IPR. The extent to which such IPR regimes shape the way, or strategy, in which individuals and firms appropriate from IPR, may not only be related to the rationale of IPR regimes, but may also be associated with variations in innovation practice, or other institutional factors. In Table 14.2 we have grouped some different rationales, mainly associated with IPR system beliefs.[4]

The IPR system of different countries is strongly historically rooted and embedded in often very different institutional structures. These institutional structures may in turn reflect the different underlying rationales that nation states have applied to the introduction and development of IPRs (see Dawson 1998). The introduction of IPR systems and their development has been associated as much with the underlying moral, ethical, social and philosophical issues of intellectual property as its direct economic ones .[5]

The rationale of the IPR regime may be found by viewing the government institution or agency under which the system is based, which is often strongly historically rooted. Table 14.3 provides examples of where the IPR system in relation to patents, trademarks and copyright is administered by national governments in each of the following major industrialised economies: the US, UK, Germany, France and Japan.

A number of points are important to highlight here. First, all countries with a developed IPR regime must be regarded as 'IPR system believers' as they accept there should be some reward for the costs and burdens of organising a variety of scientific and technical inputs and harnessing creativity to generate new ideas and knowledge. More specifically, it could be argued that patents and trademark systems in the US, Japan, as well as the entire IPR system in the UK, illustrate an overall 'economic rationale' being

Table 14.2 Key rationales of IPR systems

Moral rationales	Human rights	The law should provide remedies against those who appropriate ideas of others, and a person who has devoted time and effort to create something has a right to claim the thing as his own, and also has a right to obtain some reward to all his work.
	Business ethics	IPRs function as a safeguard for consumers against confusion of products and quality as well as deception in the marketplace (this indeed applies mostly to trademarks).
Economic investment rationale	Incentives to creativity	IPRs provide the prospect of reward which in turn encourages creative and technological advancement by increased incentives to invent, invest in, and innovate new ideas (Say 1964; Mill 1864; Clark 1907[a]).
	Increased competition	IPR helps to cover the fixed costs of inventing and producing a new product as well as protecting against new marked entry. This may stimulate a creative dynamic environment as well as strengthen and broaden continuous innovators (c.f. Schumpeter Mark I competition[b]).
Economic rationale of organising science, technology and creativity.	Order	It has been argued that 'The prizes of industrial and commercial leadership will fall to the nation which organises its scientific forces most effectively' (Elihu Root in Noble 1979: p. 110).[c]
	Increased information and spill-over	IPRs facilitates the developments and sharing of new technologies and creative efforts world wide. Patents and copyrights, when filed, provide immediate information to rivals who can incorporate such into their own knowledge bases even though they cannot make direct commercial use of it. This might create a more coherent technological and industrial development, faster spill-over in knowledge and creative efforts and technological progress which strengthens the national or global economy.
Economic rationale of organising science, technology and creativity (continued)	Increased information and better advice	An intellectual property system also offers information concerning structural changes in technological development as well as technological capabilities of industry and sectors, allowing governments to be more effectively advised on science and technology policy matters.
	Uniformity	A national system brings in national uniformity (as opposed to regional differences in IPR legislation) makes it possible to (or seeks to) promote cross-country trade in IPR and international integration of science, technology and creative efforts, stimulating prosperity world-wide.

Notes:
a More recently, Arrow (1962) and Samuelson (1954) have argued that although property rights are clearly useful for invention and investment purposes, they are nonetheless inferior to direct government investment in inventive activities.
b Schumpeter only implicitly mentioned the role of the IPR regime (Schumpeter 1939, p. 314 on the German industry). Many other evolutionary economists, such as Malerba and Orsenigo (1995) and Metcalfe (1995), have argued that the benefit of establishing a creative, dynamic environment should be the primary focus of government action, although they never discussed using the patent system as the means to reach this goal.
c This view of organising science and technology has mostly been raised with respect to establishing scientific laboratories, but we suggest here that this also apply to the creation of an adequate science and technology system organised at the nation level.

Table 14.3 Government departments under which patents, trademarks and copyright are administered

Country	US	UK	Germany	France	Japan
Patents and Trademarks	Department of Commerce	Department of Trade and Industry	Federal Ministry of Justice	Ministry of Culture and Francophone Affairs	Ministry of International Trade and Industry
Copyright	Library of Congress	Department of Trade and Industry (via the Patent Office)	Federal Ministry of Justice	Ministry of Culture and Francophone Affairs	Ministry of Education, Science, Sports and Culture

allocated under the Department of Commerce or Department of Trade and Industry. By contrast, in Germany the IPR system is administered by Federal Ministry of Justice which suggests an emphasis on a 'moral and ethical' rationale based on 'rights'. In relation to the copyright system, the US and Japan may emphasise encouragement and benefit from spill-over of creative efforts and human resources having the system administrated under the Library of Congress and Ministry of Education, Science, Sports and Culture respectively. By contrast, France, having the entire IPR system administered by the Department of Culture and Francophone Affairs, reflects its strong historical moral and ethical rationale basis of IPR protection of intellectual creativity (see also Macmillan 1998).

However, the situation is more complex than this, since all systems or regimes are dynamic and undergoing differential rates of change and direction as was indicated earlier in terms of the European situation. Within the context of patenting there has been a strong shift towards international harmonisation of patenting systems, although full global harmonisation of patenting systems is still a long way off (Carey 1994), whilst effective pan-national implementation of international standards even further away (Government Accounting Office 1993). Nonetheless, since the 1990s the three main trading and regulatory regimes in terms of pharmaceutical patenting had already sought to move towards global harmonisation of systems, after the lead taken by the US, the conciliatory follow-up by Japan and the subsequent competitive catch-up by Europe (Howells and Neary 1995, p. 165). The 'triadisation' of the patent system has been highlighted by Cameron (1997) developing the US Government Accounting Office review of patenting systems. However, the copyright system remains very much more idiosyncratic and nationally focused. National variations in copyright legislation are still very significant and even, in some cases, are still *diverging* rather than converging (for example, in relation to computer software). The IPR regimes, which many innovating service companies are having to operate in, are more nationally restricted and determined. This obviously is in part a reflection of the laggard nature of the service sector in terms of political power and policy involvement, where service trade issues and property protection have always been the last on the agenda and the last to be tackled. However, it has provided a further limiting factor on service innovation where firms find the protection of their inventions more partial and geographically more limited. A global copyright regime is still a long way off and therefore a more internationally-based service innovation system, where firms can successfully generate, exploit and defend their service innovations across the world, is still further off.

14.4 MACRO-ECONOMIC EFFICIENCY AND MICRO-ECONOMIC ASPECTS

It is presented here that IPR systems can be powerful elements in shaping wider sectoral systems of innovation, including the wider formation, and structure of, the innovation process across services. In this respect, although the IPR system has, in some senses, *flexibly* evolved to generally suit the conditions of the different types of innovation formats, most notably between physical artefacts (largely covered by the patent system) and intangible, information-based innovations (covered by copyright and trademark legislation);[6] in other respects, it has helped to *solidify* change. Thus it has contributed to the establishment of institutional and legal boundaries. It has provided a key element in the institutional governance structure surrounding and shaping service innovations since the 1960s and 1970s, that is, sectoral endowments and properties (Kitschelt 1991). This institutional governance structure is perhaps especially important in an area of new technology, such as computer software, laying out a path-dependent learning process for firms operating in these sectors.

However, much of the innovative output generated by service firms cannot be protected under the patent system, although patent restrictions were relaxed somewhat in most developed economies in the 1970s and 1980s to allow certain types of computer software to be protected by patent clauses. Thus, the US permitted patenting of certain algorithms that were previously thought to be outside the scope of patent law (although some countries do not allow computer programs per se to be patented; World Intellectual Property Organization 1987, pp. 22–23). This change may partly explain in large part why patent activity has increased by service industries (reflected also in their increased amounts of R&D expenditure[7]).

Teece (1987) noted that patents are the written articulation of certain codified aspects of the technical know-how of the firm, and copyright could also be perceived in this sense. However, because copyright does not require registration its *value* or even *existence* has not been validated by the outside world and remains contestable. Indeed copyright law has essentially been built up around case law. Much of the inherent differences between patent and copyright systems relate to differences in the economic and technical nature of intangibles and information compared with physical artefacts. Thus, for physical products, simple storage of that product does not constitute copying infringement; however, in the UK storage of a computer program can in certain instances be seen as the *reproduction* of that program, and therefore to infringe the law.

However, although the nature of the three types of intellectual property rights seems very different, a combination of them is often used. Thus once a patent has been granted with respect to an invention, other rights might be appropriate, such as a trademark if a name is applied to a product. Also in telecommunications some aspects of some software may be protected by the patent law, while other aspects can only be protected by the copyright law. Finally, in the first stage of an invention copyright may be the only means of protection. This is because, for example, under the UK Copyright, Design and Patent Act 1988, documents submitted in a patent application are open to public inspection and may be copied if not protected by the copyright law (Bainbridge 1996, p. 18). However, even before this, until the patent application is published the idea of the invention is protected by the law of confidence. Thus, each invention often goes through different stages of protection.

14.4.1   IPR Strategies and the Inclination to Copyright

Although much has been published on the appropriation of patents and the propensity to patents within the context of manufacturing firms, hardly anything concerning IPR-related aspects of such concerning services has been considered. Copyright, unlike patenting, is a relatively inexpensive form of IPR protection since it is 'there' by right and does not require registration (although this was not the case in the United States until 1 March 1979, before this date a 'copyright notice' was mandatory; United States Copyright Office 1997). Figure 14.1 below shows copyright registration in the US 1900–1995.

However, some of the evidence mentioned above may explain why IPR strategies for innovative service firms (which in turn can be linked to the wider development of the strategic assets or core competencies of such firms; Winter 1987; Prahalad and Hamel 1990) are different and more complex than

Figure 14.1 US copyright registrations 1900–95

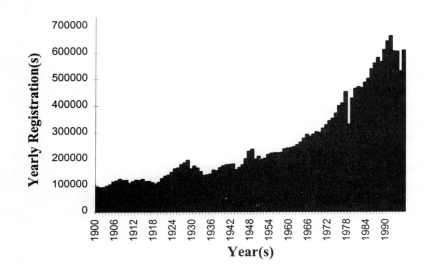

Notes: 1978: Drop in copyright registration reflects changes in reporting procedure. 1979 is the 'critical' year from which copyrights do not formally have to be registered. 1994: Approximately 65,000 claims were examined but were not assigned registration numbers in fiscal 1994 due to the conversion of the numbering operation from manual hand-stamping to an automatic optical disk system.

Source: compiled from Report of the Register of Copyrights, 1995 of the US. Copyright Office Records.

for manufacturing companies. As listed below, this may be for a number of reasons:

- IPR protection in most service innovation contexts (intangibles) is much weaker than for manufacturing innovation (as represented by artefacts and physical systems).
- IPR in services is not only weaker, but is also much harder to monitor and enforce than for manufacturing systems.[8]
- Although the copyright system compared to the patent system historically goes back a long way (in terms of published works), within the context of innovative activity its history is much more recent, less developed and, most importantly here, less well defined.

- Whereas manufacturing firms usually face a simple IPR decision of whether to patent or not to patent, for service firms the issue is to decide which is the most appropriate system for protection (patent, copyright or even trademark protection), or indeed which combination of IPR protection is the best.

The above leads to the conclusions that IPR strategies within innovating service firms will be substantially different and more complex than for innovating manufacturing firms, or (more provocatively) non-existent (see below). Certainly it is more recent and less well-developed. In the US, even partially effective cover for software programs came with the 1976 Copyright Act and only became fully effective with an amendment in 1980 to make explicit the applicability of copyright to computer programs (Braunstein 1989, p. 12). Similarly in the UK (although copyright law had been flexible in its approach) the first specifically targeted piece of legislation which dealt with computer software was the Copyright (Computer Software) Amendment Act of 1985 (soon followed by the Copyright, Designs and Patent Act 1988). It may be argued that innovative service companies have grown up with a regime that has not protected their creations and innovations properly (which become a serious problem as much copying is virtually costless (that is, low marginal costs of production in comparison to, often, high cost of creation; Sieghart 1982).

There are a number of strategies which innovative service firms are more likely to employ than their manufacturing counterparts, because of the intangible nature of their innovations and, because of the arguably weaker protection offered by the copyright system. These are:

- *Secrecy:* Thus some argue that the best IPR strategy for an innovative service firm is secrecy, or what Taylor and Silberston (1973, p. 296) have termed 'secret know-how.' How far secrecy can be sustained is questionable and it also has wider implications, such as restricting collaboration or know-how trading. It also leads to the interesting question of why an increasing number of service firms are openly seeking IPR protection for their innovations, if the best policy is to keep quiet.
- *'Ensemble' Protection:* Service firms may consider protecting their innovations through an ensemble of IPR methods, including copyright, patenting and trademark legislation. By contrast, other service companies view certain types of IPR with scepticism (often based on past experience) and do not use them in their strategic repertoire for intellectual asset protection.
- *Short Innovation Cycles:* By actually seeking to create ever shorter

innovation cycles a firm can reduce the risk of copying and imitation by reducing 'lead times' so much that by the time a potential competitor does seek to copy or imitate the innovation it is too late. Significant barriers to imitation are created by such action. Innovation cycles in the software industry are often already less than six months. However, short lead times impose considerable costs to the firm and more especially means that innovation costs have to be amortised over very short periods.

- *'Firmware':* There was much discussion in the 1980s that IPR protection was so weak for computer software that firms sought to protect their software by embedding it in microchips, coining the phrase 'firmware' or more formally 'embedded microelectronics software'. There is a variety of methods for incorporating the software (the 'microcode or 'microprograms') in the electronic circuit, but certainly a significant proportion of software is protected this way if only because all microprocessor systems must by definition incorporate their own control program (OECD 1985). Interestingly, although such microcode may be harder to copy, in the United States such code still falls within the meaning of a 'computer program' (Bainbridge 1996, p. 177).

Obviously, even these strategies are not independent of each other. Secrecy combined with short innovation cycles may offer substantial protection to a service firm and may be a preferred strategy over more formal IPR methods. One advantage that service firms reliant on the copyright system have over manufacturing companies reliant on the patent system, is that as they do not have to register the copyright (only activate it when they see it being transgressed) they do not alert potential competitors to what new technologies they are developing. This is unlike patents which offers the general public precise technical information about the product, process or molecule that has been registered.

However, it would be equally misleading to view the service sector acting similarly within one such IPR institutional shaping framework (although there may be a loosely defined IPR system that could be applied to the innovatory framework of services overall). Just as manufacturing industry varies in terms of its use and propensity to patent, so do service sectors in their ways of appropriating from the IPR system. Thus, certain service sectors may have weak IPR regimes and low levels of innovative activity; other service sectors may have an increased propensity to use copyright rather than patent protection; other segments may use few IPR protection mechanisms or none at all, but may still have relatively high levels of innovative activity. Many of these issues can only be successfully understood by examining all aspects of the use of IPRs and by positing such analysis within the wider IPR service regime.

In this context, Metcalfe (1995, p. 41) has noted that the national unit may be too broad a category to allow a clear understanding of the complete dynamics of a technological system and instead focus should be on 'a number of distinct technology-based systems each of which is geographically and institutionally localised within the nation but with links into the supporting national and international system'. Certainly the issue of why national innovation systems are necessarily dominant over sectoral or technological sectors needs to be questioned (Howells 1994, p. 94). In seeking to highlight one aspect of this, the sectoral system of innovation, it is not intended here to suggest that national systems of innovation are no longer valid. As Kitschelt (1991, p. 455) has noted, there have been a series of studies that have sought to investigate the intersection of both national and sectoral and governance regimes. Thus, for example, in relation to the copyright system, it has been illustrated that although the IPR regime protects music composers via issuing copyrights, the allocation and size of royalties generated from IPR is based upon bargaining, collaboration, networking and lobbying among various individuals and firms in the music supply chain. Hence the effect of the more informal system may undermine the purpose or rationale of the more formal IPR regime (Andersen et al 1999: Kretschmer et al 1999; Towse 1999).

14.5 COPYRIGHTS AS INDICATORS OF INNOVATION

The macro-economic efficiency of any IPR (or copyright) regime, as well as its shaping element for service innovations at the micro level, reflect the usefulness of using IPRs (or copyrights) as indicators when exploring innovation dynamics in services. That is, during the last few decades, there has been a growing interest in searching for technology indicators. This is due to the growing recognition of the importance of technology and technical change in the competitiveness and growth of firms and countries. Whereas the search for technological indicators in relation to IPR so far mainly has been in relation to the manufacturing economy, this section aims to move the search into the area of the innovating service sector. Griliches (1992) even argued that the fact that current measurement methodology may be underestimating the contribution of services to innovation and output growth, this may have prevented a clear understanding of innovation, competition and hence productivity growth in the economy as a whole.

When promoting an understanding of the rate, direction and pattern of technological change, and the evolution of corporate innovations emphasis has often been on patent data. So far, patent statistics have shown promise and some success in analysing: international patterns of innovative activities and their effects on trade and production; patterns of innovative activities amongst firms, and their effects upon their technological strength or competence as well as performance and industrial structure; rates and directions of innovative activities in different technical fields and industrial sectors; and links between science and technology (see, for example, Pavitt 1984a, 1988; Archibugi 1992; Narin 1987; Reekie 1973; Engelsman and van Raan 1992[9]). This focus on patents no doubt reflects the fact that the patent system is the most developed IPR regime (associated with the rise of corporate capitalism, noted above), which was based on production and manufacturing protected by patent rights.

Whereas patent data are probably the most long-running detailed historical record of technological activities, and are therefore very suitable to use as indicators in historical studies and approaches, the extended opportunities for the use of copyrights is much more recent due to the more recent technological trajectories of 'copyrightable' inventions within services. Hence, although it is still believed that patent data, especially in a historical perspective, are among the most comprehensively tested and used technological indicators, it has to be recognised that they do not throw a great deal of light on the evolution of new sectors within services, such as software, multimedia and audio-visual services.

Owing to the greater recognition of the importance of the service sector, which is poorly protected by patent rights, we now also have to address the merits of the use of copyright as innovation indicators. The expected increased use of service IPRs certainly provides some scope for the use of copyright data as technology indicators.

14.5.1 Possibilities and problems of using copyrights as indicators for services innovations

It is, of course, accepted that IPR data can be used and misused or abused as any other data source used in statistical studies, and that IPR data is not appropriate for all kinds of research. Possibilities and problems of patent statistics have also been discussed in many indicator studies, especially in studies by Pavitt (1984a, 1988), Griliches (1990) and Archibugi (1992). Although this chapter does not aim to contribute to the overall survey literature, it ought to be mentioned that use of copyright data is of course expected to share many of the same possibilities and problems as patent statistics, plus some different ones, as will be presented below.

From creativity and invention to innovation:
Patent data has been shown as an acceptable indicator for inventions and innovations within manufacturing by a variety of studies. Thus, Mansfield (1986) revealed that firms in his study applied for a patent in relation to about

66 per cent to 87 per cent of their patentable inventions; whilst research by Scherer et al (1959), Sanders (1964), Napolitano and Sirilli (1990) has indicated that between 40 per cent to 60 per cent of total patent applications actually progress to innovations. On this basis, the extent to which copyrights can be used as indicators in technology and innovation studies within services is critically dependant on how much firms apply for a copyright of their 'copyrightable' inventions, as well as to what extent the 'copyrightable' inventions are actually developed into further innovations. Hence, just as a patent is only a direct measure of invention and under certain conditions an indirect measure for innovation, a copyright is only a direct measure of invention of new creativity (although it does not need to satisfy the same novelty conditions; see below), and is only under certain conditions part of an innovative process.

Novelty conditions
Whereas a patent has to reflect a novelty (that is, a movement of the technological frontier) and is therefore an appropriate indicator when measuring the rate and direction of technological change, such novelty restrictions are not imposed on copyrights. However, it is still to be expected that within certain fields such as telecommunications and software you would normally only ask for a copyright where there is novelty. Although in many other disciplines within services (such as written works, performing and visual arts) the degree of novelty is not an important issue, the rate of change, as well as the structural dimensions of these changes, still reflects some institutional and cultural aspects of the frontier of the changing society.

Different Propensity to Use IPRs:
In addition, similar problems concerning the different propensity to patent across sectors, firms, industries and countries as well as over time also apply to the use of copyrights as indicators, and the problems here may be even more pronounced. First of all, as most countries have not developed a classification scheme of types of copyrights, the data cannot be broken down into sectors, which is a vital problem when investigating structural changes in patterns of specialisation. Only the US Copyright Office has broken down the copyright registration into twenty broad categories across four broad groups as presented in Table 14.4. However, these categories are still too broad for any meaningful analysis of structural changes. As copyrights in this scheme also cover sectors of very different nature (from poetry to computer programming) any inter-sectoral comparison is not very meaningful in the first place.

Nonetheless, analysis of copyright data may still be useful, albeit in a more limited and restricted way. Thus it may still be valid to investigate the changing opportunities and stock of technological capability on an intra-sectoral level. Sectors covered under 'Other Works' listed in Table 14.4, are indeed argued to represent the most interesting and dynamic innovative sectors within services and which have close parallels to those sectors that have been defined as 'technical Knowledge Intensive Business Services' (t-KIBS; as outlined by Miles et al. 1995).

When investigating the changing intra-sectoral opportunities in copyright, changes in propensity to copyright over time of course has to be investigated and adjusted for. Thus major expected changes in propensity to copyright over time (for example, the development of the information technology infrastructure is a contemporary phenomenon) is certainly likely to make an analysis of long-term patterns in 'copyrightable' innovations less meaningful, in comparison to that which has been possible with patent studies (see, for example, Andersen 1998, 2001 forthcoming). However, this does of course not rule out shorter-term analysis of 'copyrightable' innovations within services.

Criteria for 'IPRability'
Examples of how different systems approach the issue of what is patentable has been covered by a number of studies. Thus, Cheung (1986, p. 6) has noted: ' .... the troublesome question of what ideas should be granted patent protection must be faced. In one extreme, there is nothing new under the sun. In the other extreme, every different combination of ideas or every different application of an idea constitutes a new idea. In specifying the criteria of patentability, the designers of any patent system must select a position somewhere on the spectrum marked by these extremes.' The same type of question of course applies to the issue of copyrights and trademarks. What is 'copyrightable' and 'trademarkable'? 'Originality' and 'novelty' in comparison to what is a recognisable combination of the existing has become even harder with information technology, making it possible to merge and change existing compositions (this especially applies to software and music).[10] Another ambiguity is that copyright law which does not require any proven artistic merit or novelty (see above) can issue a copyright on the basis of creative effort; thus arrangements, compilations, listings, databases, and so on. are protected by copyright separately from the original material embodied in them.

The criteria for 'IPRability' differs across countries, and this hampers a direct comparison of the propensity to patent, propensity to copyright and propensity to trademark across different national systems. Archibugi (1992), for example, has mentioned how it appears there are more 'new under the suns' in Japan than in the US (to put it in Cheung's phrase) as more is

Table 14.4. US Copyright Registration Classification Scheme*

US Copyright Registration Scheme: 20 Registration Classes Sorted by 4 Broad Groups*	
Written Works (Fiction, Non-Fiction, Poetry, Prose, etc.):	• Registration of Books, Manuscripts, and Speeches • Registration of Poetry • Registration of Serials (such as Periodicals, Newspapers and Annuals)
Performing Arts (Lyrics, Music, Plays, Videos, etc.):	• Dramatic Works: Scripts, Pantomimes & Choreography • Motion Pictures including Video Tapes • Registration of Music • Musical Compositions • Musical Compositions and Sound Recordings
Visual Arts (Drawings, Photographs, Comic Strips, Sculpture, etc.)	• Registration of Visual Arts • Visual Arts • Visual Arts Deposit • Cartoons and Comic Strips • Registration of Photographs
Other Works:	• Architectural Works • Computer Programs • Games • Mask Works (Semiconductor Chips) • Multimedia Works • Recipes • Sound Recordings

Source: Compiled from http://lcweb.loc.gov/copyright/reg.html (March 2000).

patentable in Japan. This, in quantitative terms, raises Japan's propensity to patent and thus has to be adjusted for when undertaking cross-country comparisons.

14.6 CONCLUSION

This analysis has suggested how the co-evolution of IPR regimes and innovation dynamics was a combination and culmination of (i) historical consequences of the evolution of industrial structures (that is, corporate capitalism), as well as shaped by (ii) the rationales of IPR legislation, and (iii) the efficiency of the macro-economic institutional governance structure surrounding IPR, and its interaction with IPR strategies at the micro firm level. Furthermore, the macro-economic institutional governance structure surrounding IPRs has been assisted by the use of IPRs as information sources and indicators. The latter has helped IPR experts, as well as national and international policymakers, to shape new IPR regimes to cope with new technological challenges.

The institutional, legal and technical IPR framework may be critical in the formation of sectoral systems of innovation. However, this is not to suggest that there are not important (and indeed more valid) sectoral or technological systems of innovation within the service economy, either due to IPR incentives and strategies where services firms differ from manufacturing as well as differ intra-sectorally, or based upon informal sectoral collaboration, networking and bargaining undermining the rationale or intentions of the IPR regime. In order to understand the full value of the IPR regime, a closer empirical investigation needs to be undertaken, and we also need to answer the questions concerning the costs of operating such a system.

This review has emphasised that the protection of IPR afforded to service innovations has been much weaker and more recent than for manufacturing. This reflects limited extent to which IPR has played any role at all in shaping innovation dynamics within services. In part, this may reflect the problematic nature of trying to protect intangible knowledge and information products. Alternatively, it may it be that the weak IPR system covering service activity is simply a reflection of the fact that service industries are less innovative and therefore less pressure was put on the legislators do anything about it. Further, regardless of why there has been such a weak IPR system in relation to services, has this weak protection system held back innovative activity within services? In any case, the scholarly literature demonstrates that there is still very limited understanding of the macro as well as micro aspects of the IPR system with respect to the service industries.

NOTES

1. Special thanks goes to Derek Bosworth for making comments on an earlier draft of this chapter. Advice and support from the Copyright Section of UK Patent Office, in particular its Director Jonathan Startup, and the US Copyright Office are also gratefully acknowledged.
2. In particular, the growth of new information service infrastructures and technologies has generated both unprecedented challenges and important opportunities for the copyright market. Cf. 'Intellectual Property and the National Information Infrastructure': http:// www.uspto.gov/ web/ offices/ com/ doc/ ipnii/ execsum.html (March 1999). Thus, not only does the new information paradigm indicate the greater need for copyright protection, but the copyright system also needs to undergo structural changes to more efficiently satisfy the new technological opportunities being provided within the new information economy.

3. Thus, even in the UK during the 1970s, where protection afforded to computer programs was considered relatively good, this was done by treating computer programs as literary works under the Copyright Act 1956. Indeed, even under the Copyright, Designs and Patents Act of 1988 protection for computer programs still remains via the treatment as a literary work (Bainbridge 1996, p. 175). It could be argued that this delay in affording protection to computer software was because at least some of the software in the 1950s and 1960s was protected via embedding or 'hardwiring' into the computer itself, although much of the 'firmware' type of software only became more widespread with the more widespread diffusion of effective microprocessor systems in the 1970s.

4. We are obviously aware of that some do not believe that much (or any at all) value can be derived from such a system, and perhaps even find it destructive.

5. Foray (1995) has analysed the different national patent systems that exist between the Japanese D-system, centred on the more relaxed diffusion of patented material, and the US P-system, based on much stronger protection of patentable information. Although of crucial importance this study only compares two national patent systems with the context of a purely economic rationale. Also, the patent system is only a part, albeit an important part, of an IPR system, whilst the rationale for establishing and developing an IPR system is only partly based on its economic rationale and foundation.

6. However, patents and copyrights may not have been widely used in services because they are designed for industrial property protection (and thus formed a poor IPR protection mechanism for services given the design of the IPR regime). This in turn may have contributed to the illusion that services were not innovative.

7. Another factor has been the increased outsourcing and externalisation of R&D activities formerly undertaken 'in-house' within manufacturing firms and now provided externally by specialist research and technology service companies (see Howells 1997a).

8. Andersen et al (2000) is especially addressing this with respect to the music industry, concerning generating and capturing rent from IPR.

9. Earlier work in this field includes the work of Schmookler (1950; 1953; 1962; 1966), Scherer et al (1959) Scherer (1983) and Kuznets (1930, 1962).

10. The issue of what is trademarkable in the UK has been recently illustrated by the debate which arose over whether, after Lady Diana's death, the words 'Diana the Princess of Wales' should have trademark status.

15 Global Knowledge Systems in a Service Economy

Jeremy Howells and Joanne Roberts

15.1 INTRODUCTION

There has been much interest in the 'systems of innovation' approach in terms of how it shapes and transforms the innovation process in advanced industrial economies. Equally, there has been a desire to provide a better understanding of the role of knowledge in relation to the innovation process and more generally in terms of economic growth and performance. Both sets of interest have also come at a time when the spectre of globalisation of technology has been at least raised, if not wholeheartedly supported, in these modern times by many commentators. The objective of this chapter is to explore this tripartite relationship, analysing systems of knowledge creation and dissemination in an international context. Drawing on the literature concerning systems of innovation the chapter identifies and evaluates the characteristics of knowledge systems. Much effort has been directed towards national and sectoral systems of knowledge creation. However, in an increasingly global economic environment it is evident that some knowledge-creating enterprises function simultaneously in a number of national and sectoral systems. The aim of this chapter is, therefore, to examine the extent to which knowledge systems interact at an international level. The components that make up an international system are identified, and their interaction with national and sector-specific elements of knowledge systems is investigated. Globally provided services, especially knowledge-intensive business services (KIBS), are identified as having a particularly important role facilitating the transfer of knowledge between national and regional knowledge systems. The analysis presented here concludes by suggesting a number of possible theoretical frameworks in which to conceptualise the interactions of knowledge systems at an international level.

Knowledge and innovation are central to economic success of the advanced industrialised countries. Indeed, knowledge is becoming the only resource capable of offering competitive advantage and continued growth and prosperity (Drucker 1993, p. 42). Likewise, service activities concerned with the supply and management of knowledge and intangible assets, whether within the boundaries of firms or in the market, are becoming increasingly significant in facilitating knowledge creation and distribution in regional, national and international environments. In the emerging knowledge-based economy (OECD 1996) an appreciation of the creation and dissemination of knowledge is vital for policy makers and business managers. Government action can do much to promote the successful development of knowledge-based activity and the learning economy (Lundvall and Johnson 1994; Hodgson 1999). Similarly, an understanding of the dynamics of knowledge at the level of the firm, and inter-firm activity, can assist managers in their efforts to maximise efficiency and profitability, and thereby improve economic performance. Consequently, the analysis of knowledge systems presented in this chapter will prove useful to policy makers and business managers. It will also stimulate debate among academics studying the role of knowledge in innovation and economic activity.

The chapter begins with an exploration of knowledge. This is followed by the presentation of a definition of knowledge systems drawing on existing literature. A review of the systems of innovation approach is presented. A fuller exploration of knowledge systems is then provided, before knowledge systems are compared and contrasted with innovation systems. It is at this point that a conceptual analysis of knowledge systems is outlined. Attention then turns to international knowledge systems, followed by a discussion of the interaction of knowledge systems in the global service economy. Finally, conclusions are drawn and directions outlined for further research.

15.2 THINKING ABOUT KNOWLEDGE

In order to understand knowledge systems, it is necessary to have some idea of what knowledge is. Defining and comprehending knowledge is complex and problematic (Sparrow 1998, p. 24). A simple definition is that knowledge is what we know. However, more centrally knowledge is 'a mental state that bears a specific relationship to some feature of the world'. (Plotkin 1994, p. 40). Crucially knowledge has a relational characteristic, as it involves a 'knowing self' and something; that 'something' being an event or an entity.   Knowing is an active process that is mediated, situated, provisional, pragmatic and contested (Blackler 1995).   A final element in knowledge is the need for some kind of memory.   'Memory' here involves an enduring brain state that must exist in the case of knowing by the mind, and allows the bridging of the time gap between events that have occurred and any claim to know about them.   It is important to note here that memory about events in the past in turn undergoes change and therefore memory forms an unconscious, altering the form of knowing (Plotkin 1994, p. 8).

There is an important distinction to be made here between knowledge and information (Chapter 2).   Information relates to individual bits of data or data strands, whilst knowledge involves a much wider process that involves cognitive structures which can assimilate information and put it into a wider context, allowing actions to be undertaken from it.   Thus knowledge in turn combines the process of learning (Polanyi 1958, p. 369).   The take-up of learned behaviour and procedures is a critical element within knowledge acquisition, both in terms of capturing and moving it between individuals within an organisation (Kim 1993), but also in more widely diffusing such competence throughout an organisation more generally (Urlich and von Glinow 1993), between organisations and indeed within the economy as a whole.   It should be stressed that knowledge cannot be said to 'flow'; although, via information flows and mutual learning experiences which then are assembled or absorbed within a cognitive structure or framework, knowledge can be said to be 'shared' or 'transferred'.   As knowledge is transferred through the process of codification, abstraction, diffusion and absorption it acquires a dynamic quality (Boisot 1998; Nonaka and Takeuchi 1995).

In terms of technological innovation more specifically, the innovation process involves using existing knowledge but often also requires generating and acquiring new knowledge, which in turn involves learning.   Innovation also involves sharing learned knowledge.   The process of innovation by moving from existing knowledge and learning patterns to new ones through invention and discovery can be termed a 'heuristic' (defined here as a procedure or strategy for solving a problem or moving towards a solution of a problem; Plotkin 1994, p. 250).   If we accept this definition and description, it suggests that knowledge is fundamentally centred on the individual (Howells 2000 forthcoming).   Even though we may share many characteristics in our knowledge frameworks and intelligence, and in the way we learn and perceive, resulting from common social and educational experiences, knowledge it is still intrinsically. an individually-centred phenomenon.   Such a viewpoint also has important implications when we come to discuss what is meant by a knowledge system.

A great deal has been written in relation to the important distinctions between tacit and codified knowledge, and this distinction has carried through to much wider discussion at the more macro level of the economy as a whole (see, for example, Boisot 1998). The distinction between tacit and codified knowledge made by Michael Polanyi (1958, 1966, 1967) is a powerful and useful one, but has all too often been misapplied. Codified (or explicit) knowledge can be defined here as knowledge that can be written down in the form of a document, manual, blueprint or operating procedure. By contrast tacit knowledge is disembodied know-how that is acquired via the informal take-up of learned behaviour and procedures. It is presented here, therefore, that this bipolar dichotomy represents a crude characterisation of knowledge as an activity, or more generally in terms of how it should be conceived operating within a system. It in particular misrepresents Polanyi's own thinking which stressed that tacit and explicit knowledge were not divided and that explicit or codified knowledge required tacit knowledge for its interpretation. Polanyi (1966, p. 7) notes : 'While tacit knowledge can be possessed by itself, explicit knowledge must rely on being tacitly understood and applied. Hence all knowledge is *either tacit* or *rooted in tacit knowledge*. A *wholly* explicit knowledge is unthinkable.' Knowledge is therefore much more complex than this dichotomy portrays; particularly as one moves from knowledge being an individual phenomenon through to group, firm or organisation-wide process. Knowledge should be better conceived as involving a spectrum of processes ranging from what might be described as 'tacit' and 'explicit' (although indeed Polanyi 1958, p. 70 stressed that articulation would always remain incomplete and therefore on his basis one would never fully reach the 'explicit' knowledge end of the spectrum).

15.3 DEFINING KNOWLEDGE SYSTEMS

If the above defines and describes what knowledge is, how can a knowledge system be defined? Dominique Foray (1997, 64–5) defines a knowledge system:

> as a network of actors or entities that assume specific functions for the generation, transformation, transmission, and storing of knowledge.... The critical degree of cohesiveness, necessary to get a knowledge system is simply defined by some parameters describing the frequency of the knowledge interactions.

Foray (1997, p. 65) continues by noting that:

> A knowledge system includes economic agents (or learning entities) that
> assume the relevant functions of knowledge generation (by means of
> cognitive exploration and search) such as the codification and reduction of
> knowledge to information, the monitoring and perception of information
> (involving encoding, decoding, translation, filtering, and compression), the
> communication and transfer of knowledge, and its storage, retrieval, and
> reconstruction. It also includes the institutions that serve to overcome the
> market's deficiencies in the production and distribution of knowledge.

The description and definition that Foray applies to a knowledge system
covers the actors and institutions that are involved in the generation,
transformation, storage and distribution of knowledge. The knowledge
system that Foray has described is one which is highly purposeful and
specifically centred around economic agents and is framed on the basis of the
knowledge interactions between these agents, and consequent on this the
distribution of power. This specificity has indeed been highlighted by Smith
(1995, p. 82) who notes that the 'David–Foray' concept of the knowledge
system is as narrow though complex in its multi-layered approach to
scientific and technological knowledge. As Smith (1995) notes the David
and Foray (1995) approach emphasises the role of learning systems for
knowledge (see below).

Foray's definition of knowledge system, together with the way he and
Paul David have articulated this concept, is both too narrow and specific.
Thus Foray and David (1995, p. 20) specifically focus on the special
characteristics of knowledge as an economic commodity. Although much
innovation, and indeed new knowledge, comes from purposeful study,
learning and action by economic agents in a market-oriented and mediated
context, much important knowledge does not. Serendipity and non-market
situations are still highly important; social interaction and embeddedness,
past historical actions, geographical proximity, trust and chance all play a
significant role in knowledge processes. Above all care should be taken in
not taking a too *ex post* view of a knowledge system and its impact on
innovation and the wider economy. *Ex ante* the knowledge system still
remains a fragmented, highly complex and sometimes confusing world.

However, if we accept this narrow definition as a starting point, in what
way does a knowledge system differ from an innovation system? A brief
outline of the development of the systems of innovation approach is provided
below before a more detailed comparison between the two types of system in
undertaken.

15.4 SYSTEMS OF INNOVATION

The 'systems of innovation' approach has developed and evolved from the original set of 'national systems of innovation' (NSI) studies presented by Freeman (1987, 1988), Lundvall (1988, 1992) and Nelson (1992a). Freeman (1987, 1988) has identified a number of vital and distinctive elements in its national system of innovation, such as its model of competition, which could be attributed to its success in terms of innovation and economic growth. It has subsequently been applied at a variety of scales and levels, many of which have been outside the original focus of a national setting. Thus, although the national focus remains strong, and rightly so, it has been accompanied by studies seeking to analyse the notion of systems of innovation at an international, sub-national (regional or local) and sectoral or technology level. In this latter context, Carlsson (1995b) developed the 'technological systems' approach, which indicates that systems can be specific to particular technology fields or sectors. Sectors and technological systems within a nation have a powerful shaping influence on the structure and dynamic of a national innovation system, whilst national contexts have important influences on sectoral performance and conditioning (Chapter 13). Thus, prior institutional endowments of a national system may help or hinder innovative activity and performance within particular sectors of a national economy (Howells and Neary 1995).

Chris Freeman (1987, p. 1) was the first to attempt to define the concept as 'the network of institutions in the public and private sectors whose activities and interactions initiate, import, modify and diffuse new technologies'. Lundvall (1992, p. 12) makes a distinction between a narrow and broad definition of a system of innovation. In his narrow definition of a system of innovation this would include 'organisations and institutions involved in searching and exploring - such as R&D departments, technological institutes and universities'. In his broader definition, a system of innovation would include 'all parts and aspects of the economic structure and the institutional set-up affecting learning as well as searching and exploring – the production system, the marketing system and the system of finance present themselves as sub-systems in which learning takes place'.

In respect of the 'national' element, Lundvall (1992, pp. 2–3) stresses that this is not as clear-cut as is often assumed and that nation-states which the concept of 'national systems of innovation' presumes, have two dimensions: the national-cultural and the étatist-political. The ideal, abstract nation-state where these two dimensions coincide controlled by one central state authority, though, is, as Lundvall adds, difficult, if not impossible, to find in the real world. Moreover, this nationally-bounded view, at least in geographical terms, has been loosened over time. The globalisation of economic activity, resulting from the increasing cross-border flows of capital, commodities, labour and information, is bringing into question the role of nation-based structures (Ohmae 1990; Reich 1991). Although there is much debate about the extent and impact of globalisation (Hirst and Thompson 1996; Krugman 1996), it is undoubtedly transforming, however gradually, the organisations and institutions that constitute a NSI. Consequently, the role and relevance of NSI must be questioned (Nelson and Rosenberg 1993).

There is then growing recognition of the significance of supranational and international systems of innovation, and indeed some discussion of international knowledge systems including, for example, Caravcostas and Soetes (1997) examination of the European System of Innovation. As Carlsson and Stankiewicz (1991) note that the boundaries of a system depend on the particular circumstances. With this in mind, Niosi and Bellon (1994) have developed the idea of 'open national systems of innovation'. They identify three types of innovation systems, regional, national, and international that coexist and are in competition with each other. Moreover, they argue that internationalization 'does not suppress local and national networks; it modifies their functioning, however, since some previously regional or national activities are transferred to international networks' (Niosi and Bellon 1994, p. 195). The systems of innovation approach has now been widened and developed to more specifically include systems of innovation that are sectoral in dimension and those that are at a different geographical scale, both above in terms of what Freeman (1995) coined 'upper' regions ('triad' and continental regions), and below in relation to regional and local systems.

Within the context of the term 'innovation', this has a wide range of explicit and implicit definitions applied to it. Edquist (1997, p. 10) here has stressed the ambiguity and wide variation in what may be termed the ambit of the word 'innovation'. Thus, Nelson and Rosenberg (1993) and Carlsson and Stankiewicz (1991) have tended to adopt narrower definitions of innovation, mainly (though not wholly) centred on technological innovations, whilst Lundvall (1992) seeks to include what may be termed disembodied innovations, in particular institutional innovations. However, Freeman (1988, p. 339–41), in his analysis of the Japanese innovation system, also emphasised the role of social and educational innovations, whilst Carlsson and Stankiewicz (1991, p. 28), in adopting Dosi's (1988, p. 222) definition of innovation, would also seem to include the emergence and development of new organisational set-ups in their use of the word 'innovation'.

15.5 KNOWLEDGE SYSTEMS: A CONCEPTUAL ANALYSIS

The above has sought to outline some of the background to the systems of innovation approach, but how might a knowledge system be distinct from an innovation system? A number of points are put forward here, highlighting not only differences between the two types of system but also their inter-relationship. A number of problems associated with using the term 'knowledge system' as a conceptual tool are also raised.

First, interpreting a knowledge system in a wider sense than that used by Foray, a knowledge system represents a broader and less well-defined system than an innovation system. A knowledge system represents an underlying knowledge and learning framework and pool for the more specific process of innovation and hence systems of innovation. Since an innovation can broadly be seen as *application* of knowledge, knowledge represents a repository which then becomes taken up and applied to invent things and create new ways of doing things. A knowledge system on this basis is bound to be a vaguer and more nebulous system, it may include many elements which are redundant, forgotten, ignored or quite simply wrong. This notion of a knowledge system acting as the background to the foreground of an innovation system has parallels with Tassey's (1991) notion of a 'technology infrastructure'. Here Tassey envisages knowledge together with institutional frameworks as providing the basic infrastructure that acts as a resource and structuring form for technological innovation.

Secondly, education and learning will obviously be central to any knowledge system. However, Lundvall has noted the clear role that learning played in binding together production and innovation in a national system of innovation (Lundvall 1988, p. 362; Lundvall 1992, pp. 9–11) and the foundation that interactive learning provides for the competitive performance of an innovation system (Lundvall 1995, p. 39; Lundvall and Johnson 1994). Indeed much of what Lundvall lends to the role of learning in an innovation system is pertinent to a knowledge system, although more so.

Thus learning is important in Lundvall's conception of systems of innovation because, aside from it being viewed by him as being critically important in the innovation process, it is a key element in the *dynamic* of the system and is a key agent in *binding* the whole system together. Here Lundvall (1995, p. 40) notes 'many different sectors and segments of the economy contribute to the overall process of interactive learning and the specificity of the elements, as well as the linkages and modes of interaction between them, are crucial for the rate and direction of technical change'. Learning plays, therefore, a major role in the change and development of both innovation and more directly, knowledge systems, whilst forming the key element in its connectivity. In this framework learning takes place at all scales from the individual, through to the firm and organisation, on to the inter-firm and inter-organisational learning; institutional learning (Johnson 1992); cross-institutional learning and on through to the whole system, the 'learning economy'.

Thirdly, the notion of learning, however, leads to a more central concern about of how one conceives knowledge as one moves away from the individual to a more aggregate setting such as a system. Obviously in the context of learning and knowledge generation and sharing, the learning process involves a clear interactive and collective dimension. There are also inter-firm and more general institutional routines (Hodgson 1988) that can be set up through this interactive learning process. It is, however, much harder to ascribe collections of firms, organisations and institutions as having a single, clear cognitive process (involving both a decision-making and memory function) associated with the central foundation of what knowledge is (Howells 2000 forthcoming). Knowledge systems can be associated with 'learning frameworks' and parts of the system are involved in collective learning processes, but knowledge itself will reside with the individual. The authors feel that discussions about knowledge commodities and knowledge assets arise from a profound misconception about the notion of knowledge. Knowledge assets can be no more than organisational and social mechanisms for the creation, absorption, diffusion and protection of knowledge. They may, for example, result from a firm's investment in a team of workers capable of reading the code through which knowledge central to the firm's activity is codified (Cowan and Foray 1997).

Fourthly, it is useful to describe a knowledge system as *combining* the two elements of tacit and codified knowledge, although, it is argued here that it is inappropriate to describe the *separate* functioning of these two *aspects* of knowledge. It is presented here, therefore, that a knowledge system is more complex than a simple bipolar model of codified and tacit knowledge generation and transfer. As knowledge becomes more codified it becomes more like information, or quasi knowledge, and less like knowledge; however it still depends on a tacit element in its articulation, comprehension and sharing. Knowledge is also firmly rooted in the individual. Thus, as one moves further up the knowledge hierarchy (involving both geographical and socio-economic scales), knowledge radiates outward from the individual through to team/site groupings, to the whole organisation, inter-organisational, local and/sectoral, regional, national and international contexts. In doing so, it becomes more codified, more information-like, more transferable and more global in its reach but still requires interpretation at the individual level (Figure 15.1). Moving up the knowledge hierarchy, therefore, certain types of codified knowledge become essentially transmogrified into information which can then be readily transferred, but its interpretation, comprehension and absorption back into a knowledge state remains at the individual level, either as separate individuals or working through specific teams or specific local sites. Knowledge, as defined here, is then embedded within the individual and the social contexts in which individuals interact with one another.

In terms of defining a knowledge system, a distinction must be clearly drawn between individually centred knowledge and what is referred to here as quasi knowledge. A knowledge system, as defined here, consists of two sub-systems. One relates to individually centred knowledge, and can be referred to as the knowledge sub-system. Here knowledge circulates within and between individuals through social interaction. In this sub-system knowledge is shared and created in a social context, consequently the relevant institutional structures are socio-cultural (Table 15.1). Generally, this knowledge sub-system is specific to the location of the team or group within the firm. Increasingly, however, it is possible to identify such systems operating at various spatial scales. For example, R&D workers in a multinational firm may participate in a geographically dispersed team through frequent travel, enabling face-to-face contact with colleagues, together with the support of information and communication technology services, such as email and video conferencing (Howells 1995). In this instance, the knowledge sub-system is international in scope.

Figure 15.1 Knowledge: from the individual to the international context

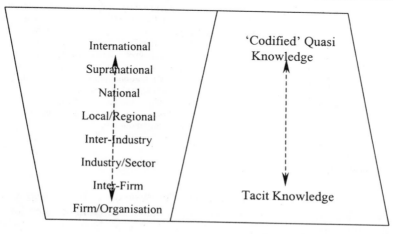

Table 15.1 Knowledge systems: institutional structure.

Institutional Factors	National *Examples:*	Supranational *Examples:*
Socio-cultural	Language; religion; levels of trust; degree of openness/insularity/toler-; ance behavioural norms	Degree of cross-cultural harmonisation; international communications through use of common language -- English.
Legal	Property rights; patent and copyright systems; employment legislation; immigration laws.	International law; international patent and copyright regulation; EU-wide employment regulations; international agreements GATT, GATS, IPR, TRIPS etc.
Political	Ideology; political structures; policy communities.	Dominant ideology – liberal democracy; the cross-border coordination of policy – OECD; IMF, World Bank, WTO, G7, EU, NAFTA, UN.
Economic environment	Level of current and prospective economic growth; business environment and industrial structure; factor endowments; mobility of factors of production.	International flows of capital, commodities, labour and information; global business environment – degree of stability and economic growth; sector structures – level of competition in international markets.
Policy measures	Competition and industrial policy; science and technology policy; trade and foreign direct investment policy; fiscal incentives: taxes and subsidies relating to innovation; educational policy.	Cross country, science and technology policies, and government-sponsored international research programmes; harmonisation of sector-wide regulation/standards – international telecommunications; education – harmonisation of syllabus content across countries and international exchange programmes for both academics and students.
Other	National trade associations; privately funded national research programmes; communication infrastructure; local, regional, national interest groups; industrial clusters and centres of excellence.	Multinational enterprises; international interest groups; joint ventures, international strategic alliances and other forms of collaborations between national and multinational firms; privately sponsored international student exchanges; international secondments within firms and international organisations; privately funded international research programmes; international private sector scientific organisations; international trade association; internationally mobile scientists and knowledge workers.

Source: Howells and Roberts (2000, p. 24).

The second sub-system within a knowledge system can be referred to as the quasi knowledge sub-system. Here knowledge is shared in codified form, and the full range of institutional factors are relevant from socio-cultural, legal, political, economic and so on viewpoint (Table 15.1). Although a distinction is being drawn here between knowledge and quasi knowledge sub-systems, they both have socio-cultural dimensions. The codification of knowledge may draw on social or cultural conventions, for example language or traditions. Moreover, as already noted, the assimilation of codified knowledge requires tacit knowledge and new tacit knowledge may arise not only from social interaction and learning, but also from the absorption and assimilation of codified knowledge. Importantly, then, the two sub-systems are inter-linked and, indeed, interdependent. However, whereas the knowledge sub-system depends on co-location and co-presence for the sharing of tacit knowledge, the quasi knowledge system is not restricted in this way. The sharing of quasi knowledge does not require co-location or co-presence between the transmitter and receiver. Consequently, when examining knowledge systems in an international context we might expect to find that the quasi knowledge sub-system has a dominant role whereas in the local context the knowledge sub-system is more significant.

A knowledge system is then clearly much broader than a system of innovation. The view of knowledge systems outlined here builds on the definition provided by Foray; in doing so, it provides a more detailed reflection of the complex institutional structures that influence the process of knowledge creation and transfer at various spatial scales. Nevertheless, it is recognised that the operationalisation of this framework would present difficulties. The value of this framework lies in its ability to complement the systems of innovation approach, providing an additional dimension for those studying innovation whether in a national or international context.

15.6 INTERNATIONAL KNOWLEDGE SYSTEMS

In today's highly internationalised world the creation of new knowledge and the innovations that transpire from such knowledge are influenced by many factors both within and beyond the boundaries of the nation. Indeed, new knowledge usually arises from the combination of existing knowledge, consequently the bringing together of knowledge from different global locations can prove to be a rich source of innovation. There are, therefore, good reasons for examining international knowledge systems.

However, before proceeding further, it is necessary to define an international knowledge system. As noted earlier, a knowledge system is broader and less well-defined than an innovation system. Moreover, a knowledge system represents an underlying knowledge and learning framework. The essential feature of an international knowledge system is that the entities from which it is formed either interact across national boundaries or in a purely supranational context (for example. EU research programmes). The various factors that make up a knowledge system at both a national and supranational level are identified in Table 15.1. For any specific international knowledge system the actual combination of relevant factors will vary depending on the nature of the knowledge being generated, transformed, transmitted or stored. It is important to note that the various elements that constitute the system can have both a positive and a negative impact on the development of knowledge. For example, regulation may stimulate or restrict knowledge creation. Equally, multinational enterprises (MNEs) may promote the development of new knowledge in competitive markets but stifle it in monopolistic markets where they may seek to prolong the economic life of obsolete knowledge.

Of central importance to any knowledge system is the interaction between the various elements, for it is these interactions that give rise to the system. As Foray (1997, p. 64) notes, it is the frequency of such interaction that determines the cohesiveness of a knowledge system. In the international context, it is possible to identify a number of channels facilitating interaction.

1. MNEs clearly have a significant role not only in the creation of new technology in an international environment but also as facilitators of international interactions of knowledge both within the boundaries of the firm and externally through trade in goods and services, and the sale of technology through licensing agreements.
2. International technical alliances give rise to knowledge interactions between firms from different countries, and between MNEs and national based firms.
3. There is international technology transfer including within the boundaries of the MNE and through the purchase of technology through licensing agreements between both MNEs and national-based firms and between national-based firms across borders.
4. There are knowledge interactions through the international trade of capital, intermediate and final goods.
5. International interactions of knowledge are embodied in labour, in particular managerial, and science and technology personnel, and are facilitated through cross border collaboration between researchers.
6. Knowledge interactions arise from joint international science projects, for example EU initiatives such as EUREKA.
7. Trade and foreign direct investment in services, such as technical and management consultancy services facilitate knowledge interactions.

8. Knowledge interaction occurs through a wide variety of social and cultural cross-border mechanisms. Given that the social and cultural characteristics of nations have been associated with their economic performance (Landes 1999; Fukuyama 1995), such mechanisms may well have an important role in the development and sustainability of international knowledge systems.

Indicators of international knowledge interactions are well advanced at a general level. They include data on the flows of technology payments, global diffusion of patents, trade in embodied technology and joint R&D consortia. According to the OECD (1997, p. 29) these indicators are increasing over time for all OECD countries, although at a different level and rate, indicating the growing significance of inputs of international knowledge to national knowledge systems. However, these indicators fail to capture all international knowledge transactions, they are more useful in terms of assessing knowledge interaction of relevance to systems of innovation. International interactions relevant to knowledge systems must include, in addition to the flows listed above, international labour mobility, cultural and social exchanges through the movement of individuals, whether permanent or temporary, and through media and ICT channels. Furthermore, knowledge diffused by international organisations such as the World Bank and the OECD, as well as non-governmental organisations, like Greenpeace, should also be included.

Knowledge-intensive business services have been identified as not only sources of new knowledge and innovation but also important facilitators of the transfer of knowledge both the regional and national contexts (Miles et al. 1995; Antonelli 1999). As earlier chapters indicate, the internationalisation of KIBS firms is well advanced (Chapters 8 and 11) and consequently they should be recognised as facilitators of the transfer of knowledge in an international context. KIBS act as an interface between 'quasi-generic' knowledge, extracted by means of repeated interactions with customers and the scientific community, and the tacit knowledge buried in the routines of firms (Antonellli 1999); consequently they perform an important functions enabling the international transfer of knowledge. Estimates of trade and FDI in the KIBS sector provide some indication of the growing level of international knowledge transfer enabled by these activities (Chapter 11).

Although it is clear that international knowledge interactions take a variety of forms, evidence and research into these interactions is limited. As noted in Chapter 11, the internationalisation of KIBS firms is connected to the development and spread of MNEs. Much research has been conducted into the role of the MNE in the context of innovation. This research can be usefully reviewed to gain an appreciation of the role of the MNE, which is regarded as a central actor in international knowledge systems (Cantwell 1995). In the late 1980s, for example, MNEs accounted for between 75 and 80 percent of the privately undertaken R&D in the world (Dunning 1993, p. 290). Although MNEs are active in international markets it is not necessarily the case that their knowledge-creating activity occurs in the same dispersed manner. Indeed, it is generally accepted that the globalisation of knowledge creation in the form of R&D activity is far from widespread (Archibugi and Michie 1995; Patel and Pavitt 1991; Pearce 1989). MNEs adopt a variety of strategies regarding the location of their R&D. These can be broadly grouped into either a centralised strategy where much of the R&D occurs in the MNE's home nation, or alternatively a decentralised strategy where R&D activity is dispersed between a number of nations. Literature on the internationalization of industrial research (Pearce and Singh 1992; Granstrand et al 1992) has suggested that innovation may be geographically dispersed within MNEs.

When MNEs adopt a centralised R&D strategy then clearly the knowledge system in its home nation will be of great significance. An international knowledge system will, however, have an impact on the innovatory activity of MNEs whether their R&D is centralised or not. Indeed, any firm that either supplies international markets, or draws resources from the international environment, may be influenced by institutions that constitute the international knowledge systems. For those MNEs that adopt a decentralised R&D strategy a number of different national knowledge systems may be of relevance and the international knowledge system may have an even more significance influence.

Of central interest to the development and operation of international knowledge systems are those MNEs that undertake R&D in a geographically dispersed manner. In many sectors the knowledge-creating process is highly internationalised. R&D teams are drawn from across the globe, perhaps working in one geographical location or alternatively, with the support of ICTs and cross-border travel, in a spatially dispersed network (Howells 1990, 1995; Boutellier et al. 1998; Roberts 2000). In such a way, MNEs develop intra-firm networks between established centres of excellence. These are complementary to external inter-firm networks, which facilitate the exchange of knowledge and occasional cooperation in learning through joint ventures. Cantwell (1995, p. 157) argues that it is in this way that technology leaders are involved in the globalisation of technology. Furthermore, MNEs outsource some R&D services to local suppliers (Chapter 13), in this way they tap into a variety of knowledge systems and acquire knowledge embedded in a diverse range of local environments.

The MNE clearly has a significant and multi-dimensional role within international knowledge systems. Knowledge is, however, shared at an international level through a variety of other institutional and organisational arrangements. To gain a full appreciation of international knowledge systems research must reach beyond the MNE to an examination of the role of other facilitators of knowledge creation and dissemination operating at an international level. Having broadly defined international knowledge systems it is now possible to explore the manner in which they interact with national, regional, local and sector-specific knowledge systems.

15.7 KNOWLEDGE SYSTEMS IN THE GLOBAL SERVICE ECONOMY

The purpose of this section is to formalise the complex web of interaction that arises from the actions of the various elements that make up an international knowledge system. Two approaches for conceptualising these interactions are outlined and compared, first the hierarchical structure and secondly the network or heterarchy structure. The hierarchical form of international knowledge system is represented in Figure 15.2(a). In this structure international actors can be viewed as determining the international knowledge system, which has an impact upon national actors and the national knowledge systems, which in turn influences regional actors and the regional knowledge systems and so on. The flow of influence is largely unidirectional. For specific knowledge-creating activity, certain elements within the hierarchy may prove to be more influential. A high level of interaction may be identified between such elements; this can be referred to as a process of 'nesting' since a sub-structure is developed within the overall hierarchical structure in order to nurture a particular knowledge activity.

The hierarchical structure may capture the essential structure of certain knowledge systems. Knowledge creation at a national level may indeed include actors that are international in scope. For example, the establishment of international regulatory bodies, such as the International Telecommunications Union (ITU) and on a pan-national level the European Medicines Evaluation Agency (EMEA), may have a significant role in the knowledge system within the telecommunications, pharmaceuticals and related sectors at both a national, regional and local level. Furthermore, MNEs with market power at an international level may also influence knowledge creation at lower spatial scales through the establishment of technical standards. For example, in the computer manufacturing and services sector IBM had such an impact from the 1960s through to the 1980s,

Figure 15.2 International knowledge systems.

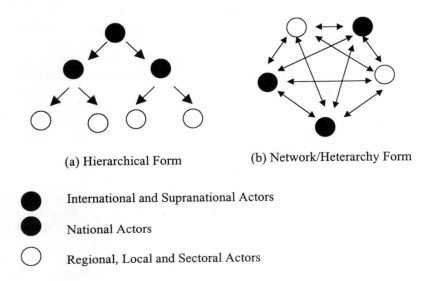

     (a) Hierarchical Form   (b) Network/Heterarchy Form

●   International and Supranational Actors

●   National Actors

○   Regional, Local and Sectoral Actors

and in the 1990s Microsoft had a central role influencing software development.

In a hierarchical international knowledge system global KIBS firms may be seen as facilitating the flow of knowledge down the hierarchy. Traditional professional KIBS may be of particular significance in such structures. For example, the global accountancy firms, like PricewaterhouseCoopers and Ernst and Young, play an important role disseminating knowledge about international and national accounting regulatory systems to their clients whether these are internationally active or nationally-based companies. Knowledge may, to a lesser extent, flow up the hierarchy structure as a result of the activities of KIBS firms, for example when they engage in lobbying national and international policy making organisations on behalf of their clients. Similarly, advertising firms play an important role transferring region- and nation-specific cultural and social knowledge to their clients. They may also, through advertising campaigns, shape cultural and social knowledge on behalf of their clients. Global KIBS firms, in a sense, provided bridges connecting different national and regional knowledge systems. KIBS may be important actors in the development of nests of activity within the hierarchical system. They can in a sense be seen as providing bridges between different national and regional knowledge systems. Global KIBS firms are particularly important in this respect, since they can provide this role for both national and multinational firms. National firms can access a wide international pool of knowledge through their links with global KIBS firms. Similarly, national-based KIBS firms enable MNEs to tap into national and regional knowledge systems that are not serviced by global KIBS firms, perhaps because they are newly emerging or simply not profitable for the attention of large KIBS firms. Indeed, global KIBS firms themselves may employ smaller KIBS firms in order to gain access to locationally specific knowledge.

The network or heterarchy structure is illustrated in Figure 15.2(b). In this structure various knowledge systems interact in their influence on the knowledge-creating, transmitting, transforming and storing process. The links between the various actors depend upon the environment in which the knowledge activity is occurring, that is, whether local, regional, national, or sector-specific. The various groups of actors overlap and interact in their influence on the knowledge-creating process. In this framework the influence of interactions is multi-directional. Certain groups of actors may dominate for periods, for example, national actors may be of most significance in the initial development of new knowledge, however, within this structure it is recognised that this dominant position is temporary. The influence of certain elements within the system clusters at specific spatial and temporal points. The network structure is highly dynamic. Consequently, KIBS, and especially new technology-based KIBS, are likely to have a particularly important role in this type of international knowledge system. They will engage in highly interactive activity enabling the flow of knowledge between various points within the network.

The characteristics of the system or the way in which it functions will depend on the nature of the knowledge created, the speed of its evolution, and the extent to which it can be internationally communicated and dispersed. For instance, in the high-technology sectors, products are developed rapidly and quickly become obsolete. In such sectors, knowledge is highly dynamic and interaction will occur through formal network structures, such as international strategic alliances and consortia, or informal network structures, for example arising from the social activities of personnel. Rapidly evolving knowledge may remain tacit becoming obsolete before it is codified. Consequently, informal networks are particularly important facilitators of knowledge transfer in high-technology sectors. Indeed, informal, uncodified information flows are seen as being important even on an international scale, allowing the multilateral exchange of information to reach into areas and sources of information well beyond the formal systems of the organisation

(Macdonald 1996, p. 224). The difficulty for many international corporations, however, is how to harness and make use of these informal information networks. The significance of international innovation networks is increasing as they expand the types of knowledge exchanged and the methods of transfer (Guinet 1997, p. 174).

In sectors with slower levels of technological change international knowledge interactions are more likely to occur within hierarchical structures. Indeed, because sectors may include a wide range of activities, some of which are more dynamic than others, it may be possible to identify relevant hierarchical and network-structured knowledge systems of relevance to a sector's knowledge activity.

15.8 CONCLUSION

This chapter has examined knowledge systems in a global service economy. Building on literature concerning systems of innovation, knowledge systems have been defined in both a national and international context. It is argued here that knowledge systems are a broader, more nebulous, concept than systems of innovation. Consequently, in their consideration it is necessary to look beyond those factors usually associated with systems of innovation. Knowledge is highly complex and cannot be separated from the individual, hence knowledge systems must give particular attention to the mechanisms through which knowledge is transferred and especially through the process of learning. More generally, though, a knowledge system includes a variety of organisational and institutional factors. Since it is argued here that knowledge is fundamentally individual centred the social context and relations are of great significance in the creation and dissemination of knowledge. A major research challenge concerns the exploration and analysis of the individual and social relations in an international context. Here interactions are complicated by the diversity in cultural and social norms between countries and regions.

This chapter presents an initial attempt to analyse knowledge systems in an international context. The frameworks developed here provide tools that can assist policy makers in their efforts to analyse knowledge systems. The chapter has highlighted the role of KIBS in the international transfer of knowledge; however, clearly further research is required to build upon the conceptual framework presented here, and empirical research is necessary to verify the analysis. Moreover, efforts to identify, measure and assess a wider range of knowledge interactions, as well as the barriers to such interactions, at a national and international level are required.

16 Understanding the New Service Economy

Jeremy Howells

16.1 OVERVIEW

Services are now 'coming of age' in terms of the economic and technological landscape (Alic 1994; Amable and Palombarini 1998). No longer can services be simply regarded as 'passive' consumers of technology and who merely 'serve' the important sectors of the economy, notably manufacturing, and individuals and households. This book has attempted to show how services, notably KIBS and private sector services, hold an increasingly dynamic and pivotal role in 'new' knowledge-based economies (Miles 1993; OECD 1996c; Chapter 2). This is not to say that services still suffer from, and are bound by, many historical and institutional legacies which still shape and, more particularly, constrain their development (Petit 1986). One such is the intellectual property system which remains much less well-defined in relation to protecting service-based innovations (Chapter 14). Related to this is the problem of how financiers value service activities and the assets associated with them which are based on more ephemeral competences surrounding knowledge and information. This was often said to make raising money for service enterprises and activities much harder in such areas as multimedia and the Internet (Chapters 5 and 6). While the 'new economy' boom at the turn of the millennium saw a stampede of capital into (often dubious) ecommerce ventures, the debate about their valuation was a very lively one.

Academics, industrialists and policy makers have been slow to realise and accept the way services have changed over the last few decades. Perceptions have been bound by old ways of thinking. Even those academics and policy makers who have realised that services do have a policy role still tend to view them as providing a supporting, infrastructural role, 'serving' the rest of the economy. This is not to deny that many knowledge-intensive services do not play a significant role as facilitators, mediators and repositories in the knowledge-based economy (see below). However, the role of Internet and web-based services and the growth in high technology environmental services (Chapters 5 and 6) indicate that certain types of KIBS industries are now taking a more proactive, lead role in the economy. The business service firms that have gained the highest profile have been associated more strongly with ICTs, and being related to new forms of transaction based on ecommerce and the Internet. These new ICT-mediated KIBS firms are becoming the new drivers in industry, even though their real value has in some instances become over-inflated. This was reflected in the stockmarket ratings of Amazon.com in the US and Freeserve and Lastminute.com in the UK. The service sector has therefore changed through the emergence of new types of entrants into the sector. These firms are doing original, innovative and sometimes unique activities, things which in many cases would not have been possible twenty or even ten years ago.

However, the service sector is changing for other reasons. This may be summed up crudely as the 'tertiarisation' of the manufacturing industry. Manufacturing firms are providing more service products. This has been seen for some time now in the computer industry where computer manufacturing firms, such as IBM and ICL, have derived an increasing proportion of their turnover from service and software activities. It is, however, also evident in other industries such as car manufacturers, for example, Ford, who have moved into finance (Ford Finance) and maintenance and spare activities (recently buying Kwikfit for some £1 billion) all closely associated with selling the manufactured product, the car, but following more deeply what consumers want in terms of support for the actual process of buying and running a car.

This is also evident in the aerospace industry with plan makers offering finance and leasing arrangements. Aero engine manufacturers not only provide finance (as well as operate major maintenance operations), General Electric (GE) has a major finance and leasing company (GE Finance), but is now providing engines not as a product (an engine) but as a service (hours of flight). This aspect of the 'servicisation' phenomenon may be termed service 'encapsulation' of manufacturing products. Thus manufactured products are not offered to consumers in their own right, but via one of two methods:

- The first is through offering the manufactured product with closely aligned service products in a single package. Thus in the case of the motor car with finance, insurance, maintenance warranties and tax all rolled into on purchased item.

- The second way is perhaps more sophisticated, in that it seeks to offer the consumer not the manufactured product itself, but rather what the purchase of the manufactured product would be seeking to ultimately fulfil. The example of the aero engine being substituted for hours of flight is a case in point. Another is the example from the computer industry of offering computer services to meet certain tasks rather than supplying the computer machines which are used in providing such a service. Demand in this sense is being satisfied at a higher, less immediate level, but in a way is more effective because it is going more directly to 'the heart of the matter' 'reaching the parts' which other competitors cannot reach so effectively.

Of course, both these encapsulation processes are being combined so that the firm in question can provide ever more complete 'solutions' to the consumer. This picks up the wider issue of outsourcing and externalisation in industry (Chapter 13). However, this process redraws the concept of what consumption is about for firms selling such products and services. Thus, in the case of the car, consumption has moved from the simple, one-off purchase of the car to the wider ongoing process of buying, using and maintaining a car over the long term. This shift in focus has major ramifications for firms selling such products and services and the 'act' of consumption in terms of how they address the needs of the consumer and satisfy the accompanying demand.

The 'reach' of the service sector is also expanding. Traditionally services were seen as being parochial and local in nature. They did not travel well. They were difficult to trade and export as for many services production had to be co-located with their consumption. To overcome this, service firms had to set up overseas operations before they could serve foreign markets, which meant much higher entry barriers for service firms when they wanted to supply overseas markets. Services therefore lagged behind in moving abroad (Chapter 11). When they did go overseas it was often in the familiar role of supporting more dynamic manufacturing firms. Manufacturing led where services followed. However, service trade has grown and service-led FDI has expanded rapidly. Services are now globalising and are no longer so strongly tied to the expansion of manufacturing activities. This is not to deny that cultural, linguistic and regulatory barriers are in many cases much higher for services and this means that to be effective internationally often requires a strong local dimension.

The global expansion of services and service firms, however, has a second important underlying feature to it. As service activity has expanded internationally it has led to the more widespread and rapid diffusion of service innovations. Service providers have become more international whilst in addition service markets have become more international in orientation. Service markets are no longer tied to their local or national roots, service consumers have become more open to international and standardised service products. Early international service products, such as airline travel, have long been similar worldwide almost from the outset because of the nature of their business. However, other services like banking are changing rapidly. Banking, even in a highly sophisticated market such as Britain, was a highly regionalised system even in the late nineteenth century and was dominated by regional banks such as the Midland Bank or the Linen Bank (Northern Ireland) or the Royal Bank of Scotland. By contrast, today, Internet banking is being offered virtually instantaneously by banks in many markets simultaneously.

Nonetheless, it should be recognised that the 'reach' and diffusion of many services, particularly more sophisticated services, remains partial. Developing countries, until recently, have remained largely outside many of the changes that have been described in this book. Developing countries remain largely information and knowledge poor (United Nations Development Programme 1999), although a number of less-developed countries, notably India, have undergone rapid growth in certain KIBS-based activities, such as computer and software services (Chapter 8). The information and knowledge rich remain concentrated in a number of major pockets scattered across the advanced, industrialised economies of the world. The global development of knowledge-based services remains highly uneven. With knowledge and information comes power and control which unfortunatley the scope of this book has not been able to explore in depth. However, one dimension of this is the corporate concentration of both the generators and repositories of knowledge and the conduits of this knowledge. The merger of AOL and TimeWarner in 2000 is just one example of this. In this wider sphere, all too often the process of innovation can be seen in a technocratic way, with wider economic and social issues 'bleached' out of the discussion or simply ignored. Many of the case studies and analyses in this book have highlighted the often subtle ways in which the growth and development of many service innovations have been influenced and shaped by these wider social conditions.

16.2 UNDERSTANDING THE NEW SERVICE ECONOMY

16.2.1 Understanding Services

This book has sought to elicit some of the current changes that are occurring within the services and knowledge economy, but it has also sought to show that services remain a neglected phenomenon of research in terms of their economic and technological impact. This neglect is evident in whole series of ways, but is particularly acute in terms of the simple lack of data available on the service sector, particularly that collected and supplied by government agencies. This inadequacy of data has a further 'knock on' effect in relation to hampering further research on services and the knowledge economy. Can increasingly knowledge- and service-based economies of the twenty-first century afford to have their key government policies and commercial strategies based on such ignorance? However, academics cannot wholly excuse themselves from blame, they have continued to accept the situation and have not stressed why policy makers within government should be more flexible and concerned about capturing changes in newer parts of the economy and society.

However, what implications and opportunities will emerging trends and changes in knowledge and the service economy have for research in this area? Perhaps the most obvious is the continued spread and intensification of services and knowledge activity within the economy overall. Within this overall pattern will be the increased technological and knowledge sophistication of a key subset of services, KIBS (Chapter 2). Some of the background to these types of services has been highlighted in the book but their size, nature and characteristics still remain clouded. This is in part a reflection of their highly dynamic quality in terms of growth and change. It is also associated with their increasing technological intensity as evident in their R&D expenditure and patenting activity. It also links in with the potentially more proactive nature of service companies in the innovation process and the lead role they now take in certain areas of technological endeavour (Chapter 10; however see below).

16.2.2 Understanding Services Innovation

This leads on to a related issue of service innovations and innovations in services. Work on services innovation still remains weak in capturing what service innovation is about. This centres on how it differs from a more artefact-based conceptualisation of innovation within manufacturing.

Conceptualisation of technological change within services is weak in its attempts at identifying new forms of innovative activity and the processes that are emerging within the services that underpin them.   In part this goes back to data problems with the existing innovation indicators researchers have in this field, but it also relates to the lack of development in generating genuinely new innovation indicators which can more adequately capture and reflect innovation within service activities. This in turn is a reflection of our still poorly articulated conceptualisation of the innovation process within a more service-oriented regime.

There is a whole strand of work that needs to be undertaken on the role of services, not as potential leaders in the innovation process, as noted above, but as intelligent and knowledgeable facilitators and supporters within the technological and industrial process. With outsourcing service companies are taking over more parts of the industrial process that manufacturing companies did themselves. This is not a new phenomenon, but its spread and reach has widened and the nature of activities involved has expanded. Outsourcing is no longer about more routine activities such as catering and cleaning, it has moved on to include IT activities, and more recently into what were considered strategic and core areas such as R&D and human resource management (Chapter 13).   The nature of the outsourcing process has tended to be described as an 'all or nothing' process. What might be described as 'complete' outsourcing does occur (although staff are still required to manage the contract and be intelligent customers), but service companies are increasingly moving into partnership with manufacturing companies (and indeed other service firms). Key functions still remain with the client company but the service company acts in partnership with the manufacturing firm, often sharing savings and profits associated with the 'outsourcing' scheme.   In this way service companies have become close partners and facilitators to help other firms achieve their strategic objectives based on their core competences. This increased focus on service companies as 'facilitators' and partners is moving away from the previous notion of service companies as 'servants'. However, much of the shift in relationship between service companies and their clients has not been fully recorded or conceptualised.

16.2.3   Understanding Services Interactions

The role of ICTs has had a major impact on all aspects of the economy and the service sector is no exception.   There are three aspects where future trends will undoubtedly impinge on how the service sector is shaped in the future, although the outcome of these trends is difficult to determine.   These factors can be examined under three main headings: the issue of 'disintermediation' associated with ecommerce and the Internet; services and 'virtualisation'; and services and the embodied. In relation to 'disintermediation' although service companies may becoming more prominent as facilitators, their role as intermediaries in some form of activities may be declining. With the rise of the ecommerce and the Internet, manufacturing firms now have the opportunity of dealing with their customers more directly, cutting out 'middlemen'. These 'middlemen' include not only retailers, but also sales agents, wholesalers, market research and marketing operators. Rather than shrinking through outsourcing, manufacturing may actually be handling and taking back certain areas of their activity. By interacting electronically with their customers, or rather their customers being able to interact with them, firms can gain more intelligence about their customers in terms of what they want, what their concerns are, and in handling their 'post-purchase' requirements.

In relation to 'virtualisation' the key issue for service companies centres on how much physical presence is required to sell and do things. The issue of online shopping is the most obvious here and how this will affect retailing in terms of the need for shops. However, this process is also affecting other major areas such as banking, insurance and other financial activities. This in turn involves the debate over location and co-location and geographical space. How far do services need to be co-located with consumption? For certain service activities the two go together, for others, such as air travel, like buying insurance, they do not. If these issues to do with consumption and selling are tied up with aspects associated with what might be termed 'front' office and shop aspects, there are also considerable changes in the 'back' part of offices and operations. 'Behind the scenes' service companies are realising they are now much more footloose in where they locate certain activities, whether it be data entry, telesales, technical support, internet activities or more general administrative activities. This has considerable implications about service location, the employment implications for service growth and in terms of the international expansion of service activities to low-cost or resource attractive (increasingly based on knowledge) sites abroad. Nevertheless physical presence via face-to-face contact will still remain important in many aspects of knowledge sharing, generation and 'co-use' (Howells 1996). The establishment of trust and indeed friendship (Roberts 2000) via face-to-face meetings will provide important platforms from which subsequent work can be done by more virtual forms of working (Howells 1995). Socialised forms of bonding will therefore remain central in setting up subsequent forms of more virtually-based interaction.

Moreover, whatever disintermediation and virtualisation does occur, will not entail that all physical activities associated with services will disappear. Many will expand. Wholesalers may come under increasing pressure, but transport distribution and logistic operators will expand to handle people and firms purchasing over the Internet and encouraged by the rise of ecommerce. Logistic firms will also benefit from the trend towards outsourcing by companies. All these types of transport and logistic support activities will continue to grow strongly. Thus although routes and activities towards service consumption may become more virtual and involve disintermediation, actual consumption of many services will have to remain physical in form.

16.2.4   Understanding Public Services

Much of the above discussion has been in terms of private sector services. How will such changes affect public and not-for-profit service sectors? The implicit, if not explicit, assumption here is that the public sector will lag behind many of these developments in terms of adoption or implementation, or will go private. Is this necessarily the case? Are there activities within the public sector which are innovative or leading the private sector in terms of service generation or delivery? Public sector services perhaps remain the darkest corner in terms of research about service innovations and the knowledge economy. Consider hospitals; although there is a huge range of important work on healthcare administration and organisation, the role of hospitals as centres of innovation or knowledge activity remain largely ignored. Perhaps that is a reflection of our concentration on technological innovation being directly tied up with the private sector and wealth creation, rather than being a wider social and economic process that cannot always be measured and evaluated in terms of direct sales or profits growth. In relation to the 'not-for-profit' areas of the economy, the relative neglect of this area should not undervalue its actual and potential worth. The growth of many Web and Internet-based communities have been established through the mutual belief in more philanthropic sharing and development of knowledge, evident in the rise of the 'gift' economy over the Web. Similarly in computer services and software, the rise of Linux and the availability of free software has established a true commonwealth of interests that has managed to grow and develop outside the more commercial environs of the software industry.

16.2.5   Understanding Services Organisation

This last discussion introduces the final main issue raised here that; of new forms of service organisation and delivery as new forms of disembodied innovations. Although disembodied innovations have longed been hailed as being important, research has not progressed much further in this area. Again the rise of the Internet and intranets will have a big impact here and this represents a unique time from which to start a base line from map and measure these potentially fundamental, paradigm-shifting changes in the service economy.

We have focused on fairly specific areas of research into services and the knowledge economy. However, there remains much to be done in basic underlying conceptual work on services, knowledge and innovation. Fundamental questions remain. What are services? Will our definition change in the future? Chapter 1 indicates that our definition and conceptualisation has changed in the past and undoubtedly our view will indeed change over the time. Other questions centre on how the trade-off between bespoke and standardised services will change over time. As some service markets break out of geographical restrictions and market delimitation, opportunities for more specialised services to be offered on a global basis will arise. These specialised services, which formerly were uneconomic to cater for when the geographical range of the market was smaller, can now be provided economically. Other services will become standardised and become more homogenous on an international basis, but this will allow for much cheaper service provision. There is also the issue of service jobs and their changing nature over time. The issue of service productivity improvements and automation has been much discussed and heralded since the mid 1970s; will this at last now properly take off within the service sector?

Lastly, but more fundamental still, is how far an identifiable service sector will still exist in the future? In part, this is a reflection of its continued growth within the economy as a whole, as more parts of the economy come under a service heading, paradoxically leading to whether the word or tag 'service' still needs to be added to discussions about the economy or industry. Identifying a distinct 'service' activity has always been difficult, but it seems to be becoming ever harder as the economy itself changes and becomes more knowledge- and service- intensive. Where does a 'manufacturing' activity end and a 'service' one begin? As services take on a more facilitating and partnership role with other parts of the economy, this blurring will potentially become more pronounced. The 'success' of services may actually lead to the decline of the term 'services' as a descriptor for economic and social analysis, as all activities take on a more 'service-like' function. The service economy will, in this sense, constitute the whole economy.

References

Accountant, The (1989), June, Lafferty Publications Limited.

Aharoni, Yair (ed.) (1993), *Coalitions and Competition: The Globalization of Professional Business Services*, London: Routledge.

Aharoni, Yair (1966), *The Foreign Investment Decision Process*, Boston, Mass.: Harvard University Press.

Ajila, S. (1995), 'Software maintenance', *Software-Practice and Experience*, **25**, 1155–81.

Alic, J. (1994), 'Technology in the service industries', *International Journal of Technology Management*, **9**, 1–14.

Alic, J. (1997), 'Knowledge, skill, and education in the new global economy', *Futures*, **29** (1), 5–16.

Alic, J. A., J. R. Miller and J. A. Hart (1991), 'Computer software: strategic industry', *Technology Analysis and Strategic Management*, **3**, 177–190.

Allen, T. J. (1977), *Managing the Flow of Technology: Technology Transfer and the Dissemination of Technological Innovation within the R&D Organization*, Cambridge, Mass.: MIT Press.

Allen, T. J. and S. D. Cohen (1969) 'Information flows in R&D labs' *Administrative Science Quarterly*, **20**, 12–19.

Altinkemer, K., A. Chaturvedi, and R. Gulati (1994), 'Information systems outsourcing: issues and evidence', *International Journal of Information Management*, **14** (4), 252–268.

Amable, B. and S. Palombarini (1998), 'Technical change and incorporated R&D in the services sector', *Research Policy*, **27**, 655–675.

Andersen, B. (1998), 'The evolution of technological trajectories: 1890-1990', *Structural Change and Economic Dynamics*, **9** (1), 5–35.

Andersen, Birgitte (2001, forthcoming) *Technological Change and The Evolution of Corporate Innovation: The Structure of Patenting* Cheltenham, UK and Brookfield, US: Edward Elgar.

Andersen, Birgitte, Zeljka Kozul and Richard Kozul-Wright (2000) Copyrights, Competition and Development: The Case of the Music Industry. *UNCTAD Discussion Paper* **145**, Geneva: UNCTAD.

Andersen, B. and I. Miles (1999), 'Orchestrating intangibles in the music sector: the Royalty Collecting Societies in the Knowledge Based Economy', CRIC-MIT Workshop on *Services and Manufacturing: How do they Differ?* Sloan School of Management, MIT, Manchester: mimeo, ESRC Centre for Research in Innovation and Competition, University of Manchester and UMIST.

Andersen, Esben S. and Bengt-Åke Lundvall (1997), 'National Innovation Systems and the dynamics of the division of labor', in Charles Edquist (ed.), *Systems of Innovation: Technologies, Institutions and Organizations*, London: Pinter, pp 242–65.

Andersen, B, Kozul, Z, and Kozul-Wright, R: 'Copyrights, competition and development: The case of the music industry ', *United Nations Discussion Paper Series,* (143)

Andriole, S. J. and P. A. Freeman (1993), 'Software systems engineering: the case for a new discipline', *Software Engineering Journal,* **10** (3), 165-179.

Antonelli, Cristiano (1999), *The Microdynamics of Technological Change*, London and New York: Routledge.

Antonelli, C. (2000, forthcoming), 'Localized technological change, new information technology and the knowledge-based economy: the European evidence', in Ian Miles and Mark Boden (eds), *Services and the Knowledge Economy*, London: Cassell.

Archibugi, D. (1992), 'Patenting as an indicator of technological innovation: a review', *Science and Public Policy,* **19** (6), 357–68.

Archibugi, Daniele and Jonathan Michie (1995), 'The globalisation of technology: a new taxonomy', *Cambridge Journal of Economics,* **19**, 155–174.

Archibugi, Daniele and Jonathan Michie (1999), 'Technological globalisation and national systems of innovation' in Daniele Archibugi and Jonathan Michie (eds.), *Technology, Globalisation and Economic Performance,* Cambridge: Cambridge University Press, pp. 1-23.

Archibugi, Daniele and Mario Pianta (1992), *The Technological Specialization of Advanced Countries*, Dordrecht: Kluwer.

Arora, A. and A. Gambardella (1990), 'Complimentarity and external linkages: the strategies of the large firms in biotechnology', *Journal of Industrial Economics,* **38**, 361–79.

Arrow, Kenneth (1962), 'Economic welfare and the allocation of resources for inventions', in National Bureau of Economic Research (ed.), *The Rate and Direction of Inventive Activity: Economic and Social Factors,* Princeton, NJ: Princeton University Press, pp. 609–627.

Arthur, B. (1989), 'Competing technologies, increasing returns, and lock-in by historical events', *The Economic Journal,* **99**, 116–31.

Ayres, R. (1988), 'Barriers and breakthroughs: an expanding frontiers' model of technology–industry life cycles', *Technovation,* **7**, 87–115.

Baark, E. (1999) 'Engineering consultancy: an assessment of IT-enabled international delivery of services', *Technology Analysis and Strategic Management*, 11, 55–74.

Baba, Y., S. Takai and Y. Mizuta (1995), 'The Japanese software industry: the "hub structure" approach', *Research Policy, 24*, 473–86.

Bagchi-Sen, S. and J. Sen (1997), 'The current state of knowledge in international business in producer services', *Environment and Planning A*, 29, 1153–74.

Bainbridge, David I. (1996), *Intellectual Property,* London: Third Edition, Pitman.

Balasubramanyam, V. N. and A. Balasubramanyam (1997), 'International trade in services: the case of India's computer software', *The World Economy, 20*, 829–43.

Baldwin, J. R., G. Gellatly, J. Johnson and V. Peters (1998), *Innovation in Dynamic Service Industries* Ottawa: Statistics Canada.

Barnett, Correlli (1986), *The Audit of War,* London: Macmillan.

Barras, R. (1986), 'Towards a theory of innovation in services', *Research Policy*, 15, 161–173.

Barras, R. (1990), 'Interactive innovation in financial and business services: the vanguard of the Service Revolution', *Research Policy*, 19, 215–237.

Bell, Daniel (1974), *The Coming of Post-Industrial Society*, London: Heinemann.

Bergen, S. A. (1990), *R&D Management: Managing Projects and New Products*, Oxford: Basil Blackwell

Bessant, J. and H. Rush (1995), 'Building bridges for innovation: the role of consultants in technology transfer', *Research Policy*, 24, 97–114.

Bilderbeek, R., P. den Hertog, W. Huntink, M. Bouman, N. Kastrinos and K. Flanagan (1994), *Case Studies in Innovative and Knowledge-Intensive Business Services*, Apeldoorn: TNO Report STB/94/041, TNO Centre for Technology and Policy Studies.

Blackler, F. (1995), 'Knowledge, knowledge work and organizations: an overview and interpretation', *Organization Studies*, 16, 1021–46.

Blalock, H. M. and A. Blalock (1959), 'Toward a clarification of system analysis in the social sciences', *Philosophy of Science, 26*, 84-92.

Boddewyn, J. J., M. Baldwin Halbrich, and A. C. Perry (1986), 'Service multinationals: conceptualization, measurement and theory', *Journal of International Business Studies*, 17, (3), 41-57.

Boisot, Max H. (1998), *Knowledge Assets: Securing Competitive Advantage in the Information Economy*, Oxford: Oxford University Press.

Bolisani, E., E. Scarso, I. Miles and M. Boden (1999), 'Electronic commerce implementation: a knowledge-based analysis', *International Journal of Electronic Commerce*, 3 (3), 53–69.

Boulding, Kenneth E. (1985), *The World as a Total System,* Beverly Hills, CA: Sage.

Boutellier, R., O. Gassmann, H. Macho and M. Roux (1998), Management of dispersed product development teams: the role of information technologies, *R&D Management,* **28** (1), 13–25.

Bowen, J. and V. Stavridou (1993), 'Safety-critical systems, formal methods and standards', *Software Engineering Journal,* **8** (4), 189–209.

Bragg, Steven M. (1998), *Outsourcing,* New York: John Wiley & Sons.

Braunstein, Y. M. (1989), 'Economics of intellectual property rights in the international arena', *Journal of the American Society for Information Science,* **40** (1), 12–16.

Breschi, Stefano and Franco Malerba (1997), 'Sectoral innovation systems: technological regimes, Schumpeterian dynamics, and spatial boundaries', in Charles Edquist (ed.), *Systems of Innovation: Technologies, Institutions and Organizations,* London: Pinter, pp. 130–56.

Broadman, H. G., (1994), 'GATS: The Uruguay Round Accord on International Trade and Investment in Services', *World Economy,* **17**, 281–92.

Brockhoff, K. (1992), 'R&D cooperation between firms – a perceived transaction cost perspective', *Management Science,* **38**, 514-24.

Brooks, F. P. (1987), 'No silver bullet: essence and accidents of software engineering', *IEEE Computer,* **20**, 5-17.

Brouwer, E. and A. Kleinecht (1995), 'An innovation survey in services; the experience with the CIS questionnaire in the Netherlands', *STI Review,* **16**, 141–48.

Bryson, J., D. Keeble, and P. Wood (1993), 'The creation, location and growth of small business service firms in the United Kingdom', *The Service Industries Journal,* **13** (2), 118–31.

Buck-Lew, M. (1992), 'To outsource or not?', *International Journal of Information Management,* **12** (2), 3-20.

Buckley, P. J. and M. Chapman (1997), 'The perception and measurement of transaction costs', *Cambridge Journal of Economics,* **21**, 127-45.

Buckley, Peter J. and Mark C. Casson (1976), *The Future of the Multinational Enterprise,* London: Macmillan.

Butchart, R. (1987), 'A new definition of high technology industries', *Economic Review,* **400**, 82–8.

Byatt, Ian C. R. (1979), *The British Electrical Industry, 1875–1914,* Oxford: Oxford University Press.

Cameron, Hugh (1997), *International Collaborative R&D and Intellectual Property Rights,* Paris: Report to the Directorate of Science, Technology and Industry, OECD.

Campaign (1989), 24. February, Haymarket Publications.

Cantwell, J. (1995), 'The globalisation of technology: what remains of the product cycle model?', *Cambridge Journal of Economics,* **19**, 155–174.

Caravcostas, Paraskevas and Luc Soete (1997), 'The building of cross-border institutions in Europe: towards a European System of Innovation?', in

Charles Edquist (ed.), *Systems of Innovation: Technologies, Institutions and Organizations*, London: Pinter, pp. 395–419.

Carey, J. (1994), 'Inching towards a borderless patent', *Business Week*, **3373–703**, 31.

Carlsson, B. and R. Stankiewicz (1991), 'On the nature, function and composition of technological systems', *Journal of Evolutionary Economics*, **1** (2), 93–118.

Carlsson, Bo (1995a), 'The technological system for factory automation: an international comparison', in Bo Carlsson (ed.), *Technological Systems and Economic Performance: The Case of Factory Automation*, Dordrecht: Kluwer, pp. 441–75.

Carlsson, Bo (ed.) (1995b). *Technological Systems and Economic Performance: The Case of Factory Automation*, Dordrecht: Kluwer.

Castells, Manuel (1996), *The Information Age: Economy, Society and Culture Volume I: The Rise of the Network Society*, Oxford: Blackwell Publishers.

Chandler, Alfred (1977), *The Visible Hand*, Cambridge, Mass.: Harvard University Press.

Charles, David and Jeremy Howells (1992), *Technology Transfer in Europe: Public and Private Networks*, London: Belhaven Press.

Chen, S–H. (1997), 'Decision-making in research and development collaboration', *Research Policy*, **26**, 121-35.

Chesbrough, H. and D. J. Teece (1996), 'When is virtual virtuous?', *Harvard Business Review*, (Jan–Feb.), 65–73.

Cheung, Steven N. S. (1986), 'Property rights and invention', in John Palmer (ed.), *Research in Law and Economics: The Economics of Patents and Copyrights*, **8**, pp. 5–18.

Chiesa, V. and R. Manzini (1997), 'Managing virtual R&D organizations: lessons from the pharmaceutical industry', *International Journal of Technology Management*, **13**, 471–85.

Clark, Colin (1957), *The Conditions of Economic Progress*, London: Macmillan.

Clark, James B. (1907), *Essentials of Economic Theory*, New York: Macmillan.

Coase, R. (1937), 'The nature of the firm', *Economica*, **4**, 386–405.

Cohen, Stephen and John Zysman (1987), *Manufacturing Matters: The Myth of the Post-Industrial Economy*, New York: Basic Books.

Computing Services Association (1989), *Computing Services Association Official Reference Book 1989*, Sterling Publications Limited.

Cooke, Phil, Frank Moulaert, Eric Swyngedouw, O. Weistein and P. Wells (1992), *Global Localisation*, London: UCL Press.

Coombs, R. (1996), 'Core competencies and the strategic management of R&D', *R&D Management*, **26**, 345–55.

Coombs, R. and R. Hull (1995), 'BPR as "IT-enabled organisational change': an assessment", *New Technology, Work and Employment*, **10** (2), 121–31.

Coombs, R. and R. Hull (1998), "Knowledge Management Practices and Path-Dependency in Innovation", *Research Policy.*

Coombs, R. and J. S. Metcalfe (1998), 'Distributed capabilities and the governance of the firm' Manchester: CRIC Discussion Paper No. 16, ESRC Centre for Research in Innovation and Competition, University of Manchester.

Coombs, Rod, Paolo Saviotti and Vivien Walsh (1992), 'Introduction', in Rod Coombs, Paolo Saviotti and Vivien Walsh (eds), *Technological Change and Company Strategies: Economic and Sociological Perspectives*, London: Academic Press.

Cooper, A. C. (1971), 'Spin-offs and technical entrepreneurship', *IEEE Transactions on Engineering Management*, **18** (1), 2–6.

Cowan, R. and D. Foray (1997), 'The economics of codification and the diffusion of knowledge', *Industrial and Corporate Change*, **6** (3), 595–622.

Crabb, S. (1995), 'Jobs for all in the global market?', *People Management*, **1** (2), 22-27.

Croisier, B. (1998), 'The governance of external research: empirical test of some transaction-cost related factors', *R&D Management*, **28**, 289–98.

Cusumano, Musamano A. (1991), *Japan's Software Factories: A Challenge to US Management*, New York: Oxford University Press.

Cusumano, M. (1992), 'Shifting economies: from craft production to flexible systems and software factories', *Research Policy*, **21**, 453–80.

Cyert, Richard M. and James G. March (1963), *A Behavioural Theory of the Firm*, New Jersey: Prentice Hall.

David, P. A. and D. Foray (1995), 'Accessing and expanding the science and technology knowledge base', *STI Review*, **16**, 13–68.

Davis, Lee (1999), 'Impact of the patent system on the innovation firm's use of knowledge', paper presented at the CISTEMA Conference on *Mobilising Knowledge in Technology Management: Competence Construction in the Strategising and Organising of Technical Change*, Copenhagen: Copenhagen Business School, October 1999.

Dawson, A. C. (1998), 'The intellectual property commons: a rationale for regulation', *Prometheus*, **16**, 275–290.

de Jong, M. W. (1994), 'Core competencies and chain relations in service industries', in *Management of Services: a Multidisciplinary Approach*, Marseilles: Proceedings of the 3rd International Research Seminar in Service Management, IAE, (Institut d'Administration des Enterprises), Université d'Aix-Marseille III.

Delaunay, Jean-Claude and Jean Gadrey (1992), *Services in Economic Thought: Three Centuries of Debate*, Boston, Dordrecht and London:

Kluwer Academic Publishers.

Den Hertog, P., R. Bilderbeek and S. Maltha (1997), 'Intangibles: the soft side of innovation', *Futures*, **29**.

Department of Trade and Industry (1986), *Intellectual Property and Innovation*, London: HMSO, Cmnd No. 9712.

Department of Trade and Industry (1997), *How EDI can work for you: a guide to implementing EDI in your business* London: DTI, URN **97/586** (available online at http:\\www.isi.gov.UK).

Department of Trade and Industry (1998), *Our Competitive Future: Building the Knowledge-Driven Economy*, London: HMSO, Cmnd No. **4176**.

Dible, Donald M. (ed.) (1978), *What Everybody Should Know About Patents, Trademarks and Copyrights*, Reston/Virginia: Reston Publishing Company Inc.

Dickson, Keith, Helen Lawton Smith and S. Smith (1990), 'The small firm perspective on inter-firm collaboration for innovation', in Dermot O'Doherty (ed.), *The Cooperation Phenomenon: Prospects for Small Firms and the Small Economies*, Graham Trotham, London, pp. 51–70.

Dik, D. (1990), 'Copyright software and tying arrangements: a fresh appreciation for per se illegality', *Computer Law Journal*, **10** (3), 413–52.

Dore, Ron (1986), *Flexible Rigidities: Industrial Policy and Structural Adjustment in the Japanese Economy: 1970–1980*, London: Athlone Press.

Drucker, Peter F. (1993), *Post-Capitalist Society*, Oxford: Butterworth-Heinemann.

Dunning, J. H. (1989), 'Multinational enterprises and the growth of services: some conceptual and theoretical issues', *The Service Industries Journal*, **9**, (1), 5–39.

Dunning, John H. (1993), *Multinational Enterprise and the Global Economy*, Wokingham: Addison Wesley.

Edquist, Charles (1997), 'Systems of innovation approaches – their emergence and characteristics', in Charles Edquist (ed.), *Systems of Innovation: Technologies, Institutions and Organizations*, London: Pinter, pp. 1–35.

Edvardsson, B., L. Edvinsson, and H. Nystrom (1993), 'Internationalisation in service companies', *The Service Industries Journal*, **13** (1), 80–97.

Elfring, T. and G. Baven (1994), 'Outsourcing technical services: stages of development', *Long Range Planning*, **27** (5), 42–51.

Elfring, Timothy and Geert Baven (1996), 'Spinning-off capabilities: competence development in knowledge-intensive services', in Ron Sanchez, Aime Heene and Howard Thomas (eds), *Dynamics of Competence-Based Competition: Theory and Practice in the New Strategic Management*, Oxford: Pergamon, pp. 209–225.

Enderwick, Peter (1992), 'The scale and scope of service sector multinationals', in Peter J. Buckley and Mark Casson (eds), *Multinational*

Enterprise in the World Economy: Essays in Honour of John Dunning, Aldershot, UK and Brookfield, US: Edward Elgar..

Engelsman, E. C. and A. F. J. van Raan (1992), 'A patent-based cartography of technology', *Research Policy,* 23, 116.

Englander, E. J. (1988), 'Technology and Oliver Williamson's transaction cost economics', *Journal of Economic Behavior and Organization,* 10, 339–53.

Erramilli, M. K. (1991), 'The experience factor in foreign market entry behaviour of service firms', *Journal of International Business Studies,* 22, (3), 479–501.

Esperanca, Jose-Paulo (1992), 'International Strategies in the European Service Sector: A Comparative Study', in Mark Casson (ed.), *International Business and Global Integration: Empirical Studies*, London: Macmillan Press.

Eurostat (1999), *Services in Europe – Data 1995–97*, Luxembourg: Office for Official Publications of the European Commission.

Evangelista, Rinaldo (1999), *Knowledge and Investment*, Cheltenham, UK and Northampton, MA, US: Edward Elgar.

Evangelista, R. and G. Sirilli (1995), 'Measuring innovation in services', Research Evaluation, 5 (3), 207–15.

Fichman, R. G. and C. F. Kemerer (1993), 'Adoption of software engineering process innovations: the case of object orientation', *Sloan Management Review,* (Winter), 7- 22.

Fisher, A. G. (1939), 'Production, primary, secondary and tertiary', *Economic Record,* 15 (June), 24-38.

Flanagan, Kieron (1999), *Innovation Networks and New Media development in Europe and the UK*, Manchester: Unpublished PhD Thesis, PREST, University of Manchester.

Flanagan, Kieron and Ian Miles (1999), 'Multimedia in the melting pot: moulding products and shaping frameworks" in Roger S. Slack, James K. Stewart and Robin A. Williams (eds.), *The Social Shaping of Multimedia*, Luxembourg: Office for Official Publications of the European Commission, pp.19-54.

Foray, Dominique (1995), 'The economics of intellectual property rights and systems of innovation: the persistence of national practices versus the new global model of innovation, in

Foray, Dominique (1997), 'Generation and distribution of technological knowledge: incentives, norms and institutions', in Charles Edquist (ed.), *Systems of Innovation: Technologies, Institutions and Organizations,* London: Pinter, pp. 64-85.

Foray, Dominique and Lundvall, Bengt-Åke, (1996), 'The Knowledge-Based Economy: from the Economics of Knowledge to the Learning Economy', in *Employment and Growth in the Knowledge-Based Economy*, Paris: OECD, pp. 11–32.

Freeman, Christopher (1987), *Technology Policy and Economic Performance: Lessons from Japan,* London: Frances Pinter.

Freeman, Christopher (1988), 'Japan: a new national system of innovation?' in Giovanni Dosi, Christopher Freeman, Richard Nelson, Gerald Silverberg and Luc Soete (eds), *Technological Change and Economic Theory,* London: Pinter, pp. 330-48.

Freeman, C. (1991), 'Networks of innovators: a synthesis of research issues', Research Policy, **20**, 499–514.

Freeman, Christopher and Luc Soete (1997), *The Economics of Industrial Innovation,* London: Pinter, Third Edition.

Freund, B., H. Konig and N. Roth (1997), 'Impact of information technologies on manufacturing', *International Journal of Technology Management,* **13** (3).

Fuchs, Victor R. (1968), *The Service Economy,* New York: National Bureau of Economic Research, Distributed by Columbia University Press.

Fukuyama, Francis (1995), *Trust: The Social Virtues and the Creation of Prosperity,* London: Penguin Books.

Gallouj, F. and O. Weinstein (1997) 'Innovation in services', *Research Policy,* **26**, 537–56.

GATT (1994), *International Trade: 1994 Trends and Statistics,* Geneva: GATT Secretariat.

Gentle, C. and J. Howells (1993), 'The European computer services industry: consolidation, rationalisation and strategic partnership', *Communications and Strategies,* **10**, 109–31.

Gershuny, Jonathan I. (1978), *After Industrial Society? The Emerging Self Service Economy,* London: Macmillan.

Gershuny, Jonathan I. and Ian D. Miles (1983), *The New Service Economy: The Transformation of Employment in Industrial Societies,* New York: Praeger Publishers.

Gibbons, Michael, Camille Limoges, Helga Nowotny, Simon Schwartzman, Peter Scott and Martin, Trow, (1994), *The New Production of Knowledge: The Dynamics of Science and Research in Contemporary Societies,* London: Sage Publications.

Glass, R. L. (1994), 'The software-research crisis', *IEEE Software,* **11** (6), 42–47.

Government Accounting Office (1993) *Intellectual Property Rights, US Companies' Patent Experience in Japan* Washington, DC: GAO/GGD-93-126, US Government Accounting Office, US Congress, Government Printing Office.

Graham, M. B. W. (1985), 'Corporate research and development: the latest transformation' *Technology in Society,* **7** (2–3), 86–102.

Graham, Stephen (1996), 'Networking the city', Manchester: Unpublished PhD Thesis, PREST, University of Manchester.

Granstrand, Ove, Lars Håkanson and Soren Sjölander (1992), *Technology Management and International Business: Internationalization of R&D and Technology*, Chichester: John Wiley & Sons.

Griffiths, G. (1994), 'CASE in the third generation', *Software Engineering Journal,* **9** (4), 159–166.

Griliches, Z. (1990), 'Patent statistics as economic indicators: a survey', *Journal of Economic Literature,* **28**,1661–707.

Griliches, Zvi (1992), *Output Measurement in the Service Sectors*, Chicago and London: The University of Chicago Press.

Grupp, H. (1995), 'Science, high technology and competitiveness of EU countries', *Cambridge Journal of Economics,* **19**, 209–23.

Guinet, Jean (1997), 'Knowledge flows in National Innovation Systems', in OECD (ed.), *Industrial Competitiveness in the Knowledge-Based Economy: The New Role of Government*, Paris: OECD.

Hagedoorn, J. and J. Schakenraad, J. (1990), Inter-firm partnerships and co-operative strategies in core technologies' in Christopher Freeman and Luc Soete (eds.), *New Explorations in the Economics of Technical Change*, London: Pinter

Hall, A. D. and R. E. Fagen (1956), 'Definition of system', *General Systems Yearbook,* **1**, 18–28.

Hall, J. A. (1990), 'Severn myths of formal methods', *IEEE Software,* **7** (5), 11-19.

Hall, Peter, Ann R. Markusen, R. Ostorn and B. Wachsman (1985), 'The American computer software industry', in Peter Hall and Ann R. Markusen (eds.), *Silicon Landscapes,* Hemel Hempstead: George Allen and Unwin, pp. 49–64.

Hall, Peter and Pascal Preston (1988), *The Carrier Wave: New Information Technology and the Geography of Innovation, 1846–2003*, London: Unwin Hyman.

Hall, R. (1992), 'The strategic analysis of intangible resources', *Strategic Management Review,* **13**, 135–44.

Haour, G. (1992), 'Stretching the knowledge-base of the enterprise through contract research', *R&D Management,* **22**, 177-82.

Häusler, J., H.W. Hohn, and S. Lütz (1994), 'Contingencies of innovative networks: a case study of successful interfirm R&D collaboration', *Research Policy,* **23**, 47–66.

Hedlund, G. and A. Kverneland (1984), *Are Establishment and Growth Patterns for Foreign Markets Changing? The Case of Swedish Investment in Japan*, Institute of International Business, Stockholm School of Economics.

Hicks, D. and J. S. Katz (1996), 'Science policy for a highly collaborative science system', *Science and Public Policy,* **23**, 39–44.

Hill, T. P. (1977), 'On goods and services', *Review of Income and Wealth,* **23**, (4), 315–38.

Hipp, C., B. S. Tether and I. Miles (2000), 'The incidence and effects of innovation in services; evidence from Germany', Manchester: mimeo, ESRC Centre for Research in Innovation and Competition, University of Manchester and UMIST.

Hirst, Paul and Graham Thompson (1996), *Globalization in Question*, Cambridge: Cambridge University Press.

Hodgson, Geoffrey (1988), *Economics and Institutions*, Cambridge: Polity Press.

Hodgson, G. M. (1994), 'Corporate Culture and the Nature of the Firm', Cambridge: Judge Institute of Management Studies Working Paper No. 14, University of Cambridge.

Hodgson, Geoffrey (1999), *Economics and Utopia: Why the Learning Economy is not the End of History*, London: Routledge.

Homburg, E. (1992), 'The emergence of research laboratories in the dyestuffs industry, 1870–1900', *British Journal of the History of Science*, 25, 91–111.

Hood, Neil and Stephen Young (1983), *Multinational Investment Strategies in the British Isles: A study of the MNEs in the Assisted Areas and the Republic of Ireland*, London: HMSO.

Howells, J. (1987), 'Developments in the location, technology and industrial organisation of computer services', *Regional Studies*, 26, 493–503.

Howells, J. (1989), *Trade in Software, Computer Services and Computerised Information Services*, Paris: DSTI/ICCP/TISP/89.16, Report to the Directorate for Science, Technology and Industry, OECD.

Howells, J. (1990) 'The internationalization of R&D and the development of global research networks', *Regional Studies*, 24, 495–512.

Howells, J. (1994), 'Innovation and the nation state' (Review of Lundvall, B.Å. (ed.) 'National Systems of Innovation') *International Review of Applied Economics*, 8, 91–4.

Howells, J. R. (1995) 'Going global: the use of ICT networks in research and development', *Research Policy*, 24, 169–84.

Howells, J. (1996), 'Tacit knowledge, innovation and technology transfer', *Technology Analysis and Strategic Management*, 8 (2), 91–106.

Howells, J. (1997a), 'Intellectual property rights, the firm and service innovations: shaping Systems of Innovation', Paper presented at the *Seventh International Forum for Technology Management*, Kyoto, Japan, 3–7 November 1997.

Howells, J. (1997b) 'Research and technology outsourcing', Manchester: CRIC Discussion Paper No. 6, ESRC Centre for Research on Innovation and Competition, Universities of Manchester and UMIST.

Howells, J. (1999a), 'Research and technology outsourcing', *Technology Analysis and Strategic Management*, 11, 591–603.

Howells, J. (1999b), 'Research and technology outsourcing and innovation systems: an exploratory analysis', *Industry and Innovation*, 6, 111–29.

Howells, Jeremy (1999c), 'Regional Innovation Systems?,' in Daniele Archibugi, Jeremy Howells and Jonathan Michie (eds), *Innovation Systems in a Global Economy,* Cambridge: Cambridge University Press, pp. 67–93.

Howells, J. (1999d), *The Role of Intellectual Property Rights in the Development of Domestic Computer Software in Developing Countries,* Geneva: Report to the United Nations Conference on Trade and Development (UNCTAD).

Howells, J. (2000, forthcoming), 'Knowledge, innovation and location, in John R. Bryson, Peter W. Daniels, Nicholas D. Henry and Jane S. Pollard (eds), *Knowledge, Space, Economy,* London: Routledge.

Howells, J. and Green, A. (1986), 'Location, technology and industrial organisation in UK services', *Progress in Planning,* **26**, 83–184.

Howells, Jeremy and Ian Neary (1995), *Intervention and Technological Innovation: Government and the Pharmaceutical Industry in the UK,* Basingstoke: Macmillan.

Hull, R, (1999) "Actor Network and Conduct: The Conduct of Knowledge Management", *Organisation,* Vol.6(3), pp.405-428.

Howells, J. and Roberts, J. (2000), 'From Innovation Systems to Knowledge Systems', Prometheus, **18**, 17-31.

Håkansson, Hakan (ed.) (1987), *Industrial Technological Development – A Network Approach,* London: Croom Helm.

Johanson, J. and J. E. Vahlne (1977), 'The internationalization process of the firm – a model of knowledge development and increasing foreign market commitments', *Journal of International Business Studies,* **8**, (1), 23-32.

Johanson, J. and F. Wiedersheim-Paul (1975), 'Internationalization of the firm – four Swedish cases', *Journal of Management Studies,* Oct., 305-22.

Johnson, Björn (1992), 'Institutional learning', in Bengt-Åke Lundvall (ed.), *National Systems of Innovation: Towards a Theory of Innovation and Interactive Learning,* London: Pinter, pp. 23–44.

Jones, C. (1994), 'Globalisation of software supply and demand', *Software Engineering Journal,* **9** (6), 235–243.

Jones, O. (1997), 'From post-it notes to post-modernism: organisations, innovation and virtual R&D', Birmingham: *Research Paper Series, 9733,* Aston Business School, Aston University.

Kastrinos, N. and I. Miles (1996), 'Patterns of entrepreneurship in the UK environmental industry', in Clara Eugenia Garcia and Luis Sanz-Menendez (eds), *Management and Technology,* Luxembourg Office for Official Publications of the European Commission, DGXII (COST A3 Social Sciences) I.

Katsoulacos, Y. and N. Tsounis (2000, forthcoming), 'Knowledge intensive business services and productivity growth: The Greek evidence', in Ian Miles and Mark Boden (eds), *Services and the Knowledge Economy,* London: Cassell.

Katz, J. S. and B. R.Martin (1997), 'What is research collaboration?', *Research Policy,* **26**, 1-18.

Kay, J. (1999), 'Business strategy in the knowledge driven economy', Paper presented to the Department of Trade and Industry, and the Centre for Economic Policy Research, London, UK, 27 January 1999.

Keeble, D., J. Bryson and P. A. Wood (1991), 'Small firms, business service growth and regional development in the UK: some empirical findings', *Regional Studies,* **25**, 439–457.

Khazam, J. and D. C. Mowery (1994), 'The commercialization of RISC: strategies for the creation of dominant designs', *Research Policy,* **23**, 89–102.

Khazam, Jonathan and David C. Mowery (1996), 'Tails that wag dogs: the influence of software-based "network externalities" on the creation of dominant designs in RISC technologies', in David C. Mowery (ed.), *The International Computer Software Industry: A Comparative Study of Industry Evolution and Structure,* Oxford: Oxford University Press, pp. 86–103

Kiesler, Sara, Douglas Wholey and Kathleen M. Carley (1994), 'Coordination as linkage: the case of software development teams' in Douglas H. Harris (ed.), *Organizational Linkages: Understanding the Productivity Paradox,* Washington, DC: National Academy Press, pp. 214–239.

Kim, D. H. (1993), 'The link between individual and organisational learning' *Sloan Management Review,* (Fall), 37–50.

Kim, J. S. and J Choi,. (1997), 'Barriers to software development in Japan: the structure of the industry and software manpower', *International Journal of Technology Management,* **13** (4), 395–412.

Kindleberger, Charles, P. (1996), *World Economic Primacy 1500-1990,* New York and Oxford: Oxford University Press.

King, S., P. Layzell and S. Williams (1994), 'CASE 2000: the future of CASE technology', *Software Engineering Journal,* **9** (4), 138–9.

Kitschelt, H. (1991), 'Industrial governance structures, innovation strategies and the case of Japan: sectoral or cross-national comparative analysis?', *Industrial Organization,* **45**, 453–93.

Kitson, M. and J. Michie (1997), 'Does manufacturing matter?' *International Journal of the Economics of Business,* **4**, 71–95.

Kluth, Michael F. and Jørn B. Andersen (1997), 'Pooling the technology base: the globalization of European research and technology organizations' in Jeremy Howells and Jonathan Michie (eds), *Technology, Innovation and Competitiveness,* Cheltenham, UK and Lyme, US: Edward Elgar, pp. 65–88.

Knight, F. (1933), *Risk, Uncertainty and Profit,* London: London School of Economics Reprints No. 16, London School of Economics.

Kreiner, K. and M Schultz, M. (1993), 'Informal collaboration in R&D: the formation of networks across organizations', *Organization Studies,* **14**, 189–209.

Kretschmer, M., G. M. Klimis and R. Wallis (1999), 'The changing location of intellectual property rights in music: A study of music publishers, collection societies and media conglomerates', *Prometheus,* **17**, 163–186.

Krugman, Paul (1996), *Pop Internationalism,* Cambridge, Mass.: MIT Press.

Kuznets, Simon S. (1930), *Secular Movements in Production and Prices: Their Nature and Their Bearing Upon Cyclical Fluctuations,* Boston: Houghton Mifflin Co., The Riverside Press.

Kuznets, Simon S. (1962), 'Inventive Activity: Problems of Definitions and Measurements', in *The Rate and Direction of Inventive Activity: Economic and Social Factors,* Princeton: Princeton University Press, pp. 19-43.

Lamberton, D. (1997) 'The knowledge-based economy: a Sisyphus model', *Prometheus,* **15**, 73-81.

Landes, David (1999), *The Wealth and Poverty of Nations,* London: Abacus.

Lane, C. (1997), 'The social regulation of inter-firm relations in Britain and Germany: market rules, legal norms and technical standards', *Cambridge Journal of Economics,* **21**, 197–215.

Leonard-Barton, Dorothy (1995), *Wellsprings of Knowledge: Building and Sustaining the Sources of Innovation,* Boston: Harvard Business School Press.

Leontief, Wiiliam (1986), *Input–Output Economics,* Oxford: Second Edition, Oxford University Press.

Leyshon, A., P. W. Daniels, and N. J. Thrift (1987), 'Internationalization of Professional Producer Services: The Case of Large Accountancy Firms', Liverpool: Working Papers on Producer Services 3, St. David's University College, Lampeter and University of Liverpool.

Licht, G., M. Kukuk, N. Janz, S. Kuhlmann, G. Münt, C. Hipp, M. Smid and D. Hess (1995), *Results of the German Service-Sector Innovation Survey,* Mannheim: ZEW, and Karlsruhe: FhG-ISI .

Licht, G., M. Kukuk, N. Janz, S. Kuhlmann, G. Münt, C. Hipp, M. Smid and D. Hess (1997), *Results of the German Service-Sector Innovation Survey,* Mannheim: ZEW and Karlsruhe: FhG-ISI.

Liebenau, J. M. (1984), 'International R&D in pharmaceutical firms in the early twentieth century', *Business History,* **26**, 329–46.

Lim, W. C. (1994), 'Effects of reuse on quality, productivity and economics', *IEEE Software,* **11** (5), 23–30.

Lundmark, M. (1995), 'Computer services in Sweden: markets, labour qualifications and patterns of location', *Geografiska Annaler,* **77 B**, 2.

Lundvall, Bengt-Åke (1988), 'Innovation as an interactive process – from user-producer interaction to National Systems of Innovation', Giovanni Dosi, Christopher Freeman, Richard Nelson, Gerald Silverberg and Luc

Soete (eds), *Technological Change and Economic Theory*, London: Pinter, pp. 349–69.

Lundvall, Bengt-Åke (1992), 'Introduction', in Bengt-Åke Lundvall (ed.), *National Systems of Innovation: Towards a Theory of Innovation and Interactive Learning*, London: Pinter, pp. 1–19.

Lundvall, Bengt-Åke (1995), 'The global unemployment problem and national systems of innovation', in Dermot P. O'Doherty (ed.), *Globalisation, Networking and Small Firm Innovation*, London: Graham & Trotman, pp. 35–48.

Lundvall, Bengt-Åke (1999), 'Technology policy in the learning economy', in Daniele Archibugi, Jeremy Howells and Jonathan Michie (eds) *Innovation Systems in a Global Economy*, Cambridge University Press, Cambridge, pp. 19–34.

Lundvall, B.A. and Johnson B. (1994), 'The Learning Economy', *Journal of Industry Studies*, 1, 23–42.

Lynch, M. (1998), 'The discursive production of uncertainty: The O. J. Simpson "Dream Team" and the sociology of knowledge machine', *Social Studies of Science*, 28 (5&6), 829–68.

Lynn, L. H, N. M. Reddy, and J.D. Aram (1996), 'Linking technology and institutions: the innovation community framework', *Research Policy*, 25, 91–106.

Macdonald, S. (1996), 'International information flow and strategy in the international firm', *International Journal of Technology Management*, 11 (1/2), 219–32.

Macdonald, S. and C. Williams (1994), 'The survival of the gatekeeper', *Research Policy*, 23, 123–32.

Machlup, Fritz (1962), *The Production and Distribution of Knowledge in the United States*, Princeton: N.J.: Princeton University Press.

Macmillan, F. (1998), 'Copyright, culture and private power', *Prometheus*, 16, 305–16.

Macneil, I. (1978), 'Contracts: adjustment of long-term economic relations under classical, neoclassical, and relational contract law', *Northwestern University Law Review*, 72, 854–906.

MacPherson, A. (1997), 'The role of producer service outsourcing in the innovation performance of New York State manufacturing firms', *Annals of the Association of American Geographers*, 87, 52–71.

Malerba, F. and L. Orsenigo, (1995), 'Schumpeterian patterns of innovation', *Cambridge Journal of Economics*, 19, 47–65.

Maid, J., (1995), 'EDS: an evolving strategy', *Financial Times* (27.05.1995).

Mansell, Robin and Uta Wehn (1998), *Knowledge Societies: Information Technology for Sustainable Development*, Oxford, New York: Oxford University Press.

Mansfield, E. (1986), 'Patents and innovation: an empirical study', *Management Science*, 32 (2), 173–81.

Marsch, U. (1994), 'Strategies for success: research organization in German chemical companies and IG Farben until 1936', *History and Technology*, **12**, 25-77.

Marshall, Alfred (1890), *Principles of Economics*, London: Macmillan Press.

Marshall, J. Neill and Peter A. Wood (1995), *Services and Space: Key Aspects of Urban and Regional Development*, Harlow: Longman.

Martin, D. (1992), 'Bull chases UK deals in India', *Computing*, 03.09.92, 3.

Martin, James and Carma McClure (1983), *Software Maintenance: The Problem and Its Solution*, Englewood Cliffs, NJ: Prentice-Hall.

Martinelli, Flavia (1991), 'A demand-orientated approach to understanding producer services', in Peter W. Daniels and Frank Moulaert (eds), *The Changing Geography of Advanced Producer Services: Theoretical and Empirical Perspectives*, London: Belhaven Press.

McGurran P, 1997, *Corporate Web Strategies in Europe: perspectives on best practice, innovation and one-to-one marketing*, Pira International: Leatherhead.

Metcalfe, J. S. (1995), 'Technology systems and technology policy in an evolutionary framework', *Cambridge Journal of Economics*, **19**, 25–46.

Metcalfe, J. Stanley and Nico de Liso (1998), 'Innovation, capabilities and knowledge: the epistemic connection', in Rod Coombs et al., (eds.) *Technology and Organisations*, Cheltenham, UK and Northampton, MA, US: Edward Elgar.

Meyer-Thurow, G. (1982), 'The industrialization of invention: a case study from the German chemical industry', *Isis*, **73**, 363-81.

Miles, I. (1993), 'Services in the New Industrial Economy', *Futures*, **25**, 653–672.

Miles, Ian (1994), 'Innovation in services', in Mark Dodgson and Roy Rothwell (eds), *Handbook of Industrial Innovations*, Aldershot, UK and Brookfield, US: Edward Elgar, pp. 243–256.

Miles, Ian (1996), *Innovation in Services: Services in Innovation*, Manchester: mimeo, Manchester Statistical Society.

Miles, I. (1998), 'Environmental services and European regulation', Paper presented at *Europeanisation and the Regulation of Risk Conference* at LSE, London, 27 March 1998.

Miles, I., B. Andersen, J. Howells and M. Boden (2000), 'Services processes and property', *International Journal of Technology Management*, **20** (1/2), 95-115.

Miles, Ian and Boden, Mark (eds) (2000), *Services and the Knowledge Economy*, London: Cassell.

Miles, I. and H. Rush (1997), 'Services and the Knowledge-Based Economy: not so peculiar after all?', Paper presented at the *Seventh International Forum for Technology Management*, Kyoto, Japan, 3-7 November 1997.

Miles, I., N. Kastrinos, K. Flanagan, R. Bilderbeek, P. Hertog, W. Huntink and M. Bouman (1995), 'Knowledge-Intensive Business Services: users, carriers and sources of innovation', Luxembourg: EIMS Publication No. 15, Innovation Programme, Directorate General for Telecommunications, Information Market and Exploitation of Research, Commission of the European Communities.

Mill, John S. (1864), *Principles of Political Economy* [1862], 2 vols, New York: D. Appleton.

Miller, R. (1994), 'Global R&D networks and large-scale innovations: the case of the automobile industry', *Research Policy, 23,* 27–46.

Mishel, L. R. (1989), 'The late great debate on deindustrialization', *Challenge,* February.

Moad, J. (1991), 'A kinder, gentler EDS?', *Datamation,* 15.02.91, 65–69.

Morgan, Bruce (1990), 'Transferring soft technology', in Richard D. Robinson (ed.), *The International Communication Technology,* New York: Taylor and Francis, pp. 149–166.

Mowery, D. C. (1983), 'The relationship between intrafirm and contractual forms of industrial research in American manufacturing, 1900–1940', *Explorations in Economic History, 20,* 351–374.

Mowery, D. C. (1984), 'Firm structure, government policy, and the organization of industrial research: Great Britain and the United States, 1900–1950', *Business History Review, 58,* 504–31.

Mowery, David C. and Nathan Rosenberg (1989), *Technology and the Pursuit of Economic Growth,* Cambridge: Cambridge University Press.

Myers, W. (1986), 'Can software for the strategic defense initiative ever be error free?', *Computer, 19* (11), 46-58.

Nairn, G. (1992), 'Software factories: industrial revolution', *Computing,* 20.08.92, 22–23.

Napolitano, G. and G. Sirilli, (1990), 'The patent system and the exploitation of inventions: results of a statistical survey conducted in Italy', *Technovation, 10,* 5-16.

Narin, F. E. Noma, and R. Perry, (1987), 'Patents as indicators of corporate technological strength', *Research Policy, 16,* 143-55.

Nelson, Richard R. (1991), 'Why do firms differ, and how does it matter?', *Strategic Management Journal, 12* (1).

Nelson, R. R. (1992a), 'National innovation systems: a retrospective on a study', *Industrial and Corporate Change,* 1 (2), 347–74.

Nelson, R. R. (1992b), 'What is commercial and what is public about technology, and what should be?', in Nathan Rosenberg (ed.), *Technology and the Wealth of Nations,* Stanford: Stanford University Press, pp.57–72.

Nelson, Richard R. (1993), 'A retrospective', in Richard R. Nelson (ed), *National Innovation Systems: A Comparative Analysis,* New York: Oxford University Press, pp. 505--23.

Nelson, Richard R. and Nathan Rosenberg (1993), 'Technical innovation and national systems', in Richard R. Nelson (ed.), *National Innovation*

Systems: A Comparative Analysis, New York: Oxford University Press, pp. 3–21.

Nelson, Richard R. and Sidney Winter (1982), *An Evolutionary Theory of Economic Change,* Cambridge, Mass: Harvard University Press.

Niosi, J. and B. Bellon (1994), 'The global interdependence of National Innovation Systems: evidence, limits and implications', *Technology in Society,* **16**, 173–197.

Noble, David F. (1979), *American by Design: Science, Technology, and the Rise of Corporate Capitalism,* New York: Alfred A. Knopf.

Nonaka, I. (1991), 'The Knowledge Creating Company', *Harvard Business Review,* **69**.

Nonaka, I. (1994), 'A dynamic theory of organizational knowledge creation', *Organization Science,* **5**, 14-37.

Nonaka, I. and N. Konno (1998), 'The concept of "Ba": building a foundation for knowledge creation', *California Management Review,* **40** (3), 40–54.

Nonaka, Ikujiro and Hirotaka Takeuchi (1995), *The Knowledge-Creating Company: How Japanese Companies Create the Dynamics of Innovation,* New York and Oxford: Oxford University Press.

Noyelle, Thierry J. and Anna B. Dutka (1988), *International Trade in Business Services,* Cambridge, Mass.: Ballinger Publishing Company.

Nusbaumer, Jacques (1987a), *The Services Economy: Leaver to Growth,* Boston: Kluwer Academic Publishers.

Nusbaumer, Jacques (1987b), *Services in the Global Market,* Boston: Kluwer Academic Publishers.

O'Farrell, P. N. (1995), 'Manufacturing demand for business services', *Cambridge Journal of Economics,* **19**, 523-543.

O'Farrell, P. N., L. Moffat and P.A. Wood (1995), 'Internationalisation by business services: a methodological critique of foreign-market entry-mode choice', *Environment and Planning A,* **27**, 683-97.

O'Farrell, P. N., and P. A. Wood (1998), 'Internationalisation by business service firms: towards a new regionally based conceptual framework', *Environment and Planning A,* **30**, 109–28.

O'Farrell, P.N., P.A. Wood, and J. Zheng (1996), 'Internationalization of business services: an interregional analysis', *Regional Studies,* **30** (2), 101–18.

OECD (1985), *Software: An Emerging Industry,* Paris: OECD, ICCP Report No. 9.

OECD (1989), *The Internationalisation of Software and Computer Services,* Paris: OECD, ICCP Report No. 9.

OECD (1993), 'The Measurement of Scientific and Technological Activities The Measurement of Scientific and Technical Activities 1993:· Standard Practice for Surveys of Research and Experimental Development' *Frascati Manual,* Paris: OECD

OECD (1995), *The OECD Input–Output Database: 1995*, Paris: OECD.

OECD (1996a), *Proposed Guidelines for Collecting and Interpreting Technological Innovation Data: The Oslo Manual*, Paris: OECD, Second Edition.

OECD (1996b), *The Environment Industry: The Washington Meeting*, Paris: OECD.

OECD (1996c), *The Knowledge-Based Economy*, Paris: OECD, OCDE/GD(96)102.

OECD (1996d), *Employment and Growth in the Knowledge-Based Economy*, Paris: OECD.

OECD (1997), *Statistics on Value Added and Employment, Services*, Paris: OECD.

OECD, (1998), *Facts and Figures*, Paris: OECD.

OECD/EUROSTAT (1999), *Services Statistics on International Transactions 1987–1996*, Paris: OECD/EUROSTAT.

Office for National Statistics (1997), *United Kingdom Balance of Payments: The Pink Book 1997*, London: HMSO.

Ohmae, Kenichi (1990), *The Borderless World: Power and Strategy in the Global Marketplace*, London: Harper Collins.

Oliver, Nick and Michelle Blakeborough (1998), 'The multi firm new product development process', in John Grieve-Smith and Jonathan Michie (eds), *Innovation, Cooperation and Growth*, Oxford: Oxford University Press, pp.151–160.

ONS (1995), *Input–Output Tables for the UK 1990*, London: Office for National Statistics (Computer files).

Ott, M. (1987), 'The growing share of services in the US Economy: degeneration or evolution?', *Review*, Federal Reserve Bank of St. Louis, June/July, 5–22.

Ouchi, W. G. (1980), 'Markets, bureaucracies and clans', *Administrative Science Quarterly*, **25**, 129–41.

Ouchi, W. G. and M. K. Bolton (1988), 'The logic of joint research and development', *California Management Review*, **30** (3), 9–19.

PA Consulting (1995), *1994 IT Sourcing Survey*, Cambridge: PA Consulting.

Papaconstantinou, G., N. Sakurai and A. Wyckoff (1996), 'Embodied technology diffusion: an empirical analysis for 10 OECD countries', *STI Working Papers* 1996/1, Paris: OECD.

Patel, P. and K. Pavitt (1991), 'Large firms in the production of the world's technology: an important case of "non-globalisation"', *Journal of International Business Studies*, **12**, 1–21.

Patel, P. and K. Pavitt (1994a), 'National innovation systems: why they are important, and how they might be measured and compared', *Economics of Innovation and New Technology*, **3**. 77–95

Patel, P. and K. Pavitt (1994b), 'The continuing, widespread (and neglected) importance of improvements in mechanical technologies', *Research Policy*, **23**, 533–45.

Patel, Pari and Keith Pavitt (1995), 'Patterns of technological activity: their measurement and interpretation', in Paul Stoneman (ed.), *Handbook of the Economics of Innovation and Technological Change*, Oxford: Blackwell Publishers, pp. 14–51.

Pavitt, K. (1984a), 'Patent statistics as indicators of innovative activities: possibilities and problems', *Scientometrics*, **7**, 77–99.

Pavitt, K. (1984b), 'Sectoral patterns of technological change: towards a taxonomy and a theory', *Research Policy*, **13**, 343–73.

Pavitt, Keith (1988), 'Uses and abuses of patent statistics', in A. van Raan (ed.) *Handbook of Qualitative Studies of Science and Technology*, Amsterdam: Elsevier, pp. 509–36.

Pearce, Robert D. (1989), *The Internationalisation of Research and Development by Multinational Enterprises*, Basingstoke: Macmillan.

Pearce, Robert D. and Satwinder Singh (1992), *Globalizing Research and Development*, Basingstoke: Macmillan.

Penrose, Edith. (1959), *The Theory of the Growth of the Firm*, Oxford: Basil Blackwell.

Perry, M. (1990), 'Business service specialization and regional economic change', *Regional Studies*, **24**, 195–209.

Perry, M. (1992), 'Flexible production, externalisation and the interpretation of business service growth', *Services Industry Journal*, **12**, 1-16.

Petit, Pascal (1986), *Slow Growth and the Service Economy*, London: Frances Pinter.

Phillips, A. (1960), 'A theory of interfirm organization', *Quarterly Journal of Economics*, **74**, 602–13.

Pianta, M. (1995), 'Technology and growth in OECD countries, 1970-1990', *Cambridge Journal of Economics*, **19**, 175–87.

Pisano, G. P. (1990), 'The R&D boundaries of the firm: an empirical analysis', *Administrative Science Quarterly*, **35**, 153–76.

Pisano, G. P., W. Shaw and D. J. Teece (1988), 'Joint ventures and collaboration in the biotechnology industry', in David C. Mowery (ed.), *International Collaborative Ventures in U.S. Manufacturing*, Cambridge, Mass.: Ballinger, pp. 182–222.

Plotkin, Henry (1994), *The Nature of Knowledge: Concerning Adaptations, Instinct and the Evolution of Intelligence*, London: Allen Lane.

Polanyi, Michael (1958), *Personal Knowledge: Towards a Post-Critical Philosophy,* London: Routledge & Kegan Paul.

Polanyi, M. (1966), 'The logic of tacit inference', *Philosophy*, **41** (155), 1–18.

Polanyi, Michael (1967), *The Tacit Dimension,* London: Routledge and Kegan Paul.

Powell, W. W. (1990), 'Neither market nor hierarchy: network forms of organization', *Research in Organizational Behaviour*, **12**, 295–336.

Prahalad, C. and G. Hamel (1990), 'The core competence of the corporation', *Harvard Business Review*, **68**, 79-91.

Preissl, Brigitte (2000), 'Service innovation: what makes it different? Empirical evidence from Germany', in J. Stanley Metcalfe and Ian Miles (ed.), *Innovation Systems in the Service Economy*, Boston, Mass.: Kluwer Academic Publishers, pp. 125-148.

Pritchard, Craig, Richard Hull, Mike Chumer and Hugh Willmott (ed.) (2000, forthcoming), *Managing Knowledge: Critical Discussions of Work and Learning*, London: Macmillan.

Quinn, J. J. and K. Dickson (1995), 'The co-location of production and distribution: emergent trends in consumer services', *Technology Analysis and Strategic Management*, **7**, 343–52.

Quinn, J. B. and P.C. Paquette (1990), 'Technology in services: creating organizational revolutions', *Sloan Management Review*, **11** (2), 67–78.

Quintas, P. (1991), 'Engineering solutions to software problems: some institutional and social factors shaping change', *Technology Analysis and Strategic Management*, **3**, 359–76.

Quintas, P. (1994), 'A product-process model of innovation in software development', *Journal of Information Technology*, **9**, 3–17.

Ramachaudran, R. (1992), 'Going it alone', *Computing* 03.09.92, 26–7.

Reddy, N. M. and M. V. H. Rao (1990), 'The industrial market as an interfirm organization', *Journal of Management Studies*, **27**, 42–59.

Reekie, W. D. (1973), 'Patent data as a guide to industrial activity', *Research Policy*, **2**, 246–64.

Reich, Robert R. (1992), *The Work of Nations: Preparing Ourselves for 21st Century Capitalism*, New York: Vintage Books.

Richardson, G. B. (1972), 'The organization of industry', *Economic Journal*, **82**, 372–83.

Riddle, Dorothy I. (1986), *Service-Led Growth: The Role of the Service Sector in World Development*, New York and London: Praeger Publishers.

Ringe, Michael J. (1992), *The Contract Research Business in the United Kingdom: The European Dimension*, Luxembourg: Report to the Directorate General for Telecommunications, Information Industries and Innovation, Commission of the European Communities.

Roberts, Joanne (1998), *Multinational Business Service Firms: The Development of Multinational Organisational Structures in the UK Business Services Sector*, Aldershot: Ashgate Publishing.

Roberts, J. (2000), 'From know-how to show-how? questioning the role of information and communication technologies in knowledge transfer', *Technology Analysis and Strategic Management*, **12** (4), (forthcoming).

Robins, J. A. (1987), 'Organizational economics: notes on the use of transaction-cost theory in the study of organizations', *Administrative Science Quarterly*, **32**, 68–86.

Romer, P. (1994), 'The origins of endogenous growth', *The Journal of Economic Perspectives*, **8**, 3-22.

Rose, A. (1997), 'Transfers of funds for research and development in Canadian industry, 1993', *Science and Technology Redesign Project Working Paper*, ST-97-05, Statistics Canada, Ottawa.

Rosenberg, Nathan (1982), *Inside the Black Box: Technology and Economics*, Cambridge: Cambridge University Press.

Rothery, Brian and Ian Robertson (1995), *The Truth About Outsourcing*, Aldershot: Gower.

Rothwell, R. (1991), 'External networking and innovation in small and medium-sized manufacturing firms in Europe', *Technovation*, **11**, 93–112.

Rothwell, R. (1992), 'Successful industrial innovation: critical success factors for the 1990s', *R&D Management*, **22** (3), 221–39.

Sako, Mari (1992), *Prices, Quality and Trust: Inter-Firm Relations in Britain and Japan*, Cambridge: Cambridge University Press.

Sampson, G. P. and R. H. Snape (1985), 'Identifying the issues in trade in services', *World Economy*, **8**, (2), 171–81.

Samuelson, P. A. (1954), 'The pure theory of public expenditure', *Review of Economics and Statistics*, **20**, 387–9.

Sanders, B. S. (1964), 'Patterns of commercial exploration of patented inventions by large and small corporations into commercial use', *Patent, Trademark, and Copyright Journal*, **8**, 51–92.

Sanderson, M. (1972), 'Research and the firm in British industry, 1919-39', *Science Studies*, **2**, 107–51.

Sandholtz, W. (1992), 'ESPRIT and the politics of international collective action', Journal of Common Market Studies, **30**, 1-21.

Saxenian, A. (1991), 'The origins and dynamics of production networks in Silicon Valley', *Research Policy*, **20**, 423–37.

Say, J. B. (1964), *A Treatise on Political Economy* [1834], New York: Augustus M. Kelly.

Scherer, Frederic. M., Sigmund Herzstein Jr., Alex W. Dreyfoos, William G. Whitney, Otte J. Bachmann, Cyril P. Pesek, Charles J. Scott, Thomas G. Kelly and James J. Galvin (1959), *Patents and the Corporation: A Report on Industrial Technology Under Changing Public Policy*, Boston, Mass.: privately published.

Scherer, F. M. (1983), 'The propensity to patent', *International Journal of Industrial Organization*, **1**, 107–28.

Schmookler, J. (1950), 'The interpretation of patent statistics', *Journal of the Patent Office Society*, **XXXII** (2), 123–46

Schmookler, J. (1953), 'The utility of patent statistics', *Journal of the Patent Office Society*, **XXXV** (6), 407–550.

Schmookler, J. (1962), 'The economics of research and development: determinants of inventive activity', *The American Economic Review,* **LII** (2), 165–76.

Schmookler, J. (1966), *Invention and Economic Growth,* Cambridge, Mass.: Harvard University Press

Schumpeter, Joseph A. (1939): *Business Cycles. A Theoretical, Historical and Statistical Analysis of The Capitalist Process* (Vol. I and II, New York: McGraw-Hill). 1989 reprint (with an introduction by Rendigs Fels) - Philadelphia: Porcupine Press Inc.

Senn, J. A. (1998), 'Expanding the reach of electronic commerce: the Internet EDI alternative', *Information Systems Management,* **15** (3), 7–15.

Sharma, D. D. and J. Johanson (1987), 'Technical consultancy in internationalisation', *International Marketing Review,* Winter, 20–29.

Shohert, S. and M. Prevezer (1996), 'UK biotechnology: institutional linkages, technology transfer and the role of intermediaries', *R&D Management,* **26**, 283–298.

Sieghart, A. (1982), 'Information technology and intellectual property', *European Intellectual Property Review,* **7**, 187–88.

Silvestrou, R., L. Fitzgerald, R. Johnston and C. Grant (1992), 'Toward a classification of service processes', *International Journal of Service Industry Management,* **3** (3), 62–75.

Simon, Herbert (1957), *Models of Man,* New York: John Wiley & Son.

Singelmann, Joachim, (1978), *From Agriculture to Services: The Transformation of Industrial Employment,* Beverly Hills and London: Sage Publications.

Sirilli, G. and R. Evangelista (1998) 'Technological innovation in services and manufacturing: results from Italian surveys', *Research Policy,* **27**, 881–9

Smith, K. (1995), 'Interactions in knowledge systems: foundations, policy implications and empirical methods', *STI Review,* **16**, 69–102.

Smith, Keith (1997), 'Economic infrastructures and innovation systems', in Charles Edquist (ed.), *Systems of Innovation: Technologies, Institutions and Organizations,* London: Pinter, pp. 86–106.

Soete, L. and M. Miozzo (1989), 'Trade and development in services: a technological perspective', Maastricht: MERIT, Working Paper 89-031.

Sowels, Nicholas (1989), *Britain's Invisible Earnings,* Aldershot: Gower.

Sparrow, John (1998), *Knowledge in Organizations: Access to Thinking at Work,* London: Sage Publications.

Stiglitz, Joseph, E. (1999), 'Public policy for a knowledge economy', Speech delivered to the Department of Trade and Industry, and the Centre for Economic Policy Research, London, UK, January...

Stopford, John M. and Louis T. Wells (1972), *Managing the Multinational Enterprise: Organization of the Firm and Ownership of the Subsidiaries,* London: Longman.

Suchman, Lucy A. (1987), *Plans and Situated Actions: The Problem of Human-Machine Communication*, Cambridge: Cambridge University Press.

Sullivan, R. J. (1989), 'England's "age of invention": The acceleration of patents and patentable invention during the industrial revolution', *Explorations in Economic History*, **26**, 424–452.

Sumon, M. P. (1999), *A Study of Innovation in the UK Environmental Management Software Industry*, Manchester: Unpublished MSc dissertation, PREST, University of Manchester.

Sundbo, J. (1997), 'Innovation in services in Denmark', Roskilde: *Service Development, Internationalisation and Competences*, Working Paper No. 2, Danish SI4S WP3-4 Report, Roskilde University, October 1997.

Sundbo, J. (1998), 'Standardisation vs. customisation in service innovations', Roskilde: *Service Development, Internationalisation and Competences*, Working Paper No. 2, Danish SI4S WP3-4 Report, Roskilde University, June 1998.

Swade, D. (1991), *Charles Babbage and his Calculating Machines*, London: Science Museum.

Swann, John P. (1989), *Academic Scientists and the Pharmaceutical Industry: Cooperative Research in Twentieth-Century America*, Boston, Mass.: John Hopkins University Press.

Tassey, G. (1991), 'The functions of technology infrastructure in a competitive economy', *Research Policy*, **20**, 345–61.

Taylor, C. T. and Z. A. Silberston (1973), *The Economic Impact of the Patent System: A Study of the British Experience*, Cambridge: Cambridge University Press.

Teece, David. J. (1987), 'Profiting from technological innovation', in David J. Teece (ed.), *The Competitive Challenge: Strategies for Industrial Innovation and Renewal*, Cambridge, Mass.: Ballinger, pp. 185–219.

Tether, B. S., C. Hipp and I. Miles (2000), 'Standardisation and specialisation in services: evidence from Germany', Manchester: mimeo, CRIC, University of Manchester and UMIST.

Thomas, Graham and Ian Miles (1989), *Telematics in Transition*, London: Longman.

Thomas, L. G. (1988), 'Multifirm strategies in the U.S. pharmaceutical industry', in David C. Mowery (ed.), *International Collaborative Ventures in U.S. Manufacturing*, Cambridge, Mass.: Ballinger, pp. 147–81.

Thorngren, B. (1970), 'How do contact systems affect regional development?', *Environment and Planning*, **A2**, 409–427.

Tierney, M. (1992), 'Software engineering standards: the "Formal Methods Debate" in the UK', *Technology Analysis and Strategic Management*, **4**, 245–78.

Tomlinson, Mark (2000, forthcoming), 'Information and technology flows from the service sector: A UK-Japan comparison' in Ian Miles and Mark Boden (eds), *Services and the Knowledge Economy*, London: Cassell.

Torrisi, Salvatore (1998), *Industrial Organisation and Innovation: An International Study of the Software Industry,* Cheltenham, UK and Northampton, MA, US: Edward Elgar.

Towse, R. (1999), 'Copyright and economic incentives: application to performers' rights in the music industry', *KYKLOS*, **52**, 369–90.

Teubal, Morris, Dominique Foray, Moshe Justman and Ehud Zuscovitch (1996), 'An introduction to technological infrastructure and technological infrastructure policy', in Morris Teubel, Dominique Foray, Moshe Justman and Ehud Zuscovitch (eds) *Technological Infrastructure Policy: An International Perspective*, Dordrecht: Kluwer, pp. 1–17.

Turnbull, Peter W. (1987), 'A challenge to the stages theory of the internationalization process', in P. J. Rosson and S. D. Reed (eds), *Managing Export Entry and Expansion*, Praeger: New York.

Turpin, T., S. Garrett-Jones and N. Rankin (1996), 'Bricoleurs and boundary riders: managing basic research and innovation knowledge networks', *R&D Management*, **26**, 267–282.

Tyler, B. B. and H. K. Steensma (1995), 'Evaluating technological collaborative opportunities: a cognitive modelling perspective', *Strategic Management Journal*, **16**, 43–70.

UNCTAD (1983), *Production and Trade in Services, Policies and Their Underlying Factors Bearing Upon International Service Transactions*, New York: United Nations (TD/B/941).

UNCTC (1990), *Transnational Corporations, Services and the Uruguay Round*, New York: United Nations.

United Nations (1999), *World Development Report 1989/99*, New York: United Nations.

United Nations Development Programme (1999), *Human Development Report: 1999*, New York and Oxford: Oxford University Press for the United Nations Development Programme (UNDP).

United States Copyright Office (1997), *U.S. Copyright Office Home Page,* http://lcweb.loc.gov/copyright/ (including clicable pages therefrom, October 1997).

Urlich, D., T. Jick and M. A. von Glinow (1993), 'High-impact learning: building and diffusing learning capability', *Organizational Dynamics*, **22** (2), 52–66.

Utterback, James (1993), *Mastering the Dynamics of Innovation*, Boston: Harvard Business School Press.

van Genchten, M. (1991), 'Why is software late? An empirical study of reasons for delay in software development', *IEEE Transactions in Software Engineering*, **21**, 582–90.

Vandermerwe, S. and M. Chadwick (1989), 'The internationalization of services', *The Service Industry Journal*, **9**, 79–93.

Veugelers, R. (1997), 'Internal R&D expenditures and external technology sourcing', *Research Policy*, **26**, 303–15.

L. Vlaar, M. Bouman with P. den Hertog & R. Bilderbeek (1998), *The Role of Technology-based Knowledge Intensive Business Services in the Dutch Environmental Production and Service Cluster (EPSC).A study of the subclusters water and waste*, Apeldoorn: TNO-SI4S report no. 6

von Emloh, D. A., A. W. Pearson and D. F. Ball (1994), 'The role of R&D in international process plant contracting', *International Journal of Technology Management*, **9** (1), 61–76.

Von Hippel, E. (1987), 'Cooperation between rivals: informal know-how trading', *Research Policy*, **16**, 291–302.

Walton, Richard E. (1987), *Innovating to Compete: Lessons for Diffusing and Managing Change in the Workplace*, San Francisco: Jossey-Bass.

Webster, A. J. (1989), 'Privatisation of public sector research: the case of the Plant Breeding Institute', *Science and Public Policy*, **16**, 224–32.

Weinstein, A. K. (1974), 'The international expansion of US multinational advertising agencies', *MSU Business Topics*, Summer, 29–35.

West, D. (1987), 'From T-Square to T-Plan: The London office of the J. Walter Thompson advertising agency 1919–70', *Business History*, **29** (2), 199–217.

Whittington, Richard (1990), 'The changing structure of R&D: from centralization to fragmentation', in Richard Loveridge and Martyn Pitt (eds), *The Strategic Management of Technological Innovation* London: Wiley, pp. 183–203.

Williams, C. C. (1997), *Consumer Services and Economic Development*, London: Routledge.

Williamson, O. E. (1973), 'Markets and hierarchies: some elementary considerations', *American Economic Review*, **63**, 316–25.

Williamson, Oliver E. (1975), *Markets and Hierarchies: Analysis and Antitrust Implications*, New York: Free Press.

Williamson, O. E. (1979), 'Transaction cost economics: the governance of contractual relations', *Journal of Law and Economics*, **22**, 233–61.

Williamson, Oliver E. (1986), *Economic Organisation: Firms, Markets and Policy Control*, New York: Harvester Wheatsheaf.

Williamson, Oliver E. (1996), *The Mechanisms of Governance*, Oxford: Oxford University Press.

Windrum, P. and M. Tomlinson (1999), 'Knowledge-intensive services and international competitiveness: a four country comparison', *Technology Analysis and Strategic Management*, **11**(3): 391–408.

Winter, Sidney (1987), 'Knowledge and competence as strategic assets', in David Teece (ed.), *The Competitive Challenge: Strategies for Industrial Innovation and Renewal*, Cambridge, Mass.: Ballinger, pp. 159–83.

Wood, P. A. (1991), 'Flexible accumulation and the rise of business services', *Transactions of the Institute of British Geographers*, **NS16**, 160–73.

World Bank (1999), *Knowledge for Development*, World Development Report, New York: Oxford University Press.

World Intellectual Property Organization (1987), *Intellectual Property and Computers*, Geneva: WO/INF/11, World Intellectual Property Organization.

Yakhlef, Ali and Miriam Salzer-Mörling (2000, forthcoming), 'Intellectual capital: managing by numbers', in Craig Pritchard, Richard Hull, Mike Chumer and Hugh Willmott (ed.), *Managing Knowledge: Critical Discussions of Work and Learning*, London: Macmillan.

Yamamoto, K. (1989), 'Japan's software industry', *Japan Computer Quarterly*, **76**, 3–25.

Young, A. (1996), 'Measuring R&D in the services', Paris: STI Working Papers, 1996/7, OECD.

Zwass, V (1996), 'Electronic Commerce: Structures and Issues', International Journal of Electronic Commerce, **1** (2), 3-23.

Index